语言的可持续性

Linguistic Sustainability

常晨光 喻常森 主 编

Edited by Chang Chenguang & Yu Changsen

中山大学出版社
SUN YAT-SEN UNIVERSITY PRESS

· 广州 ·

版权所有　翻印必究

图书在版编目（CIP）数据

语言的可持续性＝Linguistic Sustainability：汉文、英文/常晨光，喻常森主编．—广州：中山大学出版社，2020.7
ISBN 978-7-306-06879-8

Ⅰ.①语…　Ⅱ.①常…②喻…　Ⅲ.①语言学—研究—汉、英　Ⅳ.①H0

中国版本图书馆 CIP 数据核字（2020）第 084274 号

YUYAN DE KECHIXUXING

出　版　人：王天琪
策划编辑：熊锡源
责任编辑：熊锡源
封面设计：林绵华
责任校对：苏深梅
责任技编：何雅涛
出版发行：中山大学出版社
电　　话：编辑部 020-84111996，84111997
　　　　　发行部 020-84111998，84111981，84111160
地　　址：广州市新港西路 135 号
邮　　编：510275　　传　　真：020-84036565
网　　址：http://www.zsup.com.cn　E-mail：zdcbs@mail.sysu.edu.cn
印　刷　者：广州一龙印刷有限公司
规　　格：880mm×1230mm　1/32　10 印张　240 千字
版次印次：2020 年 7 月第 1 版　2020 年 7 月第 1 次印刷
定　　价：68.00 元

如发现本书因印装质量影响阅读，请与出版社发行部联系调换

鸣　谢

感谢中山大学国际翻译学院、中山大学澳大利亚研究中心、中山大学大洋洲研究中心对本书出版提供的支持。感谢各位作者的支持和耐心。责任编辑熊锡源博士为本书的出版做了大量细致的工作，特此表示感谢。

目录

Linguistic Sustainability: An Introduction
………………………………………… Chang Chenguang/ 1

从复兴语言学视角看语言的可持续性
…… Ghil'ad Zuckermann（诸葛漫） 陈　燕　金志茹/ 35

语言政策与规划研究回顾 …………… 王婴君茹　于　晖/ 66

Protecting Endangered Languages and Dialects in China
………………………………………… Chang Chenguang/ 93

Theorising Change: Culturally Responsive Digital Teaching
and Australian Aboriginal Learners
………………………………… Lester-Irabinna Rigney / 117

澳大利亚语言政策的发展变迁及其动机分析
……………………………………… 刘晓波　战　菊/ 145

中南半岛四国的语言生态与语言政策的历时演变
……………………………………… 王晋军　黄兴亚/ 160

澳门社会的语言状况与语言政策 ………… 张桂菊/ 177
从被动到主动的双语使用者
　　——青少年语言态度、身份认同转变的跟踪研究
　………………………………………… 梁斯华/ 196
生态语言学研究综观 ………… 何　伟　高　然/ 228
生态语言学与语言可持续发展 ………… 黄国文/ 260
有益性话语中的变与不变：
　　两首《洪湖水》的和谐话语分析
　………………………………… 卢　健　常晨光/ 295

Linguistic Sustainability: An Introduction

Chang Chenguang

This volume originates from the FASIC 2 Conference on "Sustainability: Social and Environmental Issues", organized by the Foundation for Australian Studies in China (FASIC) , and jointly hosted by the Centre for Australian Studies, Sun Yat-sen University, and the Centre for Oceanian Studies, Sun Yat-sen University on the university's Guangzhou campus in November 2016. The term "sustainability" was interpreted in a very broad sense at this conference, and one of the panels at this event focused on linguistic sustainability, discussing issues related to language policy, language protection, language attitude, language revival and language education. Based on the papers presented at the panel and some invited papers, we put together this volume on linguistic sustainability.

Defining sustainability

The term sustainability has been used to refer to the process of maintaining change in a balanced fashion, in which the exploitation of resources, the direction of investments, the orientation of technological development and institutional change are all in harmony and enhance both current and future potential to meet human needs and aspirations. Naturally, the term is broad enough to cover different domains, and has indeed been used in many areas. Most noticeably, for example, in order to protect our environment, activists have been demanding change in the name of sustainability for decades, and consequently, people have been increasingly aware of the crucial importance of ecological sustainability. Then the definition of sustainability has also been further extended to include economic, social and cultural domains.

Closely related to the notion of sustainability is the term sustainable development, first introduced in the *Brundtland Report* for the World Commission on Environment and Development (WCED 1987) to refer to "the development that meets the needs of the present without compromising the ability of future generations to meet their own needs". This definition of sustainable development clearly implies that we need to look after the planet we live on, our resources and our people to ensure that we can live in a sustainable manner and that we can hand down this planet to our future generations.

The 2005 World Summit on Social Development identified sustainable development goals, such as economic development, social development and environmental protection, commonly referred to as the three pillars of sustainability (United Nations General Assembly 2005). According to the Circular Ecology Website, these three pillars of sustainability may be defined as follows:

(1) Environmental Sustainability means that we are living within the means of our natural resources. To live in true environmental sustainability we need to ensure that we are consuming our natural resources, such as materials, energy fuels, land, water, etc., at a sustainable rate. Some resources are more abundant than others and therefore we need to consider material scarcity, the damage to environment from extraction of these materials and if the resource can be kept within Circular Economy

principles. Environmental sustainability should not be confused with full sustainability, which also needs to balance economic and social factors.

(2) Economic Sustainability requires that a business or country uses its resources efficiently and responsibly so that it can operate in a sustainable manner to consistently produce an operational profit. Without an operational profit a business cannot sustain its activities. Without acting responsibly and using its resources efficiently a company will not be able to sustain its activities in the long term.

(3) Social Sustainability is the ability of society, or any social system, to persistently achieve a good social wellbeing. Achieving social sustainability ensures that the social wellbeing of a country, an organisation, or a community can be maintained in the long term.

(Circular Ecology website, see http://www.circularecology.com/sustainability-and-sustainable-development.html#.W5zASUx-uLF6)

Apart from the three pillars introduced above, there is a fourth dimension, the dimension of cultural sustainability, which relates to the maintaining of cultural beliefs, cultural practices, heritage conservation, and so on. Cultural sustainability used to be subsumed under the social pillar of the three pillars of sustainability. The dimension of cultural sustainability was first mentioned in 1995, when the World Commission on Culture and Development(WCCD) defined it as "inter- and intra-generational access to cultural resources" (WCCD 1995). In 2001, a process with the aim to add culture as the fourth sustainability dimension started with the UNESCO Universal Declaration on cultural diversity (UNESCO 2001). More recently, James and Magee (2016) explicitly distinguished four domains of economic, ecological, political and cultural sustainability in their "Circles of Sustainability" approach.

As far as the dimension of cultural sustainability is concerned, there is an ongoing development from a more traditional view that focuses on material cultural heritage to a new view that includes also immaterial or intangible aspects. This indicates a more balanced emphasis on both tangible and intangible parts of cultural heritage, focusing on "the entire corpus of material signs – either artistic or symbolic – handed on by the past to each culture and, therefore, to the whole of humankind"(UNESCO 1989). In the words of Hale(1992:1), "Language loss in the modern period

[...] is part of a much larger process of loss of cultural and intellectual diversity..." As an important part of culture, language and language-related issues have increasingly entered into discussions on sustainability and sustainable development, hence the topic of our current volume.

Biodiversity, linguistic diversity and linguistic sustainability

It is apparent that notions like *linguistic diversity* and *linguistic sustainability* were patterned on, or created by analogy with, *biological diversity* (or *biodiversity*) and *ecological sustainability*. As a matter of fact, people are now approaching the question of preserving linguistic diversity and biological diversity with a certain unity of purpose. There are good reasons why scholars are increasingly turning to the metaphor of biology or ecology to discuss language-related issues. Fill and Mühlhaüsler (2001), for example, argue that the ecological metaphor contributes to our understanding of the diversity of inhabitants in an ecology and the factors that sustain that diversity. Hornberger (2002) focuses on three aspects of the metaphor: language evolution, language environment and language endangerment, and argues that, like living species, languages evolve, grow, change, live and die in relation to other languages and in relation to their environment. Like some species, they may also be endangered.

There is a widespread awareness now that biodiversity is disappearing at an alarming pace. Similarly, linguists have also been warning for decades about looming language extinctions. According to Sasse(1992:7), "about half of the known languages of the world have disappeared" in the last five centuries. Today, languages are being killed at a much faster speed than ever before in human history, and estimates have it that at least 50% of today's over 7000 spoken languages in the world may be extinct or very seriously endangered by the year 2100(Krauss 1992). *Ethnologue* (Lewis, *et al.* 2015) calculates that the rate of language loss amounts to six languages per year since 1950. More pessimistic estimate, however, even puts the figure at one language extinction every two weeks(Crystal 2000:19).

The Convention on Biological Diversity dedicated to promoting sustainable development, signed at the 1992 Rio Earth Summit, recognizes that biological diversity is about more than plants, animals and micro-organisms and their ecosystems. Instead, it is also about people and their environment, and here language is included(http://www.biodiv.org/convention/default.shtml). The

Convention subsequently also stresses the interlocking of language and ecology in traditional knowledge and its inter-generational transfer. The crucial role that languages play in the acquisition, accumulation, maintenance and transmission of human knowledge means that language loss has serious consequences for the survival of humanity's rich and diverse intellectual heritage. As is argued in the UNESCO document *Language Vitality and Endangerment*, "Language diversity is essential to the human heritage. Each and every language embodies the unique cultural wisdom of a people. The loss of any language is thus a loss for all humanity" (UNESCO 2003). Indeed, just as species loss will affect the ecosystems, the extinction of languages will also cause the irrecoverable loss of unique cultural, historical, and even ecological knowledge. Like all organisms which evolve interdependently with the others in their environment, human languages and verbal behaviours also co-evolve in conjunction with demographic, socioeconomic, political, and technological events in their different contexts and environments.

Dasmann(1968) was probably the first to advocate for the dual protection of biological and cultural diversity in a conservation perspective. Though not immediately accpeted, it eventually raised the awareness that there is an "inextricable link between cultural and biological diversity" (Maffi 2005). Similarly, Krauss (1992: 4) also explicitly emphasized the link between threats to the two realms of diversity, pointing out specifically that " language endangerment is significantly comparable to – and related to – endangerment of biological species in the natural world ". As summarized by Skutnabb-Kangas and Harmon (2018), the parallels between the biological and linguistic diversity include the following: (1) there are striking correlations between the geographical distribution of species and languages, (2) both are fundamentally evolutionary, and the histories of species and languages are both traced by similar taxonomic mathods and result in similar phylogenetic trees that reflect an evolutionary process, (3) both kinds of diversity can be classified hierarchically, (4) the quality of being restricted to or associated with a particular place or region is of special interest in both kinds of diversity, (5) the same biogeographic factors that give rise to species diversification are likely at least behind language diversification, and (6) the extinction of biological and linguistic diversity shares the same root cause: neoliberal globalization.

The languages today are the evolutionary result of the

sociolinguistic history of humanity. It is no exaggeration to say that "each language is a unique expression of the human experience of the world" (UNESCO 2003). To further elaborate on the similarities between biological and linguistic diversity, another important point to emphasize is that all the ideas, concepts and images we have created in order to survive and to improve our existence in this world, are deposited in languages, just as an organism's structure is a record of its previous structural changes and interactions. Moreover, the knowledge of any single language may even be the key to answering fundamental questions of the future. Every time a language dies, we have less evidence for understanding patterns in the structure and function of human language, human prehistory, and the maintenance of the world's diverse ecosystems. Recent research (e. g. Phillipson and Skutnabb-Kangas 1997; Harmon 2002) shows high correlations between biodiversity and linguistic and cultural diversity – "a causal relationship, or a co-evolution where biodiversity in the various ecosystems and humans through their languages and cultures have mutually influenced each other". Phillipson and Skutnabb-Kangas (1997) even make the case that terms like biodiversity, linguistic diversity and cultural diversity can be conflated in "biocultural diversity", which is essential for the long-term survival of this planet.

Among the reasons for defending linguistic diversity, the following are the most frequently mentioned: (1) Each language contains a "construction of reality" which disappears with the distinction of the language. Each language is also a unique and threatened specimen of human linguistic evolution and tradition. (2) Each language stores knowledge that should not get lost. For example, people in many indigenous and minority languages have a long-lasting connection to a certain territory, which they know so well that phenomena in the ecosystem have been lexicalized. This process of lexicalization may take hundreds of years (Mühlhaüsler 2003). Thus the knowledge about how to maintain a balanced ecosystem is encoded in these languages and is often more detailed and accurate than western science (Posey 1999). Consequently, if this knowledge about the complexities of biodiversity and how to manage ecosystems sustainably is to be maintained, the languages and cultures need to have better conditions to be transferred from one generation to the next. (3) Languages are "classifier systems" which allows us to examine how human experience is meaningfully classified and culturally structured (Nettle and Romaine 2000:

62). (4) Languages serve to identify speakers. As a result, when speakers of languages experience the loss of their languages, they are actually experiencing a loss of their original ethnic and cultural identity(Bernard 1992; Hale 1998). In addition, some scholars (e. g. Fill 2018) also suggest that linguistic diversity may also be an economic advantage for a country.

The importance of preserving endangered languages and maintaining linguistic diversity is more easily appreciated by looking at the roles of different species and organisms in the ecosystems. Given the simultaneous nature of the two phenomena, people find it tempting to transfer categories and ideas from the fields of biology and ecology to the field of linguistics, although some scholars have cautioned against making such a simple metaphoric transfer(e. g. Bastardas-Boada 2002). Nevertheless, it is still interesting to explore whether the theoretical and practical experience of preservation and recovery in biology may be an interesting analogy for the linguistic domain. Loh and Harmon (2014), for example, attempted to use methods originally developed by biologists and adapt them to measure global linguistic diversity, and found that at least 25% of the world's 7000 oral languages are threatened with extinction, compared with at least

30% of amphibians, 21% of mammals, 15% of reptiles and 13% of birds.

In any case, the ecological metaphor has stuck, and it remains, on the whole, illuminating. The concept of *ecology*, which studies " the relationships between organisms and their environment " (Brown 1995: 18), has contributed to our understanding of the existence, development and extinction of biological species. The metaphor also provides interesting insights and innovations in the linguistic field. *Language ecology*, as Haugen (1972: 325) defines it, is " the study of interactions between any given language and its environment ". Haugen then adds: "The true environment of a language is the society that uses it as one of the codes. Language exists only in the minds of its users, and it only functions in relating these users to one another and to nature, i. e. their social and natural environment. " (Haugen 1972:325) Thus, part of language's ecology is psychological, and another part of its ecology is sociological.

For Haugen, the ecological metaphor suggested analogies between languages and organisms and had useful heuristic value, but "it could not be pushed too far" (Haugen 1972:58). Yet the decision to study linguistic objects as entities interrelated multidimensionally with their context is a huge step forward. As Bastardas-Boada (1996, 1999) rightly points out, the ecological metaphor allows us to better understand "the vicissitudes of human systems of communication" and to integrate these systems holistically in the world of social interaction.

The notion of *linguistic sustainability*, therefore, derives mainly from ecological sustainability. The ecological metaphor has certainly made us aware of the importance of the maintenance and survival of language, and more efforts should be made to achieve linguistic sustainability so that the needs of our future generations will not be compromised. Both ecological sustainability and linguistic sustainability are essential for long-term planetary survival.

Ecolinguistics

As a new domain of linguistic research, ecolinguistics emerged in the 1990s, aiming to explore "the role of language in the life-sustaining interactions of humans, other species and the physical environment". With the emergence of ecolinguistics, some linguists are beginning to argue that the relationship between language and ecology may be even closer, maintaining that linguistics can be used to directly address ecological issues. In this new development, the "eco-" part is related to ecology in its more literal sense of the relationship of organisms (including humans) with other organisms and the physical environment. Language diversity is also considered as part of ecolinguistics because of the correlation between the diversity of language and biological diversity, with the ecological wisdom embedded in local cultures being the link between the two. According to the International Ecolinguistics Association, there are two aims in ecolinguistic research:

> The first aim is to develop linguistic theories which see humans not only as part of society, but also as part of the larger ecosystems that life depends on. The second aim is to show how linguistics can be used to address key ecological issues, from climate change and biodiversity loss to environmental justice.
> (The International Ecolinguistics Association, http://www. ecolinguistics-association. org)

A very important inspiration for ecolinguistic research is the work of M. A. K Halliday, whose seminal paper " New Ways of Meaning: The Challenge to Applied Linguistics " (Halliday 1990) has stimulated linguists to consider the ecological context and consequences of language. As an appliable linguistics, Halliday's systemic functional linguistics emphasizes the social accountability of linguistics and the linguist, and the importance of social intervention. Halliday takes a neo-Marxist approach towards the relationship between language and reality, maintaining that language does not only passively reflect reality, rather it actively creates reality. In this paper, Halliday urged linguists to " *interpret the grammatical construction of reality*". He gave examples of how language construes resources like air, water, soil, and mineral resources as unbounded, pointing out that this has severe consequences for humans and their environment. The challenge that Halliday put forward was to make linguistics relevant to overarching contemporary issues, particularly the widespread destruction of the ecosystems that life depends on. Halliday also gave examples of " growthism ", and the ecologically destructive consequences that this has led to. The Hallidayan approach to ecolinguistic studies is now recognized as one of the most influential approaches due to this paper, in which Halliday asked the central question to the field of ecolinguistics: "Do linguistic patterns, literally, affect the survival and wellbeing of the human species as well as other species on Earth?" (Steffensen and Fill 2014).

Currently, researchers in this new area of linguistic study draw on a wide range of linguistic tools, including critical discourse analysis, cognitive linguistics, rhetoric as well as systemic functional grammar to reveal underlying worldviews or the "stories we live by". Ecolinguists have analyzed and exposed consumerist stories, stories of economic growthism, advertising stories, stories of intensive farming, and stories which represent nature as a machine or a resource. According to Stibbe (2015), with reference to an ecosophy, the stories can be evaluated as beneficial in encouraging people to protect the ecosystems that life depends on, or destructive in encouraging behavior which damages those ecosystems. Using Positive Discourse Analysis, ecolinguistics has also searched for new stories to live by through exploring nature writing, environmental writing and indigenous forms of language around the world. Ecolinguistics attempts to make a practical difference in the world through resisting destructive stories and contributing to the search for new stories to live by (Stibbe 2015).

Ecolinguistics is still a very young, rapidly developing research area. As Fill and Penz(2018) summarize, the future of ecoliguistics must be seen at least on three levels:(1) the level of language diversity and all related topics, (2) the level of language, discourse and the environment, and(3) ecolinguistics as a trans-disciplinary science. It is to be hoped that research activity in ecolinguistics will continue to broaden and deepen, thus contributing more to maintaining linguistic sustainability.

About this volume

As mentioned at the beginning of this introduction, the chapters in this volume centre around the general theme of linguistic sustainability, covering a broad range of issues related to language policy and planning, language attitude, language protection, language revival, language education, and more broadly, ecolinguistics.

After this introductory chapter, the chapter on "Linguistic Sustainability from the Perspective of Revival Linguistics", contributed by Ghil'ad Zuckermann, Chen Yan and Jin Zhi, aims to reveal the role of language revival in linguistic sustainability with special reference to the revival of Barngarla, an aboriginal language of South Australia. One of the co-authors, Professor Zuckermann, is the founder of Revivalistics, a new trans-disciplinary field of enquiry surrounding language reclamation, revitalization and reinvigoration. He has launched, with the Barngarla Aboriginal communities of Eyre Peninsula, South Australia, the reclamation of the Barngarla language. Professor Zuckermann is elected member of the Australian Institute of Aboriginal and Torres Strait Islander Studies(AIATSIS) and the Foundation for Endangered Languages (FEL). His MOOC (Massive Open Online Course), Language Revival: Securing the Future of Endangered Languages, has attracted more than 8200 students from more than 150 countries. In this chapter, Professor Zuchermann and his co-authors argue that the loss of language is nothing new across the world, but the significance of language revival is never to be ignored from the perspectives of ethnology, ethics, aesthetics, cognitive ability, mental health, and economy. According to the authors, language revival is a continuum of revival efforts involving language reclamation, language reinvigoration and language revival; it involves huge amounts of effort from various parties. To facilitate language revival, linguists need to adopt a transdisciplinary approach to their studies on the languages to be revived and embrace the hybridity of the revived language. The revival efforts of Barngarla have proved that language revival not only changes the linguistic landscape and enhances the sustainability of the community in question, but also contributes to the development of the whole society.

Language policy and planning can have a crucial impact on linguistic diverisity and sustainability. Langauge planning involves the creation and implementation of an official policy about how the langauges and linguistic varieties of a country are to be used. Changes to and adjustment of an existing language policy essentially reflect changing social concerns. Status planning, for example, always selects among competing languages/dialects a language/dialect for a higher status and designates it for dominant and broader functions. The choices and decisions made in the process may, under certain circumstances, determine the fate of a language/dialect. In the third chapter, Wang Zhaojunru and Yu Hui provide a comprehensive review of studies on language policy and planning. Their review outlines three developmental stages of previous research as well as common research methods, which include ethnographic research, historical-structural analysis and discourse analysis. The authors categorize the most frequently explored research topics in this area into three major categories: language-in-education policy, analysis of political and legal contexts, and business as a site of language contact. This review serves as a background for discussions on language policy and planning and provides inspirations for future research.

Wang Zhaojunru and Yu Hui's review is followed by a discussion of endangered language protection, with special reference to endangered languages and dialects in China. The chapter first reiterates the importance of linguistic diversity and the protection of endangered languages. It then reviews the different criteria for the classification and description of endangered languages. The author argues that while there are common causes for language endangerment, discussion of endangered languages and dialects in China has to consider historical and local contexts. In China's case, socio-economic factors have played a more influential role in the ecology of languages and language diversity loss in recent decades. While we advocate the maintenance of linguistic diversity, it is also important to consider the costs and benefits to the relevant populations. The appropriate language policy and policy implementation, the establishment of bilingual education programs, the provision of financial support, and so on have all proved to be important measures in revitalizing endangered languages and dialects. Recently, there have been renewed efforts at endangered language protection in China, and linguists are playing an active role in the process through research. The author concludes by empahsizing the importance of habitat protection in the minority language revitalization.

The next chapter is a contribution by Lester-Irabinna Rigney. One of Australia's most respected Aboriginal educationalists, Lester-Irabinna Rigney is a descendant of the Narungga, Kaurna and Ngarrindjeri peoples of South Australia. He is an expert on Aboriginal Minority Education. He is best known for his theorisation of *Indigenist Research Epistemologies* and *Aboriginal Education*, putting him at the forefront for schooling and language rights from 1990s to the 2000s. According to Rigney's three principles of Indigenist epistemology, schools, teachers and researchers must build community partnerships and embed Aboriginal cultures as driving force for transformative, culturally responsive education. Many teachers and policy writers have been inspired by Rigney's writings that promote the idea that culturally responsive schooling is built from the experiences and abilities students bring to class. In this chapter, Rigney argues that pedagogical techniques are urgently required in Australia that assist teachers of information and communication technologies (ICTs) to respond positively to the growing need of culturally and linguistically diverse student populations. He points out that culturally responsive pedagogies (CRP) are now accepted as a hopeful strategy for improving academic achievement of First Peoples in settler colonial countries such as the USA, Canada and New Zealand. In this chapter it is argued that CRP is important for improving Aboriginal Australian schooling outcomes. The author takes a broader view to consider how teachers' approaches to ICT education in schools may be enhanced through culturally responsive pedagogies. The purpose of this chapter is to theorise new aspects of CRP applied to ICT education to open innovative spaces in which new classroom practices may be established. The insights gained could potentially enhance ICT pedagogies to benefit the learning of students from a range of cultural and linguistic diverse backgrounds.

  Language policy and planning of a country is affected by many factors. Depending on the motivating social concerns, status planning may or may not make any overt policy statement about the fate or status of the competing languages/dialects. The next chapter by Liu Xiaobo and Zhan Ju entitled "The Change of Language Policy in Australia and Analysis of Its Motivations" introduces a new development in the study of language planning and language policy: the analysis of motivations. The authors focus on the change and development of Australia's language policy by tracing the different stages in the development of Australia's language policy and analyse the motivations for language policy changes in Australia.

Wang Jinjun and Huang Xingya's contribution reviews the historical evolution of language ecology and language policies in the four countries in the Indo-China Peninsula, including Vietnam, Combodia, Myanmar and the Laos. The chapter makes a comparison between the four countries in terms of the major historical stages in language ecology and changes in language policies. It is hoped that the review and comparison may promote people-to-people communication between countries and provide useful implications for China with regard to language policy making and implementation.

In the chapter on the language status and language policy in Macau, Zhang Guiju bases her analysis on the results of four census statistics in Macau, and argues that appropriate language policy and planning are very important for solving Macau's bilingual and multilingual problems. Based on the census results, it is found that the number of speakers speaking two or more languages is increasing steadily while people speaking only one language are decreasing in number after Macao's return to China. The phenomenon of " Portuguese only " and " personal bilingualism" has been replaced by the harmonious coexistence and development of various languages and cultures. The current challenges that Macau confronts are how to make good use of critical period of learning languages and convert language resources into cultural and economic resources.

The healthy survival of a language or dialect depends partly on the attitudes of individuals and communities of speakers towards their own heritage language. Indeed, young speakers' language attitudes, language competence and language practice are often considered crucial for the sustainable development of any living language, which is why linguists are particularly concerned about the language development of bilingual children. In studies on young bilinguals in China, most findings on the trends in language use and competence are based on single or multiple cross-sessional surveys, while in-depth longitudinal studies are rare to find. The chapter by Dr Liang Sihua, "From Passive to Active: A Longitudinal Study of Young Bilingual's Language Attitude and Identity Changes", is a longitudinal case study drawing on 9 years of data from the author's linguistics ethnography on students' language attitudes, language use and identities in Guangzhou since 2009. The study finds that the participant's mobility experience from Guangzhou to Hong Kong strongly influenced the changes in his language use, language attitudes and language identity. Liang concludes that the revalorization of linguistic resources in one's linguistic repertoire, brought about by the physical movement from one place to another, underlies such changes.

The past 20 years or so have witnessed an increasing interest in ecolinguistic studies. The final three chapters are contributions in this area of research. The chapter by He Wei and Gao Ran attempts to provide an overview of the key current research issues of ecolinguistics, and to define its direction by tracing its origin, developmental stages and current research situation. It is found that early research of language diversity and the relationship between language and environment laid a foundation for the rise of ecolinguistics. Since 1970s, the Haugen Model and the Halliday Model have gradually come into being. Current studies of ecolinguistics are indicative of a trend of expansion of scope, integration of research paradigms, diversification of theories, research methods and unification of ecosophies. The authors also point out that, as a new discipline, ecolinguistics still has some unresolved problems with its research subjects, methods and scope, which are probably the main urgent issues for ecolinguists to address.

The next chaper "Ecolinguistics and Linguistic Sustainability" is a contribution from Huang Guowen, a leading figure in ecolinguistics in China, who has focused in recent years on studying the relationship between language and ecology, and particularly between the ecology of language and language in the ecosystem that life depends on. In this chapter, Huang starts with a very brief review of the different approaches to the study of ecolinguistic issues, and then takes a Hallidayan approach to addressing the issue of how our ways of meaning affect the impact we have on the environment, by analyzing a text published in *Mail Online* (14 May 2017), which tells a story of a sugar baby and her relationships with the sugar daddy, her boyfriend and her own family. Through the analysis of the language and its cultural, situational contexts, it is argued that the text is a destructive discourse which conveys an ideology that opposes and contradicts the ecosophy of ecolinguists, as the discourse encourages university students to follow the sugar baby's way of life, which would do harm to the social-cultural environment and destroy the ecosystems that life depends on in general.

In doing ecolinguistic discourse analysis, one is bound to be guided by a certain ecological philosophy, or *ecosophy* for short, which is defined by Naess(1995:8) as "a philosophy of ecological harmony". Although there is not one "correct" ecosophy that ecolinguistics should be based on, "ecosophies can be judged by whether evidence confirms or contradicts the assumptions about the state of the world that they are based on, or whether there are any internal inconsistencies" (Stibbe 2015:12). According to Stibbe (2015), based on the analyst's ecosophy, the discourses being analyzed can be classified into destructive discourses, ambivalent discourses and beneficial discourses, and the role for ecolinguistics, Stibbe argues, "consists of going beyond critiquing destructive discourses or pointing out gaps in ambivalent discourses, to searching for new discourses that convey ideologies which can actively encourage people to protect the systems that support life", i. e. beneficial discourses (2015: 30). Indeed, ecosophy, historical context and discursive acceptability should all be taken into consideration when analyzing discourses from the perspective of ecolinguistics. The final chapter in this volume by Lu Jian and Chang Chenguang analyzes the lyrics of two songs, both entitled *Honghu Lake*, within a framework of harmonious discourse analysis. It is found that the two songs, although created in different times, are both beneficial discourses in that they have construed ecologically harmonious reality through their distinctive but appropriate ways of meaning. As products of different contexts in history, they both reflect how ecology has been highly valued in different periods of time, whether unconsciously or consciously. Three dichotomies of inconsistency/consistency are discussed: the exploitation of the lake vs. the love for the lake, the ways of living vs. the pursuit of ecological harmony, and the themes of times vs. the leadership of the nation.

As a final remark, the editors, Changsen and I, acknowledge the generous support from FASIC and Sun Yat-sen university. We are extremely grateful to all the contributors for their patience and understanding in the publication of this volume, which, for various reasons, has been seriously delayed.

References

Bastardas-Boada, A. *Ecologia de les llengües. Medi, contactes i dinàmica sociolingüística.* Barcelona: Proa, 1996.

— Lingüística general y teorías de la complejidad ecológica: algunas ideas desde una transdisciplinariedad sugerente. *Lingüística para el siglo.* Salamanca: Universidad de Salamanca, 1999, XXI: 287 - 294.

— Biological and linguistic diversity: Transdisciplinary explorations for a socioecology of languages. *Diverscité langues.* Montréal, 2002. http://www.teluq.ca/diverscite/SecArtic/Arts/2002/bastarda/ftxt.htm.

Bernard, H. R. Preserving language diversity. *Human Organization*, 1992, 51 (1): 82 - 89.

Brown, James H. *Macroecology.* Chicago: University of Chicago Press, 1995.

Crystal, D. *Language Death.* Cambridge: Cambridge University Press, 2000.

Dasmann, R. F. *A Different Kind of Country.* New York: Macmillan, 1968.

Fill, A. F. The economy of language ecology: Economic aspects of minority languages. In A. F. Fill and H. Penz (eds.). *The Routledge Handbook of Ecolinguistics*. New York and London: Routledge,2018.

Fill, A. F. and P. Mühlhaüsler (eds.). *The Ecolinguistics Reader: Language,Ecology and Environment*. London:Continuum,2001.

Fill, A. F. and H. Penz. Ecolinguistics in the 21st century: New orientations and future directions. In A. F. Fill and H. Penz (eds.). *The Routledge Handbook of Ecolinguistics*. New York and London:Routledge,2018.

Hale, K. On endangered languages and the safeguarding of diversity. *Language*,1992,68(1):1 -3.

Hale,K. On endangered languages and the importance of linguistic diversity. In Lenore A. Grenoble and Lindsay J. Whaley (eds.). *Endangered Languages,Language Loss and Community Response*. Cambridge:Cambridge University Press,1998:192 -216.

Halliday,M. A. K. New ways of meaning:the challenge to applied linguistics. *Journal of Applied Linguistics*,1990 (6):7 -36.

Harmon,D. *In Light of Our Difference:How Diversity in Nature and Culture Makes Us Human*. Washington D. C. :The Smithsonian Institute Press,2002.

Haugen, E. *The Ecology of Language*. Stanford, CA: Stanford

University Press,1972.

Horberger, N. Multilingual language policies and continua of biliteracy. *Language Policy*, 2002 (1):27 –51.

The International Ecolinguistics Association. http://www. ecolinguistics-association. org. Retrieved September 30, 2018.

James,P. and L. Magee. Domains of sustainability. In A. Farazmand (ed.). *Global Encyclopedia of Public Administration*, *Public Policy and Governance.* Springer,2016:DOI 10. 1007/978 – 3 – 319 – 31816 – 5_2760 – 1.

Krauss, M. The world's languages in crisis. *Language*, 1992, 68 (1):4 – 10.

Lewis,M. P. , G. F. Simons, and C. D. Fennig. *Ethnologue*: *Languages of the World.* 18th edition. Dallas: SIL International, 2015. www. ethnologue. com.

Loh, J. and D. Harmon. *Biocultural Diversity*: *Threatened Species*, *Endangered Languages.* Zeist:WWF Netherlands,2014.

Maffi,L. Linguistic,cultural and biological diversity. *Annual Review of Anthropology*,2005, 29:599 – 617.

Mühlhaüsler, P. *Language of Environment*, *Environment of Language*: *A Course in Ecolinguistics.* London: Battlebridge, 2003.

Naess, A. The shallow and the long range, deep ecology

movement. In A. Drengson and Y. Inoue (eds.). *The Deep Ecology Movement: An Introductory Anthology.* Berkeley, CA: North Atlantic Books,1995:3 - 10.

Nettle, D. and S. Romaine. *Vanishing Voices: The Extinction of the World's Languages.* Oxford: Oxford University Press, 2000.

Phillipson, R. and T. Skutnabb-Kangas. Linguistic human rights and English in Europe. *World Englishes*, 1997,16 (1):27 -43.

Posey, D. (ed.). *Cultural and Spiritual Values of Biodiversity: A Complementary Contribution to the Global Biodiversity Assessment.* New York and Leiden: Intermediate Technologies, Leiden University, 1999.

Sasse, H. -J. Theory of language death. In M. Brenzinger (ed.). *Language Death: Factual and Theoretical Explorations with Special Reference to East Africa.* Berlin: Mouton de Gruyter, 1992: 7 - 30.

Skutnabb-Kangas, T. and David Harmon. Biological and language diversity: Parallels and differences. In A. F. Fill and H. Penz (eds.). *The Routledge Handbook of Ecolinguistics.* New York and London: Routledge, 2018.

Steffensen, S. V. and A. Fill. Ecolinguistics: the state of the art and future horizons. *Language Sciences* (special issue), 2014, 41:6 -25.

Stibbe, A. *Ecolinguistics*: *Language*, *Ecology and the Stories We Live By*. New York: Routledge, 2015.

UNESCO. *Draft Medium-Term Plan* (1990 – 1995). General Conference Twenty-fifth Session, 25 C/4. Paris: UNESCO, 1989.

UNESCO. UNESCO Universal Declaration on Cultural Diversity. Records of the general conference, 31st session, 15 October – 3 November 2001, Paris, France. Annex I, Volume 1 Resolutions. Paris: UNESCO, 2001.

UNESCO. *Cultural Landscapes*: *The Challenges of Conservation*. *Proceedings of the Workshop*, 11 – 12 November 2002, Ferrara, Italy. UNESCO World Heritage Papers, no. 7. Paris: UNESCO, 2003.

UNESCO. *The Power of Culture for Development*. Paris: UNESCO, 2010.

United Nations General Assembly. 2005 *World Summit Outcome*. Resolution A/60/1, adopted by the General Assembly on 15 September 2005. http://data.unaids.org/topics/universalaccess/worldsummitoutcome_resolution_24oct2005_en.pdf. Retrieved September 15, 2018.

WCED. *Our Common Future*. *Report of the World Commissionon Environment and Development*. New York: United Nations, 1987.

从复兴语言学视角看语言的可持续性

Ghil'ad Zuckermann(诸葛漫) 陈 燕 金志茹

一、引 言

对于语言在人类文明中的价值和意义,儿童文学作家罗素·霍本(Russel Hoban)曾经指出:"语言是古迹的载体,满载着往日的残迹,涉及僵死的过去与活着的过去,涉及消失及埋没的文明与技术。我们现在所使用的语言是一部完整的重写本,记载着人类的努力与历史。"(Haffenden 1985:138)语言是多层次的,蕴含着语言使用者的历史、传统与文化。某种语言一旦消亡,就意味着以这种语言为母语的族群失去了同历史及传统的联系,这是因为母语使用者对客观世界和人类社会的认识、对生产生活的经验、对人生的感悟和体验都凝结在母语里,而随着母语的消亡,母语者经过年深日久所积累的民族文化载体,包括神话、传说、歌谣、舞蹈、技艺等,都会因母语的消失而被摧毁。

语言濒危、语言消亡并非新近出现的现象,而是贯穿于整个人类历史,而且全球各地都有发生。澳大利亚、中南美洲、北美洲、西伯利亚等地都属于原住民语言消失较快的地区。语言杀戮(linguicide)和语言同化(glottophagy)(Zuckermann and Monaghan 2012)导致许多原住民丧失母语,澳大利亚的原住民也不例外。在1788年欧裔人殖民澳大利亚之前,原住民已经在澳大利亚繁衍生息了5.2万~6.5万年,原住民的语言多达330种,但现在仅剩13种(约4%)还处于健康状态,亦即作为母语被各个年龄段的大部分人广泛使用,而96%的原住民语言遗产消失殆尽(Australian Institute of Aboriginal and Torres Strait Islander Studies & Federation of Aboriginal and Torres Strait Islander Languages 2005; Indigenous Remote Communications Association 2013)。殖民统治的结果是原住民人口锐减,其传统的社会结构和文化也遭受前所未有的冲击和破坏。

母语的消亡不仅关乎特定群体的利益,而且关乎语言及文化的多样性,关乎社会平等和包容发展。全球6000余种语言中,约96%的语言仅由约4%的人使用,当今世界80%的网页都使用英语。随着全球化、同质化的到来,越来越多的语言面临灭绝或失去影响力。由于语言多样性反映了历史多样性和文化多样性，越来越多的人认识到保护濒危语言对保护人类文化和文明的重要性。联合国教科文组织已于 1999 年 11 月宣布将每年的 2 月 21 日定为"国际母语日"（International Mother Language Day），旨在保护世界语言和促进文化多样性的可持续发展，帮助人们进一步加深对语言传统及文化传统的认识，增进各国人民之间的相互理解。

在此背景下，越来越多的语言使用者和语言工作者认识到母语对构筑群体身份和权力、知识主权、文化自治权和精神世界的巨大作用，尤其是一些母语遭受杀戮和同化的语言使用者，非常希望借助复兴母语来恢复自己的文化自主权，增强精神主权和知识主权，提高幸福感和心理健康水平（诸葛漫、陈燕 2017）。语言复兴与否既关乎语言的可持续性，又关乎文化韧性和语言生态，因此，语言复兴应该得到越来越广泛的重视与认同。本文作者之一诸葛漫教授近 10 年来一直致力于语言复兴工作，他不仅撰文阐述自己的复兴语言学（Revival Linguistics）思想，而且积极投身于澳大利亚原住民的语言复兴实践。他在澳大利亚阿德莱德大学主讲复兴语言学课程，其慕课（大型开放性在线课堂）迄今已有 160 个国家的 1 万余人观看过。全球 100 多个国家或地区的人，比如蒙古人、托伦斯海峡岛民和库克群岛岛民，曾就语言复兴问题寻求诸葛漫教授的意见和建议。因此，本文将主要以澳大利亚的语言复兴为例，阐述语言复兴对语言可持续性的重要意义。具体而言，本文将从语言复兴的意义出发，说明语言复兴实践和复兴语言学的一些关键问题，并以邦格拉语（Barngarla）的复兴为例，充分展示语言复兴和复兴语言学为语言的可持续性所做的贡献。

二、语言复兴的意义

语言复兴包括复兴已经死亡或灭绝的语言、濒危或处于弱势的语言、休眠或沉睡的语言。语言复兴的意义主要涉及以下几个方面。

（一）民族学方面的意义

母语是特定民族的第一语言，是该民族积累知识、表达思想和感情、传承民族文化不可或缺的工具。母语如果未经记录就消失，未来的世代就无法学习和使用其祖先的语言，继而引发民族语言文化传承的衰退乃至断裂。帮助后来的世代维护或重新获得其祖先的语言，其意义远远超越重获语言本身，后代同时获得的还包括了解和继承自己的历史和文化的权利，这有助于消除种族不平等，促进社会公正与和谐。以澳大利亚为例，从更广阔的范围来看，澳大利亚的多元文化不能仅仅涉及对外来移民语言文化的包容和接受，而且必须包括对原住民语言文化的理解和尊重。

(二) 道义方面的意义

澳大利亚原住民的语言并非自然消亡,而是被殖民者人为摧毁的。从殖民初期开始,原住民就遭受语言杀戮与语言同化。Scrimgeour (2007: 16) 曾就传教士的语言实践对南澳大利亚州殖民地初期的作用做过详细研究,深刻揭示了殖民时期的语言意识形态。据她研究,在1943年9月召开的南澳大利亚州传教士协会会议上,金融家和政治家安东尼·福斯特 (Antony Forster) 多次谈到:教原住民孩子学习他们的母语的做法是错误的,更好的做法是教他们英语,因为"倘若原住民的母语灭绝,他们就会更快得到教化。受教的孩子以后就会只和白人打成一片,到那时他们的母语就毫无用处。使用母语会让他们保持偏见和劣性,那种语言是无法表达文明生活的理念的"。福斯特对原住民及其语言的蔑视和否定,代表了早期殖民者普遍的态度,有助于我们理解澳大利亚后来为什么会产生严重的语言丧失现象。

同样是在19世纪40年代,南澳大利亚州州长乔治·格雷 (George Grey) 曾是原住民语言强有力的支持者,曾经鼓励舒尔曼 (Clamor Wilhelm Schürmann) 记录下阿德莱德平原 (Adelaide Plains) 的卡尔纳语 (Kaurna) 和林肯港的邦格拉语。然而,他在夸赞伦敦商人将给澳大利亚带来的变化时却写道:"古老的民族将被扫除,过时的法律和习俗将湮灭,谋杀和迷信的根据地将被净化,福音将在无知而野蛮的人中间得到传播。那些粗鲁的语言将相继消失,到处听到的只会是英格兰的语言。"(Grey 1841:200-201)。殖民者对原住民语言的偏见和歧视,不仅给原住民语言带来了毁灭性的打击,而且给原住民的生活造成了不可挽回的局面。从欧裔人占领澳大利亚的早期开始,原住民儿童就被强制性地从他们的父母身边和社区带走。澳大利亚政府 1910—1970 年间实行的同化政策,致使 10 万余名原住民儿童被送到白人家庭或政府机构接受教育,他们就是"被偷走的孩子"(The Stolen Generations,或称 Stolen Children)。由于与自己的亲人长期分离,他们被隔绝在自己的族群之外,丧失了本族的语言、文化和传统。虽然白人政府迫使他们忘记自己的母语和文化,学习白人的语言和生活方式,但是他们无法融入白人社会。于是,他们孤立在两种文化之外,精神上无所归依,感受到深深的悲伤和痛苦,遭受到巨大的损失。

2008 年 2 月 13 日,澳大利亚时任总理陆克文在联邦议会上正式向原住民道歉,并承诺会改善他们的生活,原住民的维权意识随之不断高涨,土地所有权、母语权都是原住民的主要诉求。原住民政治家 Aden Ridgeway(2009)曾经呼吁:"语言就是力量。让我们拥有语言和力量!"诸葛漫教授认为，澳大利亚政府不仅应补偿原住民有形的土地损失，而且应赔偿他们无形的语言损失（Zuckermann, Shakuto-Neoh and Quer 2014）。立法对语言杀戮进行赔偿实际上是承认原住民有权复兴和保持他们自己的语言。如此正义道德的立法将有助于恢复原住民的权威及其对文化遗产的所有权。诸葛漫等人（同上）建议为语言损失制订赔偿计划。这种以法律为基础的补偿计划符合国际人权法的规定，即不同种族、宗教或语言的少数群体有权使用自己的语言（《公民权利和政治权利国际公约》第 27 条）。此外，这种赔偿还可以填补国际法的某些法律在澳大利亚国内法中的空缺，同时还可以确保原住民的权利，有助于他们拥有、使用、复兴自己的语言。

（三）美学方面的意义

对于语言消亡带来的后果，已故语言学家肯恩·黑尔（Ken Hale）曾形象地指出："当你失去一种语言时，你便失去了一种文化、一笔知识财富和一部艺术著作。这就像在卢浮宫博物馆上投下一枚炸弹。"（诸葛漫、徐佳 2013：101；诸葛漫、姚春林 2014：153）语言与博物馆的艺术品一样，是人类文化的瑰宝，从中可以了解整个民族的文化习俗和信仰。不同的语言用不同的方式表达思想，不同语言中的高频词也不尽相同，这些差异可以反映哪些观念在特定文化中是否重要。

语言是多姿多彩的现实世界的反映,可以反映人与世界相处的方式。世界上有一些原始文化把梦作为心灵超越的手段,比如澳大利亚曾有一些有关自然界食物来源的信息原本存储在原住民的历史或梦中,但是随着原住民语言的消亡而丧失了。Boroditsky 和 Gaby(2010)研究发现:在约克角西海岸波姆普劳(Pormpuraaw)地区的库塔语(Kuuk Thaayorre)中,没有"左""右"的概念,常用"东、西、南、北"来表示基本方位,但是讲库塔语的人总是知道自己身处何方,这种方位表达方式也影响着他们的时间意识。类似的例子在世界各地语言中比比皆是,下面再举几例加以说明。

mamihlapinatapai(微妙眼神)一词见于智利和阿根廷火地岛(Tierra del Fuego)的亚格罕语(Yaghan),指当事双方你看我、我看你,都希望对方去做双方都希望但都不愿意去做的事。这个词可以分解成更小的部分或语素:*ma-* 是反身代词/被动语态的前缀,是 *mam-* 在元音前的语素变体;*ihlapi* 的意思是"不知道下一步该做什么";*-n* 是表示状态的后缀;*-ata* 是表示完成的后缀;*-apai* 是表示双数的后缀,与 *ma-*(环缀)的含义相照应。又如,在古波斯语中,*nakhur* 指一种鼻孔被挠得发痒时才会产奶的骆驼,这说明骆驼对当时的社会非常重要,那时的人也许依靠骆驼奶才能生存。再如,在东波利尼西亚语中,*Tingo* 的意思是"从邻居家借东

西,一次借一样,直至借无可借"(De Boinod 2005)。这些看似简单的词语,竟然可以表达如此丰富而复杂的含义,我们不禁感叹:人类的想象力是多么有限。举例来说,我们在好莱坞电影里看到的所有外星人几乎都像丑陋的人类,长着两只眼睛、两个鼻孔、一张嘴。但是,如果真有外星人存在,他们看起来会像人类吗?想一想 DNA 存在了约 30 亿年,再想一想所有的基因突变,我们就觉得外星人看起来像丑陋人类的概率就像彩票中奖一样,大约只有百万分之一的可能。

如此迷人而又多层面的词汇对它们所代表的文化非常重要,并使外人反观自己的文化,这样的词汇是不应该遗失的。我们必须开展语言维护和复兴工作,如此才可以使重要的文化习俗和观念保持活力。

(四) 认知方面的意义

语言复兴不仅具有文化价值,同时还具有认知价值。多项研究表明,多语者具有许多认知方面的优势。与单语儿童相比,双语儿童有更好的非语言认知能力(Kovács and Mehler 2009),并且可以提高注意力和听觉能力;双语使用者"增强的声音体验可以使他们形成一种高效灵活的声音处理系统,这有助于他们在新的、富有挑战性的听力环境中自动对声音进行加工处理"(Krizman, *et al.* 2012:78-79)。研究表明,语言复兴的另一认知优势是:使用第二语言做决策时会减少偏差（Keysar et al. 2012：661）。

（五）心理健康方面的意义

母语丧失可能会影响心理健康。以澳大利亚为例，原住民和托雷斯海峡岛民的心理健康存在严重问题，而语言复兴运动可以使他们提高教育水平，增强自信心，提高就业率，减少犯罪（诸葛漫、陈燕 2017）。到目前为止，已经有大量的事实证明，语言复兴有助于提高使用者的幸福感和心理健康水平（Zuckermann and Walsh 2014；诸葛漫、陈燕 2017），相关数据和结论在此不再赘述。

（六）经济方面的意义

文化旅游是澳大利亚经济的重要组成部分，而了解原住民文化是许多游客游览澳大利亚的目的之一。在一些实施了语言复兴项目的地区，文化旅游业的增长尤其显著（Clark and Kostanski 2005）。原住民和托雷斯海峡岛民文化是澳大利亚海外形象的重要组成部分，我们在保护和复兴他们的语言和文化的同时，也为他们提供就业机会，促进当地经济发展。此外，经过语言复兴活动的锻炼，一些原住民可能成长为语言复兴方面的专家，之后他们可以帮助其他群体进行语言复兴，从而为更广泛的社区带来益处。总之，语言复兴有助于弥合原住民与澳大利亚白人之间的"裂痕"，刺激文化旅游消费，丰富澳大利亚的多元文化。

三、语言复兴和语言复兴研究的几个核心问题

(一) 复兴语言学是什么?

诸葛漫教授在 2009 年首次提出复兴语言学这一术语（Zuckermann 2009），旨在建立一门新的语言学学科和研究范式。复兴语言学建立在接触语言学之上，用比较的方法系统地研究全球不同社会背景下语言复兴行动的普遍机制和当地特点，并从某种语言复兴的实例中汲取经验，以此为世界各地的语言复兴运动架起一座认识论的桥梁（Zuckermann 2009；诸葛漫、姚春林 2012；诸葛漫、徐佳 2013）。在此之前，全球虽有零零星星的语言复兴实践，但是学界尚无研究者对多种语言的复兴实践开展系统的比较研究。复兴语言学将本族语习得研究与外语学习研究相结合，是语言学和应用语言学的一个分支学科，而语言复兴可以看作二语学习中最极端的情形。

2014 年，诸葛漫教授又提出语言复兴研究（Revivalistics）这一术语，用于指围绕语言收复（language reclamation）、语言复苏（language reinvigoration）和语言兴盛（language revitalization）所开展的跨学科研究（Zuckermann et al. 2014）。语言复兴研究包括复兴语言学（Revival Linguistics）和复兴组学（Revivalomics，即语言复兴的大数

据分析），其研究范围大大超过复兴语言学，其研究角度多种多样，涉及的领域包罗万象，包括法律、心理学、教育、教学法、语言学、人类学、社会学、地理学、政治学、历史学、生物学、进化论、遗传学、基因组学、殖民研究、传教研究、媒体、信息技术、考古学、气象学、戏剧、舞蹈、音乐、建筑等。比如，语言复兴的法律研究关注原住民的母语权和语言赔偿等法律问题（诸葛漫、姚春林 2014），语言复兴的心理学研究探讨语言复兴与心理健康之间的关系（诸葛漫、陈燕 2017），语言复兴的建筑学研究分析应该在什么样的建筑里开展语言复兴活动，如此等等，不一而足。总之，语言复兴研究可以从任何角度进行，而不仅仅限于语言学角度的研究。语言复兴不仅需要语言学家的参与，还需要社会工作者、精神病专家、律师、建筑师、编舞、音乐家等各行各业的人共同参与。

（二）语言复兴有哪些类别？

语言复兴活动是一个统一的连续体。根据待复兴的语言所处的状态以及复兴所需付出的努力，语言复兴活动可以分为三种不同的情形。

第一，语言收复：指"睡美人"语言的复兴，在复兴开始时，待复兴的语言已经没有母语使用者，比如希伯来语（Hebrew）、邦格拉语、卡尔纳语、万帕诺亚语（Wampanoag,

北美印第安部落语言)、西拉雅语（Siraya，台湾西拉雅族人的语言)和米阿米语（Myaamia，北美印第安人所使用的一种阿尔贡金语)。

第二，语言复苏：指严重濒危语言的复兴，在复兴开始时，待复兴的语言只有少数母语使用者，比如澳大利亚弗林德斯山区的阿尼亚玛坦哈语（Adnyamathanha)，卡鲁克语（Karuk)和瓦玛加里语（Walmajarri)。

第三，语言兴盛：指濒危语言的复兴，在复兴开始时，待复兴的语言仍然有很多儿童在使用，比如威尔士语（Welsh)、爱尔兰语（Irish)、加泰罗尼亚语和魁北克地区的法语。

（三）语言复兴研究为什么倡导跨学科研究？

让我们先以美国分子生物学家詹姆斯·沃森（James D. Watson)为例说明跨学科研究的重要性。他在1953年因与弗朗西斯·克里克（Francis Crick)、罗莎琳德·弗兰克林（Rosalind Franklin)和莫里斯·威尔金斯（Maurice Wilkins)一起发现DNA结构而获得诺贝尔奖。1950年，他获得美国印第安纳大学的生物学博士学位，但是他对生物化学、物理学和数学都有一定的了解，他正是凭借跨学科的直觉成功发现了DNA的双螺旋结构。近年来，一批又一批采用跨学科研究方法或从事跨学科研究与合作的科学家获得诺贝尔奖，一次又一次证明了跨学科研究的重要性。

跨学科研究有助于我们进行更为广阔的探索与发现。跨学科的类比有助于我们重新评估语言学（包括复兴语言学）和其他学科的假设和结论，提出新的研究方法，推动研究的进步与发展。举例来说，受爱因斯坦相对论的启发，本杰明·李·沃尔夫（Benjamin Lee Whorf）支持语言学上的语言相对论。根据沃尔夫的强势假说，语言决定思维；而根据沃尔夫的弱势假说，语言影响思维。简言之，人文科学和自然科学都可以跨学科相互学习和借鉴，比如在研究世界语言的过程中，我们可能会获得对遗传学等非语言研究学科的新理解，反之亦然。

（四）复兴语言学与文献语言学有什么区别？

作为一个新兴的跨学科研究领域，复兴语言学与业已确立的语言学分支学科文献语言学（Documentary Linguistics，又译为"记录语言学"或"语档语言学"）是互补的。文献语言学面向濒危语言，旨在赶在某一语言消亡之前，尽可能地对它进行全面记录和描写，尤其注重广泛采集大量有声语料，对语料进行充分标注和解释，以利于语料的永久保存。一些文献语言学家仅仅关注记录濒危语言的语法和词汇。他们中的一些人可能患有艾斯伯格综合征（Asperger's syndrome），而当他们只关注音素、语素时，这并不成为问题。

相比之下，复兴语言学把濒危语言的使用者而不是语言学家置于中心位置。一个患有艾斯伯格综合征的语言学家可以成为一个出色的文献语言学家或者类型学家，但很难成为一个复兴语言学家。复兴语言学家必须和社群一起工作，而这样的工作比在实验室努力分析音素、语素要繁重得多。

语言复兴好比是一对父母一起抚养孩子，语言学家只是父母双方中的一方，另一方是少数民族或原住民社群，双方必须紧密合作，才能共同推动复兴的进程。有时候，社群对待复兴的语言所做的决定在复兴语言学家看来不一定切实可行，而语言学家发挥创造力确定的拼写或者创制的新词不一定被社群所接受，这就需要双方协商和努力，但是决定权在社群一方。这种做法对患有艾斯伯格综合征的语档语言学家来说是极为困难的。

复兴语言学家既不是那种在家里的安乐椅上坐着分析语言的安乐椅语言学家（armchair linguist），也不是那种只站在走廊里观察本地人却从不参与其中的走廊语言学家（veranda linguist），更不是坐在大篷车里向本地人提问，然后等这个人累得晕倒了，再盘问下一个人的大篷车语言学家（caravan linguist）。复兴语言学家是必须在社群中工作的语言学家。有人说复兴语言学是后自闭语言学，这种语言学把它本身带回到语言学的核心——本族语使用者和他们的文化,因而能够提升幸福感,促进心理健康。

（五）为什么必须接受复兴语的混合性？

复兴后的语言与原始语言并不完全相同,比如以色列语（Israeli,即复兴后的希伯来语）是同时在几种语言基础之上产生的混杂体（诸葛漫、宋学东、韩力 2015；诸葛漫 2008）。正如克里斯特尔（Crystal 2000:62）评价卡尔纳语时所言:复兴语丢失了大量原有词汇,混合了一些来自其他语言的新词汇,发展出了新功能。为了实现语言的收复、振兴和兴盛,复兴语言学倡导摒弃纯语主义语言观,接纳复兴语的混合性。多里安（Dorian 1994）曾敏锐地洞察到,如果对外来词和语法方面的变化持保守态度,那么往往会阻碍濒危语言的复兴。

复兴语言学的语言观是现实的、非纯语主义的（诸葛漫、姚春林 2012）。复兴语言学家摒弃任何禁锢人们思想的纯语主义,帮助社区成员正确认识复兴语所发生的变化。打个比方说,如果有人喜欢蝴蝶,一只脏兮兮、受了伤的活蝴蝶要比挂在墙上的美丽的死蝴蝶好得多。复兴后的希伯来语或者卡尔纳语虽然是混合杂交而成,却是活生生的,比那些虽然真实、纯粹、完美却"死气沉沉"的希伯来语或者卡尔纳语要好得多。

（六）语言复兴是一种怎样的活动？

复兴一门语言是一项非常复杂的系统工程，需要投入大量的时间，并借助多方的帮助。我们可以用一个菱形示意图（如图1所示）形象地说明这项工程的相关主体、核心任务和相互关系。该图由四个核心部分组成，各个部分相互依存，缺一不可。下面对各个部分做具体说明。

• 语言所有者：指那些祖先以该语言为母语的语言使用者以及将来有可能以该语言为母语的人（这取决于待复兴的语言的实际状况）。通常来讲，这是语言复兴的起点（当然，菱形图的任何一部分都可以作为复兴的起点）。语言复兴始终是一个有机的过程，各部分之间彼此依存、相互促进。

• 语言学：对语言进行记录是这个过程早期的关键点，同时还需要整理或重建现有材料和资源，包括拼写、正字法、词典和语法。参与创建新媒体资源和学习资料同样也至关重要。

• 教育：包括提倡和强化将待复兴的语言用于艺术、歌曲和传统仪式，注重教育方法和策略，比如在语言复苏和兴盛（不包括业已消亡的语言的收复）的情况下，采用师生互动法进行教学。教育还包括学习、教学、学校教育和沉浸式学习。这些都是确保语言寿命的关键，尤其是在只有寥寥数人使用这种语言的时候。

● 公共领域：语言复兴的最后一个部分是把复兴的语言推广到公共领域，包括任何有意愿的公众和政府。

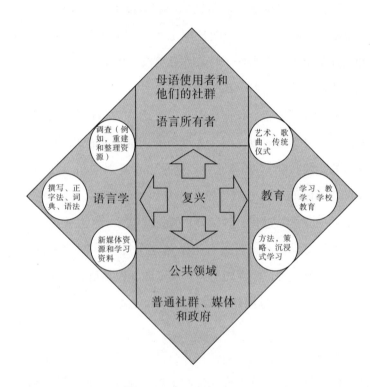

图 1　语言复兴菱形图①

---

① 更多详情，请参看 Ghil'ad Zuckermann 和 Rob Amery 2015 年开设的复兴语言学慕课，网址为 https：//www.edx.org/course/language-revival-securing-future-adelaidex-lang101x。

四、邦格拉语复兴运动的新进展

邦格拉人主要居住在澳大利亚南澳大利亚州艾尔半岛的林肯港、怀阿拉和奥古斯塔港，邦格拉语是邦格拉人的祖先所使用的语言。由于语言杀戮、殖民以及"被偷走的孩子"的影响，邦格拉语于 1960 年开始像睡美人一样陷入了沉睡。自 2011 年 9 月以来，邦格拉社区居民和诸葛漫教授紧密合作，开展了多种多样的研究、教学与宣传活动。在他们的不断努力下，邦格拉语正在慢慢苏醒：原有的一些词语被挖掘出来，新的词语在创制，邦格拉语的语法在编写。与此同时，邦格拉人的心理健康在改进，文化自信在增强（诸葛漫、陈燕 2017），语言的可持续发展带来的好处正在逐步显现。

（一）邦格拉语复兴活动的主要内容

从 2012 年起，邦格拉语复兴活动主要包括以下方面：

- 开展复兴专题讨论会。
- 加强与以史蒂芬·阿特金森（Stephen Atkinson）为主席的邦格拉语言咨询委员会的联系。
- 在艾尔半岛开展多种类型的邦格拉语复兴研讨会，例如 2017 年 8 月 22 日于林肯港以及 24 日于奥古斯塔港举办的研讨会，邦格拉族群的参会人数逾 120 人。
- 教授邦格拉语语法。

- 精心制作语法幻灯片（1000张）。
- 举办多样化的邦格拉语言咨询委员会会议，探索邦格拉语言复兴事业的未来。
- 改善并维护邦格拉网站①。
- 管理"南澳邦格拉人"脸书账号②，并吸引了500余名成员。
- 在精通邦格拉音乐的长者辞世之前，记录相关音乐。
- 在奥古斯塔港、阿德莱德以及林肯港机场举办邦格拉艺术展。
- 通过向市议员和其他参与者介绍邦格拉语符号，来改变艾尔半岛的语言面貌，例如普及"林肯港"的邦格拉语名称 Galinyala。
- 促使邦格拉人熟悉邦格拉语词典（不含宗教词汇和粗鄙词）。
- 教授邦格拉人现代邦格拉语拼写法。
- 支持林肯港（Galinyala）邦格拉青年运动（Yarniri Wilya）。
- 回答由邦格拉人及其他社群人民提出的众多关于邦格拉语的问题。

---

① 网址为http：//www.barngarla.com。
② 网址为https：//www.facebook.com/groups/Barngarla/。

- 向舒尔曼（Clamor Wilhelm Schürmann）的家人以及其他来自德国的伙伴介绍邦格拉。
- 促进位于林肯港的舒尔曼故居的考古挖掘。
- 在复兴语言学慕课①上，探讨邦格拉语复兴问题。
- 鼓励邦格拉人观看上述慕课。
- 向媒体及当地市政官员宣传邦格拉语及其他原住民语言的复兴。
- 在奥古斯塔港设立语言中心，在林肯港设立相关机构。
- 寻觅一位天赋异禀且具有雄心大志的邦格拉人到阿德莱德大学学习语言学和复兴语言学，培养其成为邦格拉语复兴运动的领导者（诸葛漫教授将为此人提供全额奖学金）。

（二）邦格拉语词典移动应用程序②

语法编写和词典编纂对语言复兴无疑是至关重要的。但是，为待复兴的语言所编写的语法和词典都必须符合语言复兴的要求，以对用户友好的方式呈现相关信息。邦格拉语留存于世的语言资料仅仅包括舒尔曼（Schürmann 1844）编写的一本邦格拉语词典和 Luise Hercus 在 1960 年代记录下来的零星资料（诸葛漫、陈燕 2017），要基于如此之少的语料去

---

① 该慕课的网址为 https：//www.edx.org/course/language-revival-securing-future-adelaidex-lang101x。
② 该程序英文名为 Barngarla Dictionary App。

复活邦格拉语的语法和词汇，相比当代词典编纂者拥有动辄达10亿词的语料库作为资源，无疑是困难重重、充满挑战的。过去的语料需要发掘和解读，新的词语必须创制出来以表现现代生活。比如，舒尔曼（Schürmann 1844）的词典录入了 *gaga-bibi*（大脑）一词，语言复兴讲习班的参与者经过商议之后，决定在其后添加 *waribirga*（电）一词，从而构成 *gagabibiwarigirga*（电脑），缩写为 *gabiwa*，这样就创造出了表示"电脑"的新词。值得注意是，*gagabibiwarigirga* 实际上是以毛利语（Māori）*rorohiko*（意为"大脑+闪电"）为依据创制的，保留了毛利语原词的结构，因此是一个仿译词（Goldsworthy 2014）。经过邦格拉社群和诸葛漫教授多年不懈的努力，他们联合开发设计的邦格拉语词典移动应用程序于2016年10月投入使用，这对邦格拉语的教学和传播将会起到巨大的作用。

与常见的词典应用程序相比，邦格拉语词典移动应用程序有着鲜明的特点。首先，应邦格拉族群长者的要求，剔除了宗教词汇和粗鄙词。其次，所有词语的语音都由邦格拉人（包括儿童）录制。此外，查询方式包括字母顺序查询，使用英语或邦格拉语查询均可，另外还提供了原住民的传统查询方式，即通过图片查询词语，而且图片中的人物通常为邦格拉人。比如，词语"困乏的"（英语 *to be sleepy*，邦格拉语

yarngoodoo）配置了邦格拉女性薇拉（Vera Richards）的女儿噶林亚拉（Galinyala）的照片，"小胡子"（英语 *moustache*，邦格拉语 *booldinooldini*）采用的是邦格拉人哈里（Harry Dare）的照片，两张图片都从某个侧面提示词语的概念意义。到目前为止，这部词典收录词语 3000 余条，其中 2000 余条是有文献记录的词语，但是收词量以后还会增加。有趣的是，即使某些词语确实出自舒尔曼（Schürmann 1844）的词典，也无法证明它们就是纯正的邦格拉语，因为舒尔曼本人在赴澳之前接受过拉丁语、英语、希腊语和希伯来语教育，这样的教育背景可能会在他记录下来的邦格拉语中留下印记，而当诸葛漫教授基于舒尔曼的词典重建邦格拉部分词汇时，又需要煞费苦心地和与邦格拉语相关的原住民语言进行比较，这样一点一点地重建邦格拉语。因此，"正如以色列语一样，复兴的邦格拉语本质上就是一种混合体，既带着诸葛漫的印记，也带着舒尔曼的印记"（Goldsworthy 2014）。这再一次证明，那种"不真实，毋宁死"（Give us authenticity or give us death）的纯语主义态度不符合语言复兴的要求，只有正视并接受复兴语的混合性，才能推动语言复兴实践的进程。

  邦格拉语词典移动应用程序的创制成功和邦格拉语的复兴不仅是对语言生态的重塑，而且是对历史错误的纠正。舒尔曼（Schürmann 1844）的那本邦格拉语词典本来是为了方便传播宗教，向"异教徒"展示基督教之光，在精神上削弱原住民，而在170余年后的今天，却帮助邦格拉人和他们的文化遗产重新联系起来（宋云谦、郭燕2017）。邦格拉语词典移动应用程序的发布，不仅便于邦格拉人随时随地查询和自学，也便于更多的族群了解邦格拉语，也许最终还会成为当地学校的教育资源。因此，这部词典不仅是邦格拉人学习母语的重要资源，也有助于他们重建文化自治、知识主权以及精神家园。

五、结　语

全球化的到来以及英语作为全球通用语地位的稳固已经对世界语言的生存、使用和分布格局产生了巨大的影响，对世界各地的语言多样性和文化多样性造成了不同程度的冲击。语言杀戮和语言同化不仅仅直接影响特定语言及其使用群体，甚至会影响整个社会的可持续性发展。澳大利亚殖民前后语言面貌的变化，尤其是原住民语言的消失，不仅给原住民的语言、文化、心理健康、生产生活等方方面面造成了严重后果，而且给澳大利亚整个国家留下了各种后遗症。即使澳大利亚政府对原住民土地和语言的丧失做出这样那样的补偿或赔偿，也无法弥合原住民与白人社会之间的裂痕。邦格拉语的复兴实践不仅给邦格拉族群带来了福祉，也给其他母语处于濒危状态的族群带来了希望和支持。虽然邦格拉语还远远没有恢复到成为邦格拉族群日常口语的地步，但是语言复兴活动对邦格拉人心理健康和幸福感的促进作用已经初步显现。事实已经证明，语言复兴运动所带来的好处目前已经远远超过了母语使用本身。从原住民的增权益能和幸福感方面来讲，当语言复兴过程结束时，即使被复兴语言的群体中并非所有成员在所有场合都使用该语言进行会话，我们也不能就此认定该语言复兴运动失败，因为复兴的过程与目标同等重要（诸葛漫、陈燕 2017）。我们相信，随着复兴活动的持续开展和深入，邦格拉人的语言生活和社会生活会逐步发生变化，复兴语言学的理论研究也将因此变得更加广阔、深入和丰富，复兴语言学的学科地位也将日益得到巩固。

参考文献

ABS（Australian Bureau of Statistics）. The health and welfare of Australia's Aboriginal and Torres Strait Islander peoples. ABS, Canberra: October 2010. (http://www.abs.gov.au/AUSSTATS/abs@.nsf/lookup/4704.0Chapter715Oct + 2010, accessed 1 December 2017)

Australian Institute of Aboriginal and Torres Strait Islander Studies & Federation of Aboriginal and Torres Strait Islander Languages.

National Indigenous Languages Survey Report 2005. Canberra: Department of Communications, Information Technology and the Arts, 2005.

Bartlett, Richard H. *Native Title in Australia*. Sydney: Butterworths, 2000.

Boroditsky, L. and A. Gaby. Remembrances of times East: Absolute spatial representations of time in an Australian Aboriginal community. *Psychological Science*, 2010, 21 (11): 1635–1639.

Clark, I. and L. Kostanski. Reintroducing indigenous place names-Lessons from Gariwerd, Victoria, Australia or how to address Toponymic dispossession in ways that celebrate cultural diversity and inclusiveness. Abstract submitted to *Names in Time and Space: Twenty Second International Congress of Onomastic Sciences*, 28 August – 4 September, 2005, Università Di Pisa, Italy.

Crystal, D. *Language Death*. Cambridge: Cambridge University Press, 2000.

De Boinod, Adam Jacot. *The Meaning of Tingo: And Other Extraordinary Words from around the World*. London: Penguin Press, 2005.

Dorian, Nancy C. Purism vs. compromise in language revitalization and language revival. *Language in Society*, 1994, 23 (4): 479 – 494.

Fishman, J. A. *Language Loyalty, Language Planning, and Language Revitalization: Recent Writings and Reflections from Joshua A. Fishman*, edited by Nancy Hornberger and Martin Pütz. Clevedon: Multilingual Matters, 2006.

Goldsworthy, A. Voices of the land. *The Monthly*, 2014 (9). https://www.themonthly.com.au/issue/2014/september/1409493600/anna-goldsworthy/voices-land, accessed 1 December 2017.

Grey, G. *Journals of Two Expeditions of Discovery in the North-west and Western Australia*. Vol. 2. London: T & W Boone, 1841.

Haffenden, J. *Novelists in Interview*. London and New York: Methuen, 1985.

Hallett, D., Michael J. Chandler and Christopher E. Lalonde. Aboriginal language knowledge and youth suicide. *Cognitive Development*, 2007 (22): 392 – 399.

Indigenous Remote Communications Association. *Language and Culture*, 2013. https://irca.net.au/resources/language-and-culture, accessed 1 December 2017.

Keysar, B., Sayuri L. Hayakawa and Sun Gyu An. The foreign-language effect: Thinking in a foreign tongue reduces decision biases. *Psychological Science*, 2012, 23 (6): 661 –668.

Kovács, Ágnes Melinda and J. Mehler. Flexible learning of multiple speech structures in bilingual infants. *Science*, 2009, 325 (5940): 611 –612.

Krizman, J., V. Marian, A. Shook, E. Skoe and N. Kraus. Subcortical encoding of sound is enhanced in bilinguals and relates to executive function advantages. *Proceedings of the National Academy of Sciences*, 2012, 109 (20): 7877 –7881.

Ridgeway, A. Language is power; let us have ours. *Sydney Morning Herald*, November 26, 2009. http://www.smh.com.au/opinion/language-is-power-let-us-have-ours-20091125-jrsb.html, accessed 1 December 2017.

Schmidt, W. *Sprachfamilien und Sprachenkreise der Erde*. Heidelberg: Carl Winters, 1927. [Atlas of 14 maps]

Scrimgeour, A. *Colonizers as Civilizers: Aboriginal Schools and the Mission to "Civilise" in South Australia, 1839 – 1845* [Ph. D. thesis]. Darwin: Charles Darwin University, 2007.

Zuckermann, Ghil'ad. Hybridity versus revivability: Multiple causation, forms and patterns. *Journal of Language Contact*, 2009

(2): 40 - 67. http://www.zuckermann.org/pdf/Hybridity_versus_Revivability.pdf, accessed 1 December 2017.

Zuckermann, Ghil'ad and Michael Walsh. Stop, revive, survive! Lessons from the Hebrew revival applicable to the reclamation, maintenance and empowerment of Aboriginal languages and cultures. *Australian Journal of Linguistics*, 2011 (31): 111 - 127. http://www.zuckermann.org/pdf/Revival_Linguistics.pdf, accessed 1 December 2017. Also published as Chapter 28 in Susan D. Blum (ed.). *Making Sense of Language: Readings in Culture and Communication*, 2nd ed. Oxford: Oxford University Press, 2012.

Zuckermann, Ghil'ad and Paul Monaghan. Revival linguistics and the new media: Talknology in the service of the Barngarla language reclamation. *Foundation for Endangered Languages XVI Conference: Language Endangerment in the 21st Century: Globalisation, Technology & New Media*. Auckland, NZ, 2012: 119 - 126. http://adelaide.academia.edu/Zuckermann/Papers/1971557/Revival_Linguistics_and_the_New_Media_Talknology_in_the_service_of_the_Barngarla_Language_Reclamation, accessed 1 December 2017.

Zuckermann, Ghil'ad and Michael Walsh. Language reclamation

and Aboriginal mental health: Breaking barriers in indigenous research and thinking. *AIATSIS 50 Years On*. Canberra, 26 – 28 March, 2014.

Zuckermann, Ghil'ad, Shiori Shakuto-Neoh and Giovanni Matteo Quer. Native tongue title: Proposed compensation for the loss of Aboriginal languages. *Australian Aboriginal Studies*, 2014 (1): 55 – 71.

Zuckermann, Ghil'ad and Rob Amery. *Massive Open Online Course (MOOC) on Language Revival*, 2015. https://www.edx.org/course/language-revival-securing-future-adelaidex-lang101x, accessed 1 December 2017.

诸葛漫, 陈燕. 原住民的语言复兴与心理健康: 以澳大利亚邦格拉语为中心 [J]. 语言战略研究, 2017 (4): 39 – 49.

宋云谦, 郭燕. 追寻远去的语言, 挖掘消失的失明——记"复兴语言学"掌门人、阿德莱德大学诸葛漫教, 2017. http://www.sohu.com/a/168855743_756019, published 4 September 2017, accessed 1 December 2017.

诸葛漫, 宋学东, 韩力. 希伯来圣经中词汇的语义世俗化 [J]. 犹太研究, 2015 (13): 30 – 40.

诸葛漫, 徐佳. 复兴语言学: 一个新的语言学分支 [J]. 语言教学与研究, 2013 (4): 100 – 106.

诸葛漫，姚春林. 试论澳大利亚原住民的母语权及语言赔偿 [J]. 北京大学学报（哲学社会科学版），2014（1）：152 - 159.

诸葛漫，姚春林. 一门新的语言学分支：复兴语言学——兼谈濒危语言和濒危方言复兴的普遍制约条件和机制 [J]. 徐佳，译. 世界民族，2012（6）：66 - 73.

诸葛漫. 混合还是复苏：以色列语的起源——多来源，形式和模式 [J]. 王晓梅，译. 南开语言学刊，2008（2）：23 - 35.

作者简介

诸葛漫（Ghil'ad Zuckermann），以色列人，牛津大学博士、剑桥大学博士。现任澳大利亚阿德莱德大学人文学院语言学和濒危语言系系主任、教授，主要研究方向：濒危语言和复兴语言学。

陈燕，厦门大学硕士、博士。现任盐城师范学院外国语学院教授，主要研究方向：词汇学、词典学。

金志茹，波兰华沙大学硕士、吉林师范大学硕士。现任吉林师范大学外国语学院教授、硕士研究生导师，主要研究方向：语言政策及语言规划。

语言政策与规划研究回顾

王曌君茹　于　晖

语言政策与规划（language policy and planning，简称 LPP）研究始于 20 世纪 60 年代。自兴起之初，该领域就是一个跨学科领域，融合语言学、社会学、政治学、人类学等多个学科的理论。LPP 研究以问题为导向，致力于解决语言政策制定、解读、应用、实施过程中遇到的问题（Hult and Johnson 2015）。近年来，LPP 越来越受到学界的关注，逐渐形成一套完整的理论体系和研究方法。本文梳理语言政策和语言规划的定义，回顾其理论发展进程，介绍语言政策的研究路径及主要话题，旨在为读者提供一个 LPP 研究的概念图景。

一、语言政策的定义

什么是语言政策？学界对此并无统一、确切的定义，更多是从目标、类型和政策范例等角度对语言政策进行阐释（Johnson 2016）。Haugen 最先将语言政策描述为"一种为规范拼写、语法和字典而准备的活动，旨在指导非同质言语社区中的书面和口头言语行为"（Haugen 1959：8）。此后，他进一步将语言政策解释为"选择"的结果，认为语言政策是人们通过选择的方式来评价语言及其变体的行为（Haugen 1966）。这一思想与 Spolsky 关于语言政策的论述有相似之处。Spolsky（2004）将言语社区中的语言政策分为三个部分：语言实践（language practice）、语言信仰或语言意识形态（language beliefs or ideology）、语言规划或语言管理（language management）。其中，语言实践是"对语言库中各种语言变体所做的习惯性的选择模式"（Spolsky 2004：5）。不同于语言管理，语言实践和语言信仰都是"没有管理者的语言政策"（Spolsky 2004：14），即语言使用者约定俗成地选择语言来做自己应该做的事。而语言管理则是带有主观意图的、通过语言干预来影响语言实践的行为。根据 Spolsky 的观点，语言实践和语言信仰是语言政策的一部分，而非语言政策的产物。Schiffman（1996）的"语言文化"（linguistic culture）观同样把语言信仰、语言态度和意识形态视作语言政策的基础，它们与语言政策之间不存在因果关系。Schiffman 指出，语言政策既是一种社会结构（social construct），也是一种文化结构（culture construct）。前者通常由权威政体颁布的语言政策文本，即显性的语言政策组成，后者则体现为与语言使用者相关的思想、价值观、意识形态等隐性的语言政策。

　　上述对"语言政策"的界定不局限于"政策"的传统意义，即由政府或权威机构颁布的关于语言使用的规章制度。语言政策包括多个层面。总体上来看，它既涉及官方的法律法规，也包含非官方的言语社区中隐含的语言态度和文化价值。鉴于此，Johnson（2016）将语言政策类型按照二分法分为"自上而下"（top-down）的语言政策和"自下而上"（bottom-up）的语言政策。"自上而下"的语言政策由管理部门或权威机构提出，是明确的（explicit）、显性的（overt）的语言政策，有以书面形式或口头形式公开表达的政策文本；"自下而上"的语言政策是由言语社区产生的、模糊的（implicit）、隐性的（covert）语言政策，没有官方的政策文本（Johnson 2016：10）。Johnson 还用"法定的"（de jure）与"实际的"（de facto）两个概念来阐释两种类型的区别。显性的语言政策是基于法律法规的，而隐性的语言政策则是客观实践中真正实施的行为。

与"语言政策"紧密相关的另一个术语是"语言规划"。两者常常同时使用,但具体意义有所不同。Haugen(1987)认为语言规划是社会规划的一部分,旨在改变社区中的言语行为。Kloss(1969)将语言规划分为"本体规划"(corpus planning)和"地位规划"(status planning)。在"本体规划"中,规划者通过干预完善语言的形式和结构,重点在语言的规范化和标准化。而"地位规划"则决定某种语言在社会交际中的地位。Rubin(1977)对语言规划的定义更具现代意义。他指出,语言规划是由专门的机构制定出来的有意图的语言改变,目的是改变语言形式(本体规划)和语言使用(地位规划),或两者兼有。同样关注语言本体和其社会影响的还有Cooper(1989),他认为语言规划是基于语言内部特征(语言习得、语言结构和功能)制定的影响人们行为的活动,体现出语言的社会属性。Hornberger(2006)在前人的基础上整合出一个总体框架,从规划类型和研究范式两个角度对语言规划进行分类:规划类型包括"本体规划""地位规划"和"习得规划"(acquisition planning);研究范式则包括国家层面的"政策规划"(policy planning)和具体教学层面的"培育规划"(cultivation planning)。关于语言规划的目的,胡壮麟(1993)认为语言规划是为了解决社会交际问题，这些问题既有语言学的，也有非语言学的。陈章太（2005）进一步指出，语言规划是为了让语言文字更好地服务于社会。

对于"语言政策"和"语言规划"的关系，研究者看法不一。Fishman（1972）认为语言政策制定先于语言规划，语言规划是语言政策的执行。与之相反，Schiffman（1996）认为语言政策是语言规划的一部分，从属于语言规划。Fettes（1997）则认为两者相互补充、相辅相成。语言规划为政策提供有效标准，语言政策检验规划的可信性。由于语言政策与语言规划在概念上有所重叠，不少学者将其合二为一，使用"语言政策与规划"（language policy and planning）这一概念（Hornberger 2006）。

二、语言政策与规划的理论发展

LPP 研究兴起于 20 世纪 60 年代。早期的语言规划研究致力于构建本学科的理论框架，明确"本体规划"和"地位规划"的区别。其中较有影响力的是 Haugen（1966，1983）提出的语言规划模型，将语言规划分为四个阶段："选择标准"（selection of a norm）、"编制标准"（codification）、"实施标准"（implementation）、"扩展标准"（elaboration）。"选择标准"和"实施标准"属于语言的地位规划，"编制标准"

和"扩展标准"则属于本体规划。其他学者也探讨过"本体规划"与"地位规划"的关联，或对 Haugen 模型进行细化和拓展（Kloss 1968；Rubin 1971；Jernudd and Das Gupta 1971）。Ricento（2000）指出早期的语言规划将"本体规划"和"地位规划"看作相对独立、意识形态中立的活动，受结构主义语言学的影响，将语言与社会文化背景区分开来。

20 世纪 80 年代到 90 年代，LPP 研究进入第二阶段。第一阶段的议题同样受到关注，但也有学者质疑早期语言规划模型的可行性。社会语言学家和批评语言学家认为语言不应该独立于历史文化和社会背景。Hymes（1972）提出的"交际能力"（communicative competence）指出语言的讨论离不开社会文化的维度，对语言政策研究影响深远。同时他提出的交际民族志（ethnography of communication）被广泛应用到语言政策与规划研究中来。例如，Hornberger（1988）用民族志研究法探究秘鲁的语言规划与双语教育，关注语言规划对学校和社区语言使用的影响。

批评语言学家则认为语言规划是一种潜在的"霸权机制"（hegemonic mechanism）（Ruiz 1984；Tollefson 1991），语言政策有明确的政治目的和意识形态。Tollefson（1991）据此提出历史—结构分析路径（historical-structural analysis），聚焦推动语言政策制定过程中的历史和社会政治因素，并结合Bourdieu（1991）、Foucault（1991）等人的批评理论，发展了"批评性语言政策"（critical language policy）（Tollefson 2006）。批评性语言政策旨在揭示语言政策创造和维持过程中的不平等现象，减少社会不平等现象，保持少数民族的语言。批评性语言政策提醒人们关注语言的社会文化背景和意识形态，为语言政策研究提供了新视角。但Johnson（2016：42）认为，批评性语言政策关注政策本身的权利，而民族志研究关注执行者的能动性，两者应该相互平衡。

20世纪末到21世纪初是LPP研究发展的第三阶段。民族志研究法和话语分析盛行，政策文本和政策话语对语言实践的影响受到关注（Davis 1994；Freeman 1998）。此外，第三阶段的语言政策研究延续批评性语言政策的思潮，融入了后现代主义理论。加上世界局势的变换，语言权利和社会意识形态问题尤其突出，语言政策的研究视角逐渐多元化，政治学、经济学和法学学科的研究方法也被应用到LPP研究中来。

Kymlicak和Pattern（2003）探讨了语言权利与政治理论的关系，认为语言在政治中扮演了重要的角色，语言政策与民主、平等、统一密切关联。许多国家都存在多民族的语言，过去普遍认为这种语言的多样化会随着现代化进程的推进而消亡。然而在国际政治中，不管是东欧出现的民族冲突，加拿大等地的民族分裂运动，还是建立泛欧洲统一体所面临的诸多困难，这一系列现象都表明，语言多样化问题不容忽视。

东欧剧变后爆发的民族冲突，部分原因是单一官方语言政策引发了少数民族语者的抗议。与东欧情况类似的还有欧洲传统的多语种国家，如比利时、西班牙、瑞士、意大利等。Kymlicak 和 Pattern（2003）指出，传统的强势主导语言与地区性语言的冲突永远存在，这种语言冲突往往会升级为民族冲突，最终成为难以愈合的民族矛盾。移民在文化融合时面临的困难很大程度也是因为语言的不同。语言迁移不可避免，因此不少移民国家通过加强语言政策的执行力度来削弱少数民族的语言权力。以美国的语言政策为例。针对日渐兴起的多元文化主义，美国采取各种举措，如加大语言培训的投入，加强语言测试的力度等，其目的就是加强英语语言的地位（Pickus 1998；Piller 2001；Rhee 1999）。同样，语言也是妨碍欧盟成为更牢固的统一体的主要障碍，因为国家的融合势必牵涉语言的融合。基于此，世界上日渐消亡的各种土语日益受到语言学者的重视。这些问题都涉及语言的权利，但Kymlicak 和 Pattern（2003）也承认，语言权利的界定难以把握。少数民族语言的保护问题将长期存在，围绕语言政策的规范化问题仍需进一步研究。

从 20 世纪 60 年代兴起到现在，LPP 领域的发展日渐成熟，研究从多个层面阐释语言现象，从关注语言本体规划到探究语言的社会背景及潜在的意识形态。语言政策理论框架不断完善，但 Ricento（2006）认为，语言政策与规划依旧缺乏宏大的理论。尤其在特定语言政策的制定和实施方面还存在不足。语言政策与规划需要"跨学科"发展，从其他领域（政策、法律、教育等）的理论和实践中汲取经验。

三、语言政策与规划的研究方法

语言政策与规划的研究角度众多，并无统一具体的方法论指导，但不同的研究范式从不同维度揭示了语言政策的制定、解读及实施过程。早期的语言规划研究以实证观察法和历史回顾法为主（Johnson 2016）。研究者通过理论观察，描写特定语言项目，分析政策执行策略等来呈现某个政体特定的语言政策。Hornberger（2006）回顾了早期语言政策研究，整合出语言政策研究的概念框架。其中，Hornberger 指出，"政策规划"注重语言在社会中的形式，规划内容包括语言国家化、语言官方化、在不同地点（学校、宗教、媒体、职场等）的语言标准等。"培育规划"则关注语言在社会中的功能，包括语言保持、语言传播以及语言习得过程中的听说读写问题（Hornberger 2006：28）。Hornberger 的框架尽管并非研究方法，但突出了语言政策研究的重点，为后续研究奠定了基础。

本节将重点介绍 LPP 研究中常用的几种方法，包括民族志研究、历史—结构分析和话语分析。

(一) 民族志研究

受社会语言学家 Hymes "交际民族志"的影响，民族志研究成为语言政策研究的主要方法。Wolcott（2008）认为，民族志研究就是透过"滤镜"揭示人类文明的方式，整个过程扎根于长期一手的田野调查，人们通过社会实践建构自己对文化的解读。就语言政策而言，民族志研究者将政策视为一种社会文化进程，包括影响人们日常语言选择的社会实践、意识形态、语言态度等机制（McCarty 2011：xii）。Wolcott（2008：48）将民族志研究分为三个阶段：从参与或观察中体验；在正式或非正式访谈中提问；在政策文献和文化分析中核查。Hornberger 和 Johnson（2007）推出"语言政策民族志研究"，以规划文件和政策文本为单位，提出调查问题，直接关注语言政策的制定过程。McCarty，Romeo-Little 和 Zepeda（2006）用民族志研究法研究了美国一所印第安学校学生的母语迁移和保持情况。研究者通过观察和访谈等方式，发现学生对本族语有强烈的兴趣和学习意愿，但文化压制和种族歧视使他们对母语的使用充满怀疑与不确定性。除了传统的田野调查，叙事分析、话语分析、社交地图等方法在语言政策的民族志研究中也较为常见。Ricento & Hornberger（1996）用洋葱来比喻语言政策与规划的多层次：洋葱的"外表皮"代表语言政策与规划的进程，而洋葱的"中心"则代表基层言语社区日常语言实践中对政策的实施、否决和改变。民族志研究就是将"洋葱"层层剥开，探究语言政策这一有机体的各个层面。

（二）历史—结构分析

受批评理论的影响，历史—结构分析也成为语言政策研究的重要研究方法。Tollefson（1991）对语言政策研究的"新古典主义方法"（neoclassical approach）和历史—结构分析法进行对比。新古典主义方法关注国家层面的语言政策，特别是后殖民时代多语国家的少数民族语言教育，对国家语言政策在社会文化融合和经济发展中所起的作用持积极态度。与之相反，历史—结构分析关注的是语言规划中的不公平现象，包括经济资源和政治权利的不平等分配。历史—结构分析包括"历史"和"结构"两个层面。语言政策所处的历史背景各不相同，例如，殖民主义是后殖民时代的主要特点，由此引发的殖民国语言和本族语言的冲突是语言政策研究关注的问题。语言政策关注与之相关的历史进程是如何导致语言地位的不平等的。"结构"则与研究者的意识形态相关。历史—结构分析法的核心是权利（power），包括政体权利、意识形态权利和话语权利。相关研究围绕权利分配展开：涉及宏观层面的研究，如政策中涉及的民族、种族、性别问题（Tollefson 2011）以及语言在社会政治中扮演的角色（Forester 1985）；也涉及微观层面的话语交流、身份构建等问题，例如Pérez-Milan（2013）研究了语言课堂中的历史—结构因素，旨在理解教师与学生在政策规范和意识形态作用下社会身份的建构。McCarty（2011）提出历史—结构分析（也叫历史—话语分析、历史—文本分析）的概念框架，列举了与"本体规划""地位规划""习得规划"三种类型对应的历史—结构分析内容。"本体规划"包括诸如教育标准化、规范化、权威性及文化认同等话题。"地位规划"则关注语言帝国主义（linguistic imperialism）、就业市场语言分级、语言与国家认同等。"习得规划"聚焦资源公平性对教学和教师培训的影响、全球化与英语语言政策以及英语语言的工具性等问题。

然而历史—结构分析法也存在不足之处（Johnson 2016）。一方面，该研究方法更依赖于研究者对文本的主观解读，容易先入为主。另一方面，历史—结构分析的"微观"层面，即基层对语言政策的解读和实践研究还有所欠缺。

（三）话语分析

很多语言政策分析实质上是话语分析，围绕着各种书面的或口头的政策文本展开。与政策文本相关的话语（新闻媒体、课堂话语、法律话语等）也成为研究对象。Barakos 和 Unger（2016）认为语言政策是一种多维度的意识形态现象，对语言使用者的信念及价值观的构建、改变和重塑有重要影响。话语研究融合了不同的理论框架和研究方法，为语言政策和规划的多个层面提供了新的阐释途径。

对于"话语"的定义，Jaworski & Coupland（1999）认为话语既指语言的使用，也是基于社会情景构建世界的实践手段。因此，语言政策研究的话语路径旨在对语言政策及相关社会实践进行文本、语境和社会历史分析（Barakos & Unger 2016：3）。话语路径转向要求政策分析超越文本层面，从时间和空间维度上探究政策的形成过程，充分关注政策制定过程中的参与者，以及政策在社会情景下的历时和共时变化。

批评话语分析是语言政策话语分析的主要方法。批评话语分析关注权利，基本思想是：语言可以塑造社会，社会反过来也可以塑造语言（Johnson 2016）。这与语言政策理论发展对语言权利和意识形态的凸显相契合。用于政策分析的批评话语分析理论主要有 Fairclough 的"三维模型"（Fairclough 1995）和 Wodak 的"话语—历史分析法"（the discourse-historical approach）（Wodak & Meyer 2001）。Fairclough（1995）指出，对于话语事件，可以从文本、话语实践和社会实践三个层面进行分析。文本即自身的内容和形式，可能包括词汇、语法、衔接等；话语实践即文本的生成、传播和消费；社会实践则指话语的社会文化背景。Fairclough 的模型对语言政策的研究适用性较强，因为语言政策是话语实践的产物，应该从话语的多个方面进行探究。Wodak 提出的"话语—历史分析法"结合语言数据及其社会背景，从四个维度进行话语分析：①语篇内部分析，包括语篇主题、词汇语法、语用策略等；②语篇互文性和互语性分析；③语篇外部的社会变体和社会情景分析；④社会政治和历史情景分析（Wodak & Meyer 2001：67）。

批评话语分析既照顾到话语内部特征，也关注了话语的社会文化背景。应用批评话语分析研究语言政策可以涵盖语言政策的多个层面：既对政策文本本身进行阐释，也呈现社会实践与社会文化之间的关联。

采用什么样的研究范式和研究方法应当根据语言政策的研究问题和研究对象来决定。Johnson（2016）根据语言政策制定的不同阶段，归纳了主要的研究方法（见表1）。

表1　语言政策分析研究方法（Johnson 2016：160）

语言政策与语言规划活动	行为主体	研究方法
政策制定	政策制定者。例如，国会议员和其他政要、商界领袖、法官和律师、多语和单语的倡导者和活动家、学区管理人员和教师	历史—文本分析法；民族志研究，包括局内人的描述（访谈）和政策制定过程中的参与式观察；对政治和政策辩论及其形成过程的话语分析；宏观层次的文献收集
政策阐释	政策阐释者。例如，政策制定者（即他们如何解释自己制定的政策），以及那些负责政策援用的人员，尤其是教师、雇主和教育管理者	关于话语实践阐释的话语分析（话语的产出和解释过程）；访谈和参与式观察；中观层次的文献收集
政策援用	政策援用者，以及语言政策的受影响者。主要包括教师和学生、雇主和雇员、家长和孩子	参与式观察；访谈；互动过程的话语分析（通过音频和视频录制采集）；微观层次的文献收集
政策实施	政策实施者。包括教师、学生和社区成员	教室和社区中的参与式观察；教室和社区中互动过程的话语分析

从政策制定到具体实施，Johnson 归纳的研究方法围绕整个语言规划过程展开。语言政策与规划是一个"跨学科"领域。单一的研究方法无法适用于语言政策研究的多个层面。因此，多种研究方法相互借鉴、相互补充，才能更加全面地探究语言政策与规划的各个维度。

四、语言政策与规划研究的主要话题

（一）语言教育政策研究

20 世纪 90 年代起，有大批学者致力于双语或多语的教育话语分析（Arthur 1996；Heller 1999；Heller & Martin-Jones 2001；Lin & Martin 2005）。研究关注语言教育政策（language education policy）中的语言权利分配、少数民族双语教育的有效性以及宏观的语言政策是如何被解读、被转换到学校的语境中来的。

双语教育是实现语言转化的主要工具。从国家宏观调控政策看，双语教育的目的通常是使少数民族尽快融入主流文化和团体；从另一方面来看，双语教育也是帮助语言复兴和逆袭的重要途径。少数民族仅凭家庭中的语言输入和输出往往不够，双语教育就成为促进语言保持和帮助语言复兴的重要手段。然而从语言宏观调控看，双语教育并非是放之四海皆准的灵药，双语教育的有效性也不仅仅是因为在课堂上使用了两种语言。人们对双语教育的效果往往会有过于乐观的预期，双语教育自身很难独自承担重任，需要社会、文化、宗教等机构团体的一致努力。

双语教育往往与国家的宏观政策调控相关，这就决定了双语教育的政治属性，而这种语言实践往往会制造少数民族与主体民族之间的不平等关系。Tollefson（2002）研究教育机构自上而下的语言政策，认为语言权利存在不平等现象，少数民族语言及其使用者往往被排斥在外。而 García 和 Menken（2010）则认为语言政策执行者有自主性和主观能动性，在自上而下的政策话语生成过程中，可以通过协商，在具体实践中创造性地引用政策内容。课堂话语由此成为研究政策解读和实践的对象。例如，Rojo（2010）结合民族志研究法，对西班牙的双语教育课堂进行话语分析。研究发现，能接受双语教育项目的少数民族群体有限，双语教育对少数民族群体包容性不强。Cincotta-Segi（2011）则调查了老挝北部的三所小学，对双语课堂进行了详细的话语分析。研究结果显示，尽管教师缺乏足够的训练，但他们会通过极富创造性的方式对语言政策进行阐释，同时满足学生的需求。

基于课堂的话语研究从实施层面和意识形态层面为双语教育政策执行提供了空间，促进了政策制定者和实施者的对话。与民族志研究相结合的课堂话语分析为语言政策的解读和应用研究提供了有效的途径。

（二）政治和法律环境分析

语言政策与规划同样受到政治和法律学家们的关注。从政治、法律的角度分析语言政策，旨在揭示政策制定过程中，政治和法律环境对其产生的影响或语言政策在政治组织和司法系统中的作用。研究通常围绕与政策相关的历史文本、法律文献、司法判决、官方政策等文件展开。

语言在任何司法程序中都起到至关重要的作用，有时法律过程也是操控语言的过程。Eades（2003）回顾了语言在法律程序中的应用，发现现有研究大多聚焦庭审中的语言，对其他司法程序中的场景甚少涉及。1966年联合国制定的《公民权利和政治权利国际公约》明确规定，被告有权通过他所懂的语言获悉所受指控。然而在实践中，单语倾向、对移民和土著的歧视往往影响了司法的公正性。法律中的这些语言现象促使语言学者研究和思考相关的问题，诸如二语者有哪些翻译需求，这些需求如何满足。另外，与语言政策相关的法律及司法判决程序如何尽可能地保障少数民族语言权利、维护政策分配公平性、实现双语教育的有效性也成为语言政策研究者关注的话题。

语言同样影响国家认同和公民身份的构建。特别是在移民和归化问题愈演愈烈的今天，国家的语言政策与国家统一息息相关。例如，法国通过标准化法语实现"一个国家，一种语言"的意识形态（Piller 2001）；但García（1997）指出，在"欧盟身份"的建构上，欧盟的多语制也可能实现力量的统一。语言之外的因素，包括共同文化和共同价值观也是一致的基础。Blommaert（1999）以斯瓦希里语为例，探究了语言政策对恢复国家认同的重要意义。20世纪60年代中期，为了重新构建国家认同，坦桑尼亚将本族语定为国家语言，而在这之前，坦桑尼亚的官方语言是殖民国的语言——英语。斯瓦希里语很快成为政治、教育、媒体等各个领域的主要用语。Blommaert（1999）认为坦桑尼亚的国家认同并不在于种族或文化因素，而是基于政治意识形态和语言政策的施行。

（三）商业话语中的语言接触

随着全球化进程的日益推进，英语在世界各地广泛传播，英语已成为世界上使用最广泛的通用语言。英语作为国际语言在全世界各个领域得到了广泛应用。在多个领域，如商务、技术、科学、互联网、娱乐、体育、学术会议等，英语都成为首选语言。对商业话语的语言规划研究，聚焦于英语的主导地位是否会造成文化地位的不平等。Harris & Bargiela-Chiappini（2003）探讨了商业背景下的语言接触，指出研究者应当考虑如何平衡以英语为代表的西方文化与其他弱势文化的地位。与此同时，有关跨文化商务语言的研究多以英文发表，以其他语言发表的相关著作的影响力较小，但这些研究文献为跨文化分析提供了研究基础。

广告也是商业话语中重要的研究对象。全球化的推进促使多语现象成为广告语言的主要手段，呈现出渐强的态势。早期对广告语言的研究多关注借词的使用或广告用词的形态。20世纪80年代以来，研究开始关注广告中通过各种语言的身份构建及与之相关的典型民族文化形象，如英语的使用常常与"国际认可、可靠、自信、高质量、实用"等特点相连，法语的使用则被视为"优雅、精致、迷人"的典范，德语代表"可靠、精准、卓越的技术"（Kelly-Holmes 2000）。以美国为代表的英语国家在国际市场和广告界占据无可争议的引领地位，英语在广告中不再体现民族文化形象，而是代表一种社会典型形象，即现代、进步和全球化。在美国品牌所代表的价值和品位向世界各个角落输出的同时，一些超级品牌却反其道而行之，采用去英语手段实现其多元化营销策略（Klein 2001）。语言接触作为语言政策研究的重要话题，关注不同语言、文化在不同场合的交流与融合。语言接触引起的双语或多语现象需要语言规划来协调。如何保持语言的多样性，实现主要语言和少数民族语言地位发展的平衡是语言政策研究者需要继续深入研究的课题。

五、结　语

本文讨论语言政策与规划研究,追溯"语言政策"和"语言规划"的定义,回顾了语言政策与规划研究的发展历程。同时结合研究案例,介绍了语言政策研究常用的方法,包括民族志研究、历史—结构分析和话语分析几种主要途径。语言政策涉及的话题较广,文中围绕语言教育政策、政治和法律文本以及商业话语中的语言接触,呈现了语言政策与规划研究的多个层面。随着理论不断完善,未来该领域研究将呈多元化态势,逐步由"交叉学科向超学科过渡发展"(张天伟 2016:46)。研究者将融合多学科研究手段,对语言政策的宏观和微观层面进行更加细致、深入的探究。

参考文献

Arthur, J. Codeswitching and collusion: Classroom interaction in Botswana primary schools. *Linguistics and Education*, 1996, 8(1): 17–34.

Barakos, E. and J. Unger. *Discursive Approaches to Language Policy*. London: Palgrave Macmillan, 2016.

Blommaert, J. *State Ideology and Language in Tanzan*ia. Cologne: Köppe, 1999.

Bourdieu, P. *Language and Symbolic Power*. Cambridge, MA: Harvard University Press, 1991.

Cincotta-Segi, A. R. Signaling L2 centrality, maintaining L1 dominance: Teacher language choice in an ethnic minority primary classroom in the Lao PDR. *Language and Education*, 2011, 25 (1): 19 –31.

Cooper, R. L. *Language Planning and Social Change.* Cambridge: Cambridge University Press, 1989.

Davis, K. A. *Language Planning in Multilingual Contexts: Policies, Communities, and Schools in Luxembourg.* Amsterdam and Philadelphia: John Benjamins, 1994.

Davis, K. A. Dynamics of indigenous language maintenance. In T. Huebner and K. A. Davis (eds.). *Sociopolitical Perspectives on Language Policy and Planning in the USA.* Amsterdam and Philadelphia: John Benjamins, 1999: 67 –89.

Eades, D. Participation of second language and second dialectspeakers in the legal system. In M. McGroarty (ed.). *Language Contact and Change.* Beijing: The Commercial Press, 2003: 250 –272.

Fairclough, N. *Critical Discourse Analysis: The Critical Study of Language.* London and New York: Longman, 1995.

Fettes, M. Language planning and education. In R. Wodak and D. D. Corson (eds.). *Language Policy and Political Issues in Education.* Dordrecht: Kluwer Academic, 1997: 13 –34.

Fishman, J. A. Domains and relationship between micro and macro Sociolinguistics. In J. J. Gumperz and D. Hymes (eds.). *Directions in Sociolinguistics.* New York: Holt Rinehart and Winston, 1972: 345 –367.

Forester, J. *Critical Theory and Public Life.* Cambridge, MA: MIT Press, 1985.

Foucault, M. Governmentality. In G. Burchell, C. Cordon and P. Miller (eds.). *The Foucault Effect: Studies in Governmentality*. Chicago: The University of Chicago Press, 1991: 5 – 22.

Freeman, R. D. *Bilingual Education and Social Change*. Clevedon: Multilingual Matters, 1998.

García, S. European Union identity andcitizenship: Some challenges. In M. Roche and R. van Berkel (eds.). *European Citizenship and Social Exclusion*. Aldershot: Ashgate, 1997: 47 – 68.

García, O. and K. Menken. Stirring the onion: Educators and the dynamics of language education policies (looking ahead). In K. Menken and O. García (eds.). *Negotiating Language Policies in Schools: Educators as Policymakers*. London and New York: Routledge, 2010: 132 – 146.

Harris, S. and F. Bargiela-Chiappini. Business as a site of language contact. In M. McGroarty (ed.). *Language Contact and Change*. Beijing: The Commercial Press, 2003: 290 – 310.

Haugen, E. Planning for a standard language in Norway. *Anthropological Linguistics*, 1959, 1 (3): 8 – 21.

Haugen, E. Linguistics and language planning. In W. Bright (ed.). *Sociolinguistics*. The Hague: Mouton, 1966: 50 – 71.

Haugen, E. The implementation of corpus planning: Theory and practice. In J. Cobarrubias and J. A. Fishman (eds.). *Progress in Language Planning: International Perspectives*. Berlin: Mouton de Gruyter, 1983: 269 – 291.

Haugen, E. *Blessing of Babel: Bilingualism and Language*

Planning. Berlin and New York: Mouton de Gruyter, 1987.

Heller, M. *Linguistic Minorities and Modernity*. London: Longman, 1999.

Heller, M. and M. Martin-Jones. *Voices of Authority: Education and Linguistic Difference*. Westport, CT: Ablex, 2001.

Hornberger, N. H. *Bilingual Education and Language Maintenance*. Dordrecht: Foris Publications, 1988.

—— Frameworks and models in language policy and planning. In T. Ricento (ed.). *An Introduction to Language Policy: Theory and Method*. Malden: Blackwell Publishing, 2006: 24–43.

Hornberger, N. H. and D. C. Johnson. Slicing the onion ethnographically: Layers and spaces in multilingual language education policy and practice. *TESOL Quarterly*, 2007, 41 (3): 509–532.

Hult, F. M. and D. C. Johnson (eds.). *Research Methods in Language Policy and Planning: A Practical Guide*. Hoboken, NJ: Wiley-Blackwell, 2015.

Hymes, D. On communicative competence. In J. B. Pride and J. Holmes (eds.). *Sociolinguistics: Selected Readings*. Harmondsworth: Penguin Books, 1972: 269–293.

Jaworski, A. and N. Coupland. *The Discourse Reader*. London and New York: Routledge, 1999.

Jernudd, B. and J. Das Gupta. Towards a theory of language planning. In J. Rubin and B. Jernudd (eds.). *Can Language Be Planned? Sociolinguistic Theory and Practice for Developing Nations*. Honolulu: The University Press of Hawaii, 1971: 195–215.

Johnson, D. C. *Language Policy*. Trans. Fang Xiaobing. Beijing: Foreign Language Teaching and Research Press, 2016.

Kelly-Holmes, H. Bier, Parfum, Kaas: Language fetish in European advertising. *European Journal of Cultural Studies*, 2000 (3): 67 -82.

Klein, N. *No Logo*. London: HarperCollins, 2001.

Kloss, H. Notes concerning a language-nation typology. In J. Fishman, C. Freguson, and J. Das Gupta (eds.). *Language Problems of Developing Nations*. New York: John Wiley and Sons, 1968: 69 -85.

Kloss, H. *Research Possibilities on Group Bilingualism: A Report*. Quebec: International Center for Research on Bilingualism, 1969.

Kymlicak, W. and A. Pattern. Language rights and political theory. In M. McGroarty (ed.). *Language Contact and Change*. Beijing: The Commercial Press, 2003: 35 -58.

Lin, A. M. Y. and P. W. Martin. *Decolonization, Globalization: Language-in-Education Policy and Practice*. Clevedon, UK: Multilingual Matters, 2005.

McCarty, T. L. Preface. In T. L. McCarty (ed.). *Ethnography and Language Policy*. New York: Routledge, 2011.

McCarty, T. L., M. E. Romeo-Little and O. Zepeda. Native American youth discourse on language shift and retention: Ideological cross-currents and their implications for language planning. *International Journal of Bilingual Education and Bilingualism*, 2006 (9): 659 -677.

Pérez-Milan, M. *Urban Schools and English Language Education* in Late Modern China: A Critical Sociolinguistic Ethnography. New York: Routledge, 2013.

Pickus, N. To make natural: Creating citizensfor the twenty-first century. In N. Pickus (ed.). *Immigration and Citizenship in the 21st Century.* Lanham, MD: Rowman and Littlefield, 1998: 143 – 167.

Piller, I. Naturalization language testing and its basis in ideologies of national identity and citizenship. *International Journal of Bilingualism*, 2001 (5): 259 – 277.

Rhee, J. Theories of citizenship and their role in the bilingual education debate. *Columbia Journal of Law and Social Problem*, 1999 (33): 33 – 83.

Ricento, T. and N. H. Hornberger. Unpeeling the onion: Language planning and policy and the ELT professional. *TESOL Quarterly*, 1996 (4): 196 – 213.

Ricento, T. Historical and theoretical perspectives inlanguage policy and planning. *Journal of Sociolinguistics*, 2000, 4 (2): 196 – 213.

— *An Introduction to Language Policy: Theory and Method.* Malden, MA: Blackwell Publishing, 2006.

Rojo, M. *Constructing Inequality in Multilingual Classrooms.* Berlin: Mouton de Gruyter, 2010.

Rubin, J. Evaluation and language planning. In J. Rubin and B. H. Jernudd (eds.). *Can Language Be Planned? Sociolinguistic Theory and Practice for Developing Nations.* Honolulu: The University Press of Hawaii, 1971: 277 – 279.

Rubin, J. Bilingual education and language planning. In B. Spolsky and R. L. Cooper (eds.). *Frontiers of Bilingual Education*. Rowley, MA: Newbury House Publishers, 1977: 21-40.

Ruiz, R. Orientations in language planning. *NABE Journal*, 1984, 8 (2): 15-34.

Schiffman, H. F. *Linguistic Culture and Language Policy*. London and New York: Routledge, 1996.

Spolsky, B. *Language Policy: Key Topics in Sociolinguistics*. Cambridge: Cambridge University Press, 2004.

Tollefson, J. W. *Planning Language, Planning Inequality: Language Policy in the Community*. London: Longman, 1991.

—*Language Policies in Education: Critical Issues*. Mahwah, NJ: Lawrence Erlbaum Publishers, 2002.

— Critical theory in language policy. In T. Ricento (ed.). *An Introduction to Language Policy: Theory and Method*. Malden: Blackwell Publishing, 2006: 42-59.

—Language planning and Language policy. In R. Mesthrie (ed.). *The Cambridge Handbook of Sociolinguistics*. Cambridge: Cambridge University Press, 2011: 43-55.

United Nations. *International Covenant on Civil and Political Rights*, 1966. https://en.wikipedia.org/wiki/International_Covenant_on_Civil_and_Political_Rights.

Wodak, R. and M. Meyer. *Methods of Critical Discourse Analysis*. London: Sage Publications, 2001.

Wolcott, H. F. *Ethnography: A Way of Seeing*. Lanham, MD:

AltaMira Press, 2008.
陈章太. 语言规划研究 [M]. 北京：商务印书馆, 2005.
胡壮麟. 语言规划 [J]. 语言文字应用, 1993 (2): 11-20.
张天伟. 语言规划与政策研究 [J]. 外语电化教学, 2016 (168): 40-47.

作者简介：

王罂君茹，北京师范大学外文学院硕士研究生，主要研究方向：系统功能语言学、语篇分析。

于晖，中山大学博士。现任北京师范大学外文学院语言学教授，主要研究方向：系统功能语言学、语篇分析。

Protecting Endangered Languages and Dialects in China

Chang Chenguang

Language endangerment

Although there is still some debate about the exact number of languages spoken in the world today, most scholars in the linguistic sciences agree that the total number is well over 6,000. Whatever the exact number, this number is diminishing, and it is doing so at an alarming rate. As Crystal (1997: 17) estimates, "80% of the world's 6,000 or so living languages will die" within the 21st century. Apparently this should worry anyone who regards linguistic diversity and linguistic sustainability as healthy phenomena in the same way that we may worry about biodiversity and ecological sustainability.

Fortunately, there has been growing awareness of endangered language protection, at least among linguists. In fact, according to Nettle and Romaine (2000: 23), language endangerment is increasingly seen as a topic that primarily concerns linguists. We have also seen the increase in the number of international organizations formed to record endangered languages and to regulate and promote the linguistic rights of minority language communities. In the past few decades, there have been various initiatives to foster awareness of the accelerating rate of language diversity loss. The UNESCO Red Book, for example, was a pioneering effort in this direction. Then, in 1995, a Clearing House for endangered languages was set up at the University of Tokyo, its emphasis being on recording newly discovered instances of disappearing languages. In the same year, the Endangered Languages Fund (ELF) was created in the USA, and a similar activist group, the Foundation for Endangered Languages (FEL) was formed in Britain. In 2002, the first chair position in the subject of endangered languages was created by the Rausing Foundation at the School of Oriental and African Studies (SOAS) at the University of London. These initiatives have played an important role in our attempt at protecting endangered languages and preserving linguistic diversity.

Why do we need to protect endangered languages? Most importantly, language, culture and identity are intricately interrelated. Language reflects our affective relation to the perceived cosmos. Ever since the work of the American linguist Benjamin Lee Whorf on the Hopi world-view, linguists have come to appreciate the importance of linguistic diversity more and more. As we discussed in the introduction chapter of this volume, linguistic diversity and biodiversity are closely related. It has been found, for example, that speakers of languages indigenous to a particular area tend to have a unique and intimate knowledge of the flora and fauna and the natural resources of their own habitat. Links are also made between languages and ecological knowledge associated with forest conservation and the use of medicinal plants. In addition, human relations are uniquely reflected in language. A typical example is kinship terminology, which is remarkably diverse from one language group to another. There are also close links between languages and spiritual beliefs. So it is not surprising that there has been a rapid growth in research interest in endangered language protection and language revitalization so that linguistic diversity can be maintained.

Language vitality and endangered languages

What, then, is an endangered language? An endangered language may be roughly defined as a language that may soon vanish, ceasing to be used as a vehicle of communication, perhaps even disappearing completely from human history. This definition is broad enough to cover different degrees of language endangerment, but it obviously fails to provide clear and operable criteria on which to base our descriptions.

Attempts have been made to further refine this definition. Dai and Deng (2002), for example, propose a set of dynamic and quantified "comprehensive parameters systems" to define the endangered languages. The core parameters they identify include the following:

(1) the proportion of population who have lost the heritage language,

(2) the age group of people who still use the heritage language,

(3) heritage language ability.

According to this system, an endangered language should meet the following three conditions: (1) 80% of the population have shifted to use the dominant language and the number is still increasing, (2) the heritage language is only used by the middle-aged and senior population, and (3) the heritage language users only have listening ability and have lost speaking ability. These three criteria complement each other, and if a language meets these three conditions, it can be defined as an endangered language.

Another important attempt applies the IUCN's (International Union for Conservation of Nature) Red List criteria for species endangerment to languages, highlighting speaker numbers as a crucial indicator, as reproduced in the following table.

Table 1 IUCN's Red List Criteria Applied to Language Endangerment (Cited in Romaine 2018)

Least concern	Speakers are widespread and abundant
Near threatened	Not currently threatened, but likely to be in near future

(continued)

Vulnerable	Speakers observed or projected to decline by 30% or more in three generations (75 years), or number less than 10,000 and declining by 10% or more in three generations, or speakers' number less than 1,000
Endangered	Speakers observed or projected to decline by 50% or more in three generations, or number less than 2,500 and declining by 20% or more in two generations (50 years), or speakers' number less than 250
Critically endangered	Speakers observed or projected to decline by 80% or more in three generations, or number less than 250 and declining by 25% or more in one generation (25 years), or speakers' number less than 50
Extinct	No speakers remain

But as Romaine (2018) rightly points out, speaker numbers may be a crucial indicator for vulnerability and small languages can disappear much faster than large ones, but this is not the only one – size alone does not tell the whole story. If there is successful intergenerational transmission, even small communities may enjoy strong language vitality over time.

In March 2003, the UNESCO Intangible Cultural Heritage Unit convened an Ad Hoc Expert Group on Endangered Languages. In the document *Language Vitality and Endangerment* (UNESCO 2003), this expert group detailed a set of nine determining factors to measure the vitality of a language. The document was intended as a guideline adaptable to a variety of local situations, and most factors have 6 grades (0 through 5), where zero represents complete shift to another language (termed extinct), and five represents vitality of a language for that factor (termed safe). This index is reproduced in the table below, and to exemplify how each factor can be further specified, six possible degrees of endangerment for the second factor "intergenerational transmission" are highlighted.

Table 2 UNESCO's Language Vitality and Endangerment

1. Absolute number of speakers
2. Intergenerational transmission
   Degree of endangerment

5 safe	spoken by all generations
4 vulnerable	spoken by most children, but may be restricted to certain domains
3 definitely endangered	no longer learned at home
2 severely endangered	spoken by grandparents and older generations, but not used with children
1 critically endangered	youngest speakers are grandparents and older, use the language partially and infrequently
0 extinct	no speakers left

3. Community members' attitude towards their own language
4. Shifts in domains of language use

(continued)

5. Governmental and institutional language attitudes and policies, including official status and use
6. Type and quality of documentation
7. Response to new domains and media
8. Availability of materials for language education and literacy
9. Proportion of speakers within the total population

Other attempts include Wurm (2002), who proposes a five-grade scale, ranging from potentially endangered, to endangered, seriously/severely endangered, moribund and extinct, which are further detailed as follows:

(1) Potentially endangered: lack of prestige in the home country, economic deprivation, pressure from larger languages in the public sphere and social fragmentation in the private, to the extent that the language is not being systematically passed on in the education system;

(2) Endangered: where the youngest fluent speakers tend to be young adults, and there is a disjunction in passing on the language to children, especially in the school but even in the home environment;

(3) Seriously/severely endangered: with the youngest fluent speakers being among the older generation aged fifty and over, implying a loss of prestige and social value over a generation ago;

(4) Moribund: with only a tiny proportion of the ethnic

group speaking the language, mostly the very aged;

(5) Extinct, where no speakers remain.

Lewis, *et al.* (2013) use The Expanded Graded Intergenerational Disruption Scale designed by Lewis and Simons (2010) for reporting language status in the *Ethnologue* (Lewis, *et al.* 2013). This scale identifies the following levels:

0. International: The language is widely used between nations in trade, knowledge exchange, and international policy.

1. National: The language is used in education, work, mass media, and government at the national level.

2. Provincial: The language is used in education, work, mass media, and government within major administrative subdivisions of a nation.

3. Wider Communication: The language is used in work and the mass media without official status to transcend language differences across a region.

4. Educational: The language is in vigorous use, with standardization and literature being sustained through a widespread system of institutionally supported education.

5. Developing: The language is in vigorous use, with literature in a standardized form being used by some, though this is not yet widespread or sustainable.

6. (a) Vigorous: The language is used for face-to-face communication by all generations and the situation is sustainable.

(b) Threatened: The language is used for face-to-face communication within all generations, but it is losing users.

7. Shifting: The child-bearing generation can use the language among themselves, but it is not being transmitted to children.

8. (a) Moribund: The only remaining active users of the language are members of the grandparent generation and older.

(b) Nearly Extinct: The only remaining users of the language are members of the grandparent generation or older who have little opportunity to use the language.

9. Dormant: The language serves as a reminder of heritage identity for an ethnic community, but no one has more than symbolic proficiency.

10. Extinct: The language is no longer used and no one retains a sense of ethnic identity associated with the language.

As can be seen from the review above, most researchers agree that there are many factors to consider when deciding if a particular language is endangered, and there are different degrees of endangerment. Whatever scale or criteria we adopt to examine the status of a language, it is clear that an endangered language is not necessarily a minority language, and not every minority language is necessarily endangered. But since speaker number is a very crucial factor, there is a high probability that with time a minority language, if neglected, will become endangered.

Endangered languages in China

Chinese population is comprised of one majority Han group and 55 ethnic minority groups. The Han Chinese nationality, constituting the 92 percent majority in China, also includes over 300 million speakers of non-Mandarin varieties of Chinese. While these varieties all share the same characters for writing and are classified as one language, in many areas, the differences in the spoken versions can be quite extreme, so much so that they may not be intelligible to speakers of Mandarin. These non-Mandarin varieties, dialects of Chinese (*fangyan*), include the following:

(1) Wu (90 million plus, around Shanghai and Zhejiang Province),

(2) Yue or Cantonese (55 million plus, in Guangdong, eastern Guangxi, Hong Kong and Macao),

(3) Hakka (around 45 million, scattered in southeastern China),

(4) Min (around 70 million, mainly in Fujian Province, Taiwan Province and Hainan Province),

(5) Gan (around 42 million, in Jiangxi Province),

(6) Xiang (around 38 million, in Hunan Province).

These varieties each have very large internal diversity, with many subvarieties. In addition, the majority of overseas Chinese up until quite recently came from the Min, Yue and Hakka regions of the southeastern coast of China.

The minority population occupies about 8% of the total Chinese population. It is estimated that there are some 120 spoken languages among these ethnic groups, and many of these minority languages in China were already in crisis at the beginning of this century (Bradley 2007). As Li (2006) puts it, about half of these languages are known to be used by less than ten thousand people. Based on Dai and Deng's (2002) system introduced above, more than 20 of these languages are in serious danger. Examples of these seriously endangered minority languages are scattered in different parts of China, for example,

(1) Naxi and Hani in Yunnan Province,
(2) Maonan in Guizhou Province,
(3) Tujia in Hunan Province,
(4) Yi in Sichuan Province,
(5) Manchu, Erluanchuan, Hezhe in Northeast China.

It is estimated that more than 20% of these languages will disappear within half a century at most. In the case of Manchu language, for example, there are currently only a handful of senior people who can speak the language in Heilongjiang Province, in the northeast of China. They are all over 80 years old. Once these elderly speakers pass away, the Manchu language will become extinct, totally disappearing from this planet. This will be a great loss for our culture, since a huge number of books and documents were written by Manchu and more than 200,000 pieces still exist today.

Another example of an endangered Chinese language is the language of the She minority group of eastern Guangxi and Guangdong in China, with an estimated 700,000 plus members. Among these people, only about 1,000 still use the language in two small areas near Huizhou in eastern Guangdong Province. The majority of the She people mainly speak Hakka and

Cantonese Chinese, and many of them also know Mandarin Chinese. While there has been some work done on She, additional descriptive work is needed before it disappears.

According to a more recent study by Hirsh (2013: 38), an estimated 108 languages in China are endangered in different degrees, including the following nine most critically endangered languages, with a recent estimate of remaining number of native speakers provided (sourced from Lewis, *et al.* 2013):

  A'ou (50),
  Ayizi (50),
  Gelao, Re (a few speakers),
  Khakas (10 in China),
  Lawu (50),
  Manchu (20),
  Mulao (a few elderly speakers),
  Nanai (40 in China),
  Qabiao (18 in China).

In the cases of other minority languages, the endangerment is not quite so terminal, and small numbers of children are still learning the languages. Such is the case for the two languages within the Tujia ethnic group. As Bradley (2007) points out, most such languages are fairly well documented, and the choice to stop using them is one which has been made by the speech community themselves for a variety of reasons.

Apart from the minority languages, the non-Mandarin dialects (*fangyan*) in China have also been affected, in different degrees, with the promotion of *Putonghua* (common speech) in schools and more and more public domains. Although other local domains remain for these dialects, the use of *Putonghua* is becoming more widespread, especially among young people. There is some loss of local differences within Chinese , " as regional subvarieties absorb the local speech of parts of their hinterlands with the expansion of cities" (Bradley 2007).

Causes of language endangerment

Many factors conspire to bring about the endangerment of languages. Globally, colonialization, foreign occupation, natural calamities, epidemic disease, socio-economic change, etc. have all been identified as causes for language endangerment. For example, a language maybe facing a crisis when the community of speakers become endangered through sickness, conflict or subjugation. When people lose their homes, their traditional land, or even their right to live, their language may become extinct. Languages can become endangered due to language contact. When speakers of one language come into contact with another language used by a more dominant, or developed society, language shift towards the new language may happen. Language endangerment can also happen when a language loses its traditional domains or is not used in new domains (Hirsh 2013: 124).

Historically, colonialism has had a huge global impact on many languages, resulting in the marginalization of and a rapid decline in the use of indigenous and minority languages. Today, globalization, the growth of the Internet and web-based information is having a direct and detrimental impact on minority languages and linguistic diversity (United Nations 2013).

In general, as Wendel and Heinrich (2012) argue, language endangerment is the result of changes in language ecologies caused by transformations of the socio-economic organization of communities. They maintain that two major waves of language diversity loss can be attested. The first one began 11,000 years ago when agrarian societies expanded into the territories of hunter-gatherer communities, whose cultures are primarily oral. One of the serious limitations of speakers of unwritten languages is that their strategies for structuring knowledge is limited, as expression in oral cultures is typically additive, aggregative, and contextualized in the here-and-now. They are unable to organize knowledge in the elaborate and abstract taxonomies, as is possible with writing (see Halliday 2008, for a detailed discussion on the differences between spoken and written language). The shift of the socioeconomic system from hunting and gathering to farming resulted in previously unknown types of social conditions, a transition which such oral cultures found extremely difficult to cope with. The second wave was initiated by the French Revolution, which led to the transformation "from dynastic realms into modern states". As modernization is closely linked with industrialization, urbanization, and social mobility, the value and utility of minority languages were undermined. The result is language diversity loss.

In China, socio-economic factors have certainly played a more influential role in the ecology of languages and language diversity loss in recent decades. In a sense, urbanization has been the biggest killer of languages, especially when rapid economic changes take place over one or two generations, as is the case in China, where a large number of rural population are attracted to urban centres for better employment. As Wendel and Heinrich (2012) point out, efforts aiming at upward social mobility often lead to the adaptation to dominant language and culture. Since the 1980s, with the opening-up and reform of China, millions of migrant workers from the countryside have been attracted to the big cities in central and coastal areas of China in search of work. In the beginning, these young migrant workers often left their families behind, with grandparents helping take care of the children in countryside villages. Later in the new century, with the provision of more and more favorable working and living conditions by local governments to attract migrant workforce, the workers can now afford to bring their children with them to the cities, where the migrant children are allowed to attend schools. *Putonghua* becomes the medium of instruction in the schools for these children. Moreover, it is also predominantly used in their daily communication instead of minority languages or dialects. Consequently, intergenerational transmission of the minority languages and dialects is gradually weakened. As Fishman (1997) has rightly pointed out, languages become endangered often because "they lack informal intergenerational transmission and informal daily life support".

Instead of being resisted, the language shift among the younger speakers towards the dominant *Putonghua* is often embraced by the migrant workers and their children in most cases, as this shift is seen to be beneficial for upward social mobility. This is easily understandable, and we should not ignore their aspirations for a better, more decent life. The pressures of the new socio-economic systems have made it increasingly difficult to practice their ancestral languages, and lack of practice will eventually lead to language loss. Mufwene (2002) calls our attention to "a moral dilemma" here. The loss of ancestral languages is a consequence of changes in the socio-economic ecologies of speakers. While we advocate the maintenance of cultural heritage and linguistic diversity, we also need to consider the costs and benefits to the relevant populations. After all, the reality is that *Putonghua*, as the national language, is essential for participation in modern national life. As a common language, it serves to facilitate communication and break down the language barriers between speakers of different minority languages and dialects. As Pennycook (1998) argues, we can not assume that the promotion of local languages instead of a dominant language, or the promotion of a dominant language at the expense of a local language, are in themselves good or bad. Instead, we need to understand both their location historically and their location contextually. As linguists, we should certainly not "work against the aspirations of the affected populations and exhort them to hold on to their languages and cultures only in the interest of a kind of diversity that should benefit our disciplines" (Mufwene 2002).

Language policy and planning is another very important factor that can have great impact on the maintenance of language diversity. As summarized by Mair (2004), the main goals of language planning in China may be divided up under the following headings:

(1) simplification and standardization of the sinographic script

(2) promotion of *Putonghua*(Mandarin) as the national language

(3) the design and refinement of *Pinyin* (the romanized spelling of *Putonghua*) and its adoption for appropriate applications

(4) identification and mapping of languages, topolects (*fangyan*), and dialects – both Sinitic and non-Sinitic

(5) recognition and description of languages meriting official "minority" (*shaoshuminzu*) status

(6) creation of scripts for languages that lack them and the streamlining of traditional non-Sinitic writing systems

(7) translation of words, names, and technical terms from other languages

(8) pedagogical issues, including methods for elementary instruction, uniform testing at higher levels, and the teaching of Mandarin to speakers of topolects and non-Sinitic languages within China, as well as to foreigners abroad

(9) bilingualism

(10) foreign language instruction and applications within China

The language policy in China has been, in general,

supportive of minority language maintenance, although there are inconsistencies in its implementation. An oft-cited analysis is Zhou (2000, 2001), which breaks down China's minority language policy since 1949 into three stages: the first pluralistic stage (1949 – 1957), the Chinese monopolistic stage (1958 – 1977), and the second pluralistic stage (1978 – present). The first stage is characterized by accommodation and official promotion of linguistic pluralism, when the government identified minorities' language rights, established infrastructures for minority education, and developed prototypes of bilingual education. From 1958 to 1977, however, largely due to the influence of the "Cultural Revolution", the policy seemed to have been shifted away from the first stage and Mandarin education was promoted over minority languages in education and bilingual education in minority schools was also scaled down. The negative impact of policy change in this stage on the minority languages can still be felt today. In the third stage, the so-called second pluralistic stage since 1978, the emphasis has been on the promotion of both Putonghua and minority languages. Bilingual education is revived, and minority groups' rights and those of language use are protected through legislation.

Of course, there is a lot more that needs to be done. Although minority groups are officially guaranteed the use of their native languages in ethnic autonomous regions, discrepancies between policy and policy implementation are significant (Zhou 2004). Of course, there are also many practical difficulties in the implementation of minority language policy, such as poverty, lack of qualified bilingual teachers, discriminatory views toward minority languages, which all need to be addressed to ensure the implementation of the policy.

Endangered language protection

In terms of the efforts in endangered language protection and achievements so far, the following are worth mentioning. First of all, on the legislative level, the Chinese government has issued relevant laws and regulations to protect the use and enrichment of minority languages. Minority autonomous regions in China are authorized to build their schools, design their school curricula, choose languages used as the medium of instruction in schools, and provide teacher training programs. Although the survival of endangered languages cannot depend on legislation as the main support, legal provisions certainly allow speakers of endangered languages to claim some public space for their languages (Romaine 2002).

Secondly, bilingual education has been emphasized and promoted in minority areas. More than 10,000 schools have been set up where bilingual education are conducted in the minority autonomous regions and some provinces with concentrations of minority groups. In fact, education has been identified as a key factor in language survival, and today there is growing appreciation of the important role school-based education can play in language maintenance and language revitalization. As Hirsh

(2013: 125) points out, through bilingual, multilingual, immersion and mother tongue-based forms of education, children can be exposed in schools to heritage languages and languages used in the wider community, with a positive effect overall on cognitive development and engagement with learning for children from minority language backgrounds.

Thirdly, special financial support has been provided to minority groups to develop minority education. For example, many special funds and projects such as the Ethnic Minorities Education Aid Special Fund, Project Hope, and the Border Areas Aid Fund have helped many minority students receive education in school.

Finally, Chinese researchers have been active in academic research on endangered languages, in an effort to reverse previous patterns of language loss over time, and to safeguard the knowledge and beliefs held within the languages. Of course, linguistic research in itself is not sufficient, and the publication of scholarly studies in academic journals is really only the first step in the complex process. Working closely with specific communities of speakers, Chinese linguists have collaborated with the international community, often leading the way in programs of language documentation, language attitude surveys, and language revitalization. More significantly, through their efforts, people's awareness of the importance of language diversity and endangered language protection has been raised.

More recently, there have been renewed efforts at the protection of endangered languages and dialects in China. One of such attempts is the language resources protection project, launched in 2015 by the Ministry of Education and the National Language Commission of China, aiming to survey, protect, display and develop language resources. The project involves 4,500 linguists from over 350 universities and research institutions worldwide. An online platform was established by the ministry and the commission in 2017 to collect and demonstrate Chinese dialects and ethnic minority languages for purposes of academic research and language promotion. A promotional video can be accessed at the following link: http://moe.edu.cn/s78/A19/moe_814/201607/t20160721_272527.html. at the Ministry of Education website.

In September 2018, China hosted the first international conference on linguistic diversity protection in Changsha, Hunan Province. An important document, Protection and Promotion of Linguistic Diversity of the World Yuelu Proclamation, was jointly issued by the Ministry of Education of China, UNESCO, the State Language Commission and the Chinese National Commission for UNESCO. The document stresses once again the crucial role of linguistic diversity for the sustainable development of mankind. The document also emphasizes the necessity to combine protection with advanced science and technology.

The role of linguists in endangered language protection is indispensible. There is still an urgent need for the participation of linguists in longitudinal research and projects connected to single communities for the study and revitalization of endangered languages and dialects. However, ultimately changes need to be made from inside. Language rescue cannot be imposed from outside. More importantly, we must help minority language communities help themselves, with targeted measures in poverty alleviation to improve their living conditions, education and employment opportunities and general well-being, so that the endangered languages can be revived in their own habitat. After all, habitat protection may be one of the best ways to protect minority languages.

References

Bradley, D. East and Southeast Asia. In Christopher Moseley (ed.). *Encyclopedia of the World's Endangered Languages*. London and New York: Routledge, 2007.

Crystal, D. *English as a Global Language*. Cambridge: Cambridge University Press, 1997.

Dai, Q. X. and Y. L. Deng. Reflection on qualitative questions in endangered language research. *Journal of China Minority University*, 2002 (2): 120 – 125.

Fishman, J. A. Maintaining languages: What works and what doesn't. In Gina Cantoni (ed.). *Stabilizing Indigenous Languages*. Flagstaff, Arizona: Northern Arizona University Press, 1997.

Halliday, M. A. K. *Complementarities in Language*. Shanghai: The Commercial Press, 2008.

Hirsh, D. *Endangered Languages, Knowledge Systems and Belief Systems*. Bern: Peter Lang, 2013.

Lewis, P. and G. Simons. *Assessing Endangerment: Expanding Fisherman's GIDS*, 2010. http://www.lingv.ro/resources/scm_images/RRL022010Lewis.pdf.

Lewis, M. P., et al. (eds.). *Ethnologue: Languages of the World*, 17th edition. Dallas, TX: SIL International, 2013. http://www.ethnologue.com.

Li, J. F. *Research on Endangered Languages in Southwest of China*. Beijing: Central University for Nationalities Press, 2006.

Mair, V. H. Foreword. In M. L. Zhou (ed.). *Language Policy in the People's Republic of China: Theory and Practice Since 1949*. Boston: Kluwer Academic Publishers, 2004.

Mufwene, S. S. Colonisation, globalisation, and the future of languages in the twenty-first century. *International Journal on Multicultural Societies (IJMS)*, 2002, 4 (2): 162 – 193.

Nettle, D. and S. Romaine. *Vanishing Voices: The Extinction of the World's Languages*. Oxford: Oxford University Press, 2000.

Pennycook, A. *English and the Discourses of Colonialism*. London and New York: Routledge, 1998.

Romaine, S. The impact of language policy on endangered languages. *International Journal on Multicultural Societies (IJMS)*, 2002, 4 (2): 194 – 212.

Romaine, S. Language endangerment and language death: The future of language diversity. In A. F. Fill and H. Penz (eds.). *The Routledge Handbook of Ecolinguistics*. New York and London: Routledge, 2018.

UNESCO Ad Hoc Expert Group on Endangered Languages. *Language Vitality and Endangerment.* Document submitted to the International Expert Meeting on UNESCO Programme Safeguarding of Endangered Languages, Paris, March 2003. http://www.unesco.org/culture/ich/doc/src/00120 - EN.pdf.

United Nations. Protection of minority languages is a human rights obligation, UN expert says. *UN News*, 12 March 2013.

Wendel, J. and P. Heinrich. A framework for language endangerment dynamics: The effects of contact and social change on language ecologies and language diversity. *International Journal of the Sociology of Language*, 2012, 218: 145 - 166. DOI 10.1515/ijsl - 2012 - 0062.

Wurm, S. A. Strategies for language maintenance and revival. In David Bradely and Maya Bradely (eds.). *Language Endangerment and Language Maintenance.* London: Routledge, 2002.

Zhou, M. Language policy and illiteracy in ethnic minority communities in China. *Journal of Multilingual and Multicultural Development*, 2000, 21 (2): 129 - 148.

Zhou, M. The politics of bilingual education in the People's Republic of China Since 1949. *Bilingual Research Journal*, 2001, 25 (1&2).

Zhou, M. (ed.). *Language Policy in the People's Republic of China: Theory and Practice Since* 1949. Boston: Kluwer Academic Publishers, 2004.

Theorising Change: Culturally Responsive Digital Teaching and Australian Aboriginal Learners

Lester-Irabinna Rigney

Introduction

In Australia, pedagogical techniques are urgently required that assist teachers of information and communication technologies (ICTs) to respond positively to the growing need of culturally and linguistically diverse student populations. The 2017 *Australian Digital Inclusion Index* highlights that ICT digital skills are central to empowerment and are crucial to participation in education and social life (Thomas, *et al.* 2017). The *Digital Index* confirms that far too many Aboriginal Australians are excluded from accessing ICT and have a lower level of digital inclusion than most Australians. Low ICT accessibility and use inhibits individual capacity building. School tensions also exist regarding the inability of government to close the gap on Aboriginal disadvantage in education attainment despite a decade of strategy (Commonwealth of Australia 2017). For both Aboriginal Australians and Indigenous peoples globally there is a pressing need to improve equity, transform digital access and improve schooling outcomes for Indigenous students.

A growing body of evidence indicates that culturally responsive pedagogies *do* improve the academic success of First Nations peoples (Castagno and Brayboy 2008). Culturally responsive pedagogies (CRP) are now accepted as a hopeful strategy for improving academic achievement of First Peoples in settler colonial countries such as the USA, Canada and New Zealand (Castagno and Brayboy 2008; Dick, Estell and McCarty 1994; Smith 2003; Moll and González 2004; Bishop, *et al.* 2007). By way of a working definition, the term culturally responsive pedagogy refers to set of specific teacher pedagogies that "emphasises and respects student identities and backgrounds as meaningful sources for optimal learning" (Klump and McNair 2005: 3). In this chapter it is argued that CRP is important for improving Aboriginal Australian schooling outcomes. In the past decade in Australia there have been many Aboriginal schooling initiatives including *Dare to Lead*, *What Works*, *Stronger Smarter*, and the Cape York Institute, all with varied and uneven effects (Craven and Price 2009; Sarra 2007; Rigney 2011a; Price and Hughes 2009; Buckskin, *et al.* 2010). Research into the experiences of Aboriginal students has too often focused on the challenges teachers face and the need to improve teacher quality

(Ma Rhea, Anderson and Atkinson 2012; Rigney, *et al.* 1998; Craven, *et al.* 2005; Rigney 2011a, 2011b; Price 2012). Unfortunately, the theory and practice of CRP in Australia is only weakly developed and has had no significant peer evaluated reviews (Perso 2012; Krakouer 2015; Radoll 2015). Despite a few productive advocates (e. g. Worby, Rigney and Tur 2006; Sarra 2007; Yunkaporta and McGinty 2009; Nakata 2011; Rahman 2013; Rigney 2018), CRP has yet to seriously engage the curriculum and pedagogical reform projects of the state and federal jurisdictions.

As yet, little attention has been given to the intersection of CRP and ICT education in Australian public school classrooms. There is presently no empirically substantiated Australian version of CPR and ICT education available to Australian educators working in schools, or to those preparing new teachers. It is not intended here to consider pedagogies for specific technologies or devices (laptop computers, phones, desk-top computers). This chapter takes a broader view to consider how teachers' approaches to ICT education in schools may be enhanced through culturally responsive pedagogies. The purpose of this chapter is to theorise new aspects of CRP applied to ICT education to open innovative spaces in which new classroom practices may be established. The insights gained could potentially enhance ICT pedagogies to benefit the learning of students from a range of cultural and linguistic diverse backgrounds.

Teacher challenges

Australian teachers are required to teach Technology as one of eight core learning areas in the Australian Curriculum (ACARA 2018a). In addition to the core learning areas, the General Capabilities require the teacher to assess skills in "ICT capability" and "intercultural understandings" through each content descriptor (ACARA 2018b). Aboriginal Histories and Cultures, considered non-core content as one of three Cross-curriculum Priorities, offer the teacher opportunities to add depth and richness to the Technology core curriculum and, indeed, any core curriculum, where required. While at first glance the Cross-Curriculum Priority Aboriginal Histories and Cultures seems to lend itself to CRP, nowhere in the Australian Curriculum website is there any mention of CRP or hyperlinks to relevant resources. Likewise, apart from Western Australia (see Government of WA 2018), no state or territory Education Department website provides any CRP teacher resources for enacting the Australian curriculum, whether in relation to Technology or any other learning area. Not surprisingly, debates on factors affecting ICT teachers' pedagogy to enact the Australian Curriculum are far from settled. These challenges include: lack of ICT support and infrastructure (Bate 2010); inhibitive school leadership and culture (Somekh 2007, 2009); and teachers' values derived from their socio-cultural context that impact on their pedagogy (Goos 2005). Research by Aboriginal scholars on the impact of Aboriginal pedagogy and ICT on student outcomes is thin and mainly consists of case studies and program descriptions. Donovan (2007) argues that Aboriginal pedagogies of learning through experimentation, localising curriculum and ensuring flexible delivery are all compatible with ICT pedagogy. Radoll (2015) calls for greater investment in ICT teacher pedagogies, affordable ICT access cyber-safety tools, and digital literacies that meet Aboriginal self-determination. Rigney (2011b, 2011c, 2018; Rigney, et al. 2013) discusses the importance of Aboriginal parent voices and their digital aspirations for their children. He claims that Aboriginal perspectives on digital technologies are under-theorised in Australia and that little is known of suitable pedagogies to integrate ICT into non-English speaking Aboriginal communities. Rigney (2018) also argues for CRP to decolonise education structures toward democratic inclusion and remove deficit orientated approaches to schooling. For Rigney, CRP pedagogies are emancipatory and address unequal power relations, promote reform, and pursue democratic inclusion.

The brief analysis here of pedagogical challenges to ICT teaching in Australia means that Australian teachers, schools and state departments are caught between high demand on one side for transformational change to the Aboriginal digital classroom experience, while on the other side, only a few CRP projects have been reported in this space. This is problematic when the Australian curriculum is dependent on teachers enacting responsive ICT content to improve the disparity between Aboriginal and non-

Aboriginal academic performance and educational outcomes.

Constructing culturally responsive ICT pedagogies

Teachers-including those using ICT with their students and those teaching Technology as a core curriculum learning area-need tools to help make CRP normative in their classroom. Three primary literature archives provide the conceptual framework: (1) New Pedagogy Studies; (2) Indigenous Australian Epistemologies; (3) Culturally Responsive Pedagogies Theory. While these approaches do not explicitly deal with teaching for equality in ICT studies to students from diverse backgrounds, they do lend themselves to what the author considers to be good inclusive teaching adaptable to ICT curriculum content.

New pedagogy studies

In Australia, research about equity in schools has shifted to a focus on "New Pedagogy Studies" (Green 2003: 18). For theorists of New Pedagogy Studies, the urgent public school sector challenge is how to improve learning outcomes in so-called "disadvantaged" schools, many of which include Aboriginal students. The need to improve classroom practice is greatest in high poverty, cultural and linguistically diverse contexts. Here, the "standard" classroom practice tends to be inadequate without complementary teacher pedagogies that account for the social determinants (transiency, health issues, poverty) that can influence learning (Teese 2011). The social determinants of schooling are the conditions in which students are born, grow, live and work. These elements are shaped by access to housing, jobs, internet, income and social power. In communities characterised by poverty, social determinants of schooling are primarily responsible for education inequities that require fit-for-purpose localised pedagogies. Comber (2016) argues for the need to support (via professional development) both novice teachers and leaders with "common" and "new innovative" teaching practices to deal with these social determinants, which include high staff and student turnover (Comber 2016: 253). In contrast, Hayes, Johnston and King argue that "the key issue is not what kinds of pedagogies improve educational outcomes but how to support the development of the kinds of pedagogies that we have good reason to believe will work" (2009: 253). For these scholars, improving learning in disadvantaged schools is dependent on pedagogies localised to the community context and requires student and teachers to be ethnographers and knowers of community challenges and aspirations (Hattam, Zipin, Brennan and Comber 2009). ICT curriculum content needs to be integrated with appropriate pedagogies in order to improve learning and ultimately enhance community wellbeing. Simply put, public schools serving highly diverse student cohorts need to support teachers' engagement in the process of redesigning and producing sustainable pedagogical and curriculum change (Comber and Kamler 2006; Hayes, *et al.* 2006; Bokhorst-Heng , *et al.*

2006; Lingard 2007).

Indigenous Australian Epistemologies

The Australian theoretical fields of Indigenous Epistemologies, Aboriginal Education, Aboriginal and Torres Strait Islander Studies point to strategies in three main areas that have been shown to be effective in schools for increasing Aboriginals student engagement and success: a school culture and leadership supportive of local Indigenous student identities, knowledges and epistemologies (Rigney 2006, 2011a; Price 2015); school-wide strategies that improve teacher quality (Nakata 2007); and student centred learning strategies (Craven and Price 2009; Ma Rhea 2015; Moreton-Robinson, *et al.* 2012). Other scholars argue for pedagogies that promote anti-racism by including Indigenous knowledges (Moreton-Robinson 2000; Arbon 2008; Martin 2008; Rigney 2011a, 2011b; Aveling 2012; White, *et al.* 2013). In relation to digital technologies, connecting ICT pedagogy to culture, identity and aspirations is central to Aboriginal wellbeing and needs to be embedded across all curriculum learning areas. To promote learning, schools must support teacher with long-term, coordinated, placed-based approaches that honour community priorities and embed their participation.

Culturally Responsive Pedagogies Theory

Culture, identity and linguistic repertoire have the greatest influence on Aboriginal students' sense of self and all of these strengths come from outside the classroom. Bishop (2011) refers to the educational experiences of Māori children, which in many ways parallel the experiences of Australian Aboriginal students. Māori students are frustrated when the teacher "pathologizes Māori students" lived experiences by explaining their lack of educational achievement in deficit terms, either as being within the child or their home, or within the structure of the school (Bishop 2011: 36). Bishop notes that some teachers with low expectations of Māori tended to "blame someone or something else outside of their area of influence" and as a result they have "very little responsibility for the outcomes of these infuences" (Bishop 2011: 36). The consequence of such deficit views, according to Bishop, is a breakdown in the "quality of teachers" relationships with Māori students"; a "fatalistic" logic creates a "downward spiralling, self-fulfilling prophecy of Māori student achievement and failure" (Bishop 2011: 36). The pedagogy used and its responsiveness to culture are rarely questioned.

Gay (2010: 26) defines CRP as teaching "to and through [students'] personal and cultural strengths, their intellectual capabilities and their prior accomplishments". Culturally responsive pedagogies work with marginalised students by validating the cultural and linguistic identities they bring to school from home. Research on culturally responsive teaching approaches date as far back as Freire (1971) who worked with oppressed populations seeking liberation from injustice via schooling. Contemporary versions of child-centred pedagogies, including the

Reggio Emilia educational philosophy, use social constructivist approaches to advocate for children's rights to language and culture (Rinaldi 2006; Gardner 1999; Bruner 1996; Dahlberg, Moss and Pence 1999).

Recent transnational work across colonial/settler countries that address culturally responsive approaches to the unique learning needs of minority students are summarised below. These examples hold potential for teaching ICT and include:

(1) Gloria Ladson-Billings (1995: 160) advocates a version of culturally responsive pedagogy for improving learning the outcomes of African-American children. She articulates three main principles: "Students must experience academic success; students must develop and/or maintain cultural competence; and students must develop a critical consciousness to challenge the status quo of the current social order."

(2) Moll and González (2004: 700) argue that orthodox classroom pedagogies and practices underestimate and constrain the intellectual strengths of Latino students. They refer to funds of knowledge (FoK) as the strengths a child brings to class. To improve literacy, the teacher should draw upon the hidden, home and community knowledge bases of their students. Research using FoK approaches offer insights into ICT teaching as they demonstrate how family networks of knowledge and activities such as food preparation, agriculture, mechanics and cooking make excellent resources to students and teachers to support ICT learning.

(3) Villegas and Lucas (2002: 21) advocate CRP to promote more inclusive classrooms and to help bilingual and minority children achieve authentic literacy. A culturally responsive teacher: is socio-culturally conscious; has affirming views of students from diverse backgrounds; is capable of transformative change toward making responsive schooling for all students; is capable of promoting learners' knowledge construction; knows about the lives of students; and uses knowledge of students' lives to design instruction that builds on what they already know while stretching them beyond the familiar.

(4) Russell Bishop and colleagues (Bishop, et al. 2007: 15) in New Zealand argue for Kaupapa Māori Culturally Responsive Pedagogy of Relations that is underpinned by the principles: power is shared; culture counts; learning is interactive and dialogic; connectedness is fundamental to relations, and there is a common vision of excellence for Māori in education (Sleeter 2011).

(5) The Assembly of Alaska Native Educators (1999) outline Eight Alaskan Culturally Responsive Teacher Standards for culturally responsive teacher pedagogies. These include: a teaching philosophy that encompasses multiple worldviews; understanding how students learn; teaching for diversity; content related to local community; providing instruction and assessment that builds on student's cultures; creating a learning environment that utilises local sites; involving family and community as partners; and ongoing professional development.

This literature on CRP is far from exhaustive, but provides a snapshot of the principles which can be adapted for ICT purposes. This body of knowledge would urge ICT teachers to respond to localised contexts and invite to class the student's social and community networks of knowledge as resources for learning, change and improvement.

High intellectual challenge and high expectations of all students are critical in culturally responsive classrooms. CRP uses strength-based approaches to build more positive classroom relations that move beyond deficit views of minorities. Teachers will foster a culturally rich and diverse sense of classroom belonging that helps bilingual and bi-cultural children gain access to both their own knowledges and those of the dominant culture.

Mobilising funds of knowledge: teaching ICT using culturally responsive pedagogies

CRP theory has tremendous promise for Aboriginal students and other culturallyand linguistically diverse groups. The Australian *Digital Inclusion Index* report calls for "urgency to address digital inclusion" as the benefits for social cohesion, "businesses and governments are overwhelming" (Thomas, *et. al.* 2017: 3). Digital equality for the disadvantaged is crucial for participation in economic and social life. Yet three million Australians are still not online and have limited capacity to use ICT. Many Australians are "missing out on the education, health, and social benefits associated with being connected"

(*Thomas*, *et al.* 2017: 3). For Aboriginal students, inclusive ICT teacher pedagogies responsive to student's funds of knowledge have the potential to improve their educational achievement, yet such approaches are poorly developed in Australia. By way of small beginning to this urgent work, key ICT teacher pedagogies and their characteristics are drawn from CRP theory that frames educating for digital democratic citizenship.

Culturally Responsive ICT for Schools and Teachers:

(1) Creating learning environments that recognise all children are intelligent and have citizenry rights at birth:

a. Using a whole of school approach to establish learning environments for students to realise their rights.

b. The curriculum offerings provide pathways to celebrate the student's sense of identity, history, language and culture and their connection to Australian citizenship.

c. ICT learning environments seek solutions to local challenges including digital exclusion, digital divide, digital literacy and numeracy.

d. Opportunities to recognise and celebrate the cultural capital that all students bring with them to class.

e. Promote and sustain strong student voice in schools.

f. Opportunities for engagement with local community organisations such as foodbanks, women's groups, Amnesty International, NGOs, businesses, hospitals, police and other essential services.

(2) Creating learning environments and assessment tasks

that are high in intellectual challenge:

a. Setting high expectation for academic learning across the curriculum.

b. Designing challenging yet achievable learning programs based on the learning strengths and needs of students and drawing on their linguistic and/or cultural and/or religious and/or socioeconomic backgrounds.

(3) Creating a strength-based approach to culture:

a. Validating Aboriginal identities, cultures, languages and funds of knowledge.

b. Conceptualising culture as an asset to learning rather than an inhibitor.

c. Affirming Australian Aboriginal cultures as the oldest living cultures in the world.

d. Recognising that culture is central to Aboriginal student physical and digital wellbeing and ensuring that it is embedded in curriculum as enabler to improve learning achievement.

e. Practicing a pedagogy that accommodates multiple world views, knowledges, values and aspirations.

f. Incorporating local community values in all aspects of ICT teaching, learning, school systems and student support structures

g. Affirming students' home language, while linking it to standard English.

h. Providing opportunities for all students to learn about other cultures and multicultural Australia.

i. Abandoning deficit-orientated approaches to teaching,

learning and assessment. Moving beyond compensatory education.

(4) Creating strong community engagement:

a. Valuing parent, family and community leaders as the network of knowledge for students. They are an ideal intellectual resource for school and should be regularly invited to participate in ICT classes.

b. Building and maintaining respectful learning relationships through genuine partnerships with Aboriginal community.

c. Providing cultural awareness training for staff and students. Provide staff with community ethnographies that are relevant to the school's catchment area.

d. Providing staff professional development, induction and resources for engaging with the concepts and practices of CRP in order to enable professional growth.

e. Ensuring that school leadership supports and funds initiatives in CRP.

f. Developing staff accountability systems to ensure that CRP is embedded sustainably across the whole institution.

(5) Embed Aboriginal knowledges, perspectives and languages:

a. Incorporating and reinforcing the integrity of the cultural knowledge and experiences of all students.

b. Creating learning environments that use the local community as an extension of the classroom.

c. Using multimedia resources to build a sense of in Aboriginal history, achievements and milestones.

d. Evaluating out-dated multimedia teaching resources for cultural appropriateness.

　　e. Adopting bi-lingual or bi-cultural approaches to knowledge, ICT curriculum and assessment.

　　f. Recognising that Aboriginal knowledges and cultures are dynamic and adaptive and are enabled and supported through art, song, spirituality, stories, dance, kinship and connection to land and Country, and through self-determination.

　　g. Recognising that Aboriginal perspectives of ICT come in the form of personal and family experiences, linguistic affiliations, music, poetry, film, media, and Aboriginal standpoints.

　　h. Drawing upon Aboriginal multimedia, television, radio and social media.

　　i. Developing a culturally-responsive ICT curriculum that situates local knowledge and actions in a global context.

　　(6) Creating school learning that promotes cyber safety as cultural safety:

　　a. Offering learning that encompasses cyber-safety as cultural safety, including topics such as sexting, cyber-crime, and protection of cultural and intellectual property.

　　b. Tailoring ICT curriculum to the specific ICT challenges of the surrounding community.

　　c. Encouraging Aboriginal students to articulate their digital aspirations and those of their community, and connect these to their ICT learning.

d. Developing culturally safe classrooms that support positive student identities.

ICT teachers who are responsible for helping to bring about change in educational outcomes of Aboriginal students would do well to create classroom relations and interactions that are explicit in terms of a culturally responsive framework. Modern 21st century learning requires new spaces that are culturally safe, coherent and consistent. Such spaces do not override Aboriginal cultures but draw upon them as a source of learning and a foundation on which to build new digital learning structures. They connect school, home, Aboriginal country and community to learning in successful ways.

Conclusion

As ICT teachers seek culturally responsive pedagogies to improve educational achievement and equity, and to meet the requirements of the Australian curriculum, they require tools to help them effectively engage in this work. The theoretical analysis here suggests that teachers can engage in purposeful pedagogical discussions that focus on ICT content while drawing on the students' funds of knowledge and cultural strengths. This chapter begins a much-needed Australian schooling conversation by providing some criteria, definitions and characteristics that shift CRP from theory into genuine practice. As the Australian Curriculum demands effective teacher enactment of ICT content to an ever increasing culturally, ethnically, and linguistically diverse student population, CRP theory provides a timely and useful tool for teachers to pursue.

References

Arbon, V. *Arlathirnda ngurkarnda ityirnda: Being-knowing-doing: De-colonising Indigenous tertiary education.* Teneriffe, QLD: Post Press, 2008.

ACARA (Australian Curriculum Assessment and Reporting Authority). *Learning Areas*, 2018a. https://www.australian-cur-riculum.edu.au/f-10-curriculum/learning-areas/.

—— *General Capabilities*, 2018b. https://www.australiancur-ric-ulum.edu.au/f-10-curriculum/general-capabilities/.

Assembly of Alaska Native Educators. *Guidelines for preparing culturally responsive teachers for Alaska's schools.* Anchorage, AK, 1999. Retrieved 30 January 2018 from http://ankn.uaf.edu/Publications/teacher.pdf.

Aveling, N. Indigenous studies: A matter of social justice; a matter of urgency. *Diaspora, Indigenous, and Minority Education*, 2012, 6 (2): 99-114.

Bate, F. A bridge too far? Explaining beginning teachers' use of ICT in Australian schools. *Australasian Journal of Educational Technology*, 2010, 26 (7): 1042-1061.

Bishop, R. Te Kotahitanga: Kaupapa Māori in mainstream classrooms. In C. Sleeter (ed.). *Professional Development for Culturally Responsive Relationship Based Pedagogy.* New York: Peter Lang, 2011: 23-46.

Bishop, R., M. Berryman, T. Cavanagh and L. Teddy. *Te Kōtahitanga Phase 3: Whānaungatanga: Establishing a Culturally Responsive Pedagogy of Relations in Mainstream Secondary School Classrooms*. The Ministry of Education, New Zealand, 2007.

Bokhorst-Heng, W., M. D. Osbourne and K. Lee (eds.). *Redesigning Pedagogy: Reflections on Theory and Praxis*. Rotterdam: Sense, 2006.

Bruner, J. S. *The Culture of Education*. Cambridge, MA.: Harvard University Press, 1996.

Buckskin, P., P. Hughes, K. Price, L. -I. Rigney, C. Sarra, I. Adams, and C. Hayward. *Review of Australian Directions in Indigenous Education, 2005 - 2008 for MCEECDYA*. Perth: MCEECDYA Reference Group on Indigenous Education, Department of Education and Training, Government of Western Australia, 2010.

Castagno, A. and B. Brayboy. Culturally responsive schooling for indigenous youth: A review of the literature. *Review of Educational Research*, 2008, 78 (4): 941 - 993.

Comber, B. *Literacy, Place, and Pedagogies of Possibility*. London: Routledge, 2016.

Comber, B. and B. Kamler. Redesigning literacy pedagogies: The complexities of producing sustainable change. In W. Bokhorst-Heng, M. Osbourne and K. Lee (eds.). *Redesigning Pedagogy: Reflections on Theory and Praxis*. Rotterdam: Sense, 2006: 19 -32.

Commonwealth of Australia. *Closing the Gap: Prime Minister's Report* 2017. Canberra, ACT: Department of the Prime Minister and Cabinet, Commonwealth of Australia, 2017.

Craven, R. G., C. Halse, H. W. Marsh, J. Mooney and J. Wilson-Miller. *Teaching the Teachers Aboriginal Studies: Recent Successful Strategies*. Vols 1 & 2. Canberra, ACT: Department of Education, Science and Training, Commonwealth of Australia, 2005.

Craven, R. G. and K. Price. The literature. In K. Price and P. Hughes (eds.). *What Works. The Work Program. Stepping Up: What Works in Pre-service Teacher Education*. Canberra, ACT: National Curriculum Services and the Australian Curriculum Studies Association, Commonwealth of Australia, 2009: 1 – 6.

Dahlberg, G., P. Moss and A. Pence. *Beyond Quality in Early Childhood Education and Care: Postmodern Perspectives*. London: Falmer Press, 1999.

Dick, G., D. Estell and T. McCarty. Saad kaakih bee'enootiilji na'alkaa: Restructuring the teaching of language and literacy in a Navajo community school. *Journal of American Indian Education*, 1994, 33 (3): 31 – 46.

Donovan, M. Can information communication technology tools be used to suit Aboriginal learning pedagogies? In L. E. Dyson, M. Hendriks and S. Grant (eds.). *Information Technology and Indigenous Peoples*. Melbourne, VIC.: Information Science Publishing, 2007.

Freire, P. *Pedagogy of the Oppressed*. New York: Seabury Press, 1971.

Gardner, H. *The Disciplined Mind. What All Students Should Understand*. New York: Simon & Schuster, 1999.

Gay, G. *Culturally Responsive Teaching: Theory, Research, and Practice*. New York: Teachers College Press, 2010.

Goos, M. A sociocultural analysis of the development of pre-service and beginning teachers' pedagogical identities as users of technology. *Journal of Mathematics Teacher Education*, 2005 (8): 35 –59.

Government of Western Australia. *Leading a Culturally Responsive School*, 2018. http: //det. wa. edu. au/professionallearning/ detcms/professionallearning/professional-learning – website/for-school-leaders/leading-a-culturally-responsive-school. en ?cat – id = 10850889.

Green, B. An unfinished project? Garth Boomer and the pedagogical imagination. *Opinion: Journal of the South Australian English Teachers' Association*, 2003, 47 (2): 13 –24.

Hattam, R. , L. Zipin, M. Brennan and B. Comber. Researching for social justice: Contextual, conceptual and methodological challenges. *Discourse: Studies in the Cultural Politics of Education*, 2009, 30 (3): 303 –316.

Hayes, D. , K. Johnston, and A. King. Creating enabling classroom practices in high poverty contexts: The disruptive possibilities of looking in classrooms. *Pedagogy, Culture & Society*, 2009, 17 (3): 251 –264.

Hayes, D., M. Mills, P. Christie and B. Lingard. *Teachers and Schooling Making a Difference: Productive Pedagogies, Assessment and Performance.* Crows Nest, NSW: Allen & Unwin, 2006.

Klump, J. and G. McNair. *Culturally Responsive Practices for Student Success: A Regional Sampler*, 2005. Retrieved 17 October 2006 from www.nwrel.org/request/2005 june/textonly.html.

Krakouer, J. *Literature Review Relating to the Current Context and Discourse on Indigenous Cultural Awareness in the Teaching Space: Critical Pedagogies and Improving Indigenous Learning Outcomes Through Cultural Responsiveness.* Melbourne, VIC.: ACER, 2015.

Ladson-Billings, G. Toward a theory of culturally relevant pedagogy. *American Educational Research Journal*, 1995, 32 (3): 465–491.

Lingard, B. Pedagogies of indifference. *International Journal of Inclusive Education*, 2007, 11 (3): 245–266.

Ma Rhea, Z. *Leading and Managing Indigenous Education in the Postcolonial World.* Oxon: Routledge, 2015.

Ma Rhea, Z., P. Anderson and B. Atkinson. *Improving Teaching in Aboriginal and Torres Strait Islander Education: Australian Professional Standards for Teachers.* Melbourne, VIC.: Australian Institute for Teaching and School Leadership, 2012.

Martin, K. *Please Knock Before You Enter: Aboriginal Regulation of Outsiders and the Implications for Researchers.* Teneriffe,

QLD: Post Press, 2008.

Moll, L. and N. González. Engaging life: A funds-of-knowledge approach to multicultural education. In J. A. Banks and C. A. Banks (eds.). *Handbook of Research on Multicultural Education.* San Francisco, CA.: Jossey-Bass, 2004: 699 –715.

Moreton-Robinson, A. *Talkin' Up to the White Woman: Indigenous Women and Feminism.* Brisbane, QLD: University of Queensland Press, 2000.

Moreton-Robinson, A., D. Singh, J. Kolopenuk and A. Robinson. *Learning the Lessons? Pre-service Teacher Preparation for Teaching Aboriginal and Torres Strait Islander Students.* Melbourne, VIC.: Australian Institute for Teaching and School Leadership, 2012.

Nakata, M. *Disciplining the Savages-Savaging the Disciplines.* Canberra, ACT: Aboriginal Studies Press, 2007.

Nakata, M. Pathways for Indigenous education in the Australian curriculum framework. *Indigenous Education*, 2011, 40: 1 –8.

Perso, T. F. *Cultural Responsiveness and School Education: With Particular Focus on Australia's First Peoples: A Review snd Synthesis of the Literature.* Darwin, NT: Menzies School of Health Research, Centre for Child Development and Education, 2012.

Price, K. (ed.). *Aboriginal and Torres Strait Islander Education: An Introduction for the Teaching Profession.* Port Melbourne, VIC.: Cambridge University Press, 2012.

— (ed.). *Aboriginal and Torres Strait Islander Education: An Introduction for the Teaching Profession.* Port Melbourne,

VIC.: Cambridge University Press, 2015.

Price, K. and P. Hughes (eds.). *What Works. The Work Program. Stepping Up: What Works in Pre-service Teacher Education*. Canberra, ACT: National Curriculum Services and the Australian Curriculum Studies Association, Commonwealth of Australia, 2009.

Radoll, P. Information and communication technologies in the classroom: Implications and considerations. In K. Price (ed.). *Aboriginal and Torres Strait Islander Education: An Introduction for the Teaching Profession*. Port Melbourne, VIC.: Cambridge University Press, 2015: 121 – 139.

Rahman, K. Belonging and learning to belong in school: The implications of the hidden curriculum for Indigenous students. *Discourse: Studies in the Cultural Politics of Education*, 2013, 34 (5): 660 – 672.

Rigney, D., L.-I. Rigney and P. Hughes. *Report of Aboriginal Students and the South Australian Certificate of Education (SACE) for the Senior Secondary Assessment Board of South Australia (SSABSA)*. Bedford Park, SA: Yunggorendi, First Nations Centre for Higher Education and Research, Flinders University, 1998.

Rigney, L.-I. Indigenist research and Aboriginal Australia. In J. E. Kunnie and N. I. Goduka (eds.). *Indigenous People's Wisdoms and Power: Affirming Our Knowledges Through Narrative*. London: Ashgate Publishing, 2006: 32 – 50.

— Social inclusion in education. In D. Bottrell and S. Goodwin (eds.). *Schools, Communities and Social Inclusion.* South Yarra, VIC.: Palgrave Macmillan, 2011a: 38 –49.

— Indigenous education and tomorrow's classroom: Three questions, three answers. In N. Purdie, G. Milgate and H. R. Bell (eds.). *Two-Way Teaching and Learning: Toward Culturally Reflective and Relevant Education.* Camberwell, VIC.: ACER Press, 2011b: 35 –48.

— *Indigenous Education: Creating Classrooms of Tomorrow Today*, 2011c. Retrieved 28 January 2018 from https://research.acer.edu.au/cgi/viewcontent.cgi? article = 1107& context = research_conference.

— Defining culturally responsive digital education for classrooms: Writing from Oceania to build Indigenous Pacific futures. In E. McKinley and L. Smith (eds.). *Handbook of Indigenous Education.* Singapore: Springer, 2018: 1 –17.

Rigney, L.-I., K. Falkner, P. Radoll and M. Wimore. Digital inclusion and Aboriginal and Torres Strait Islander Peoples: A discussion paper. Unpublished Report. Telstra Foundation, 2013.

Rinaldi, C. *In Dialogue with Reggio Emilia: Listening, Researching and Learning.* Oxon: Routledge, 2006.

Sarra, C. Young, black and deadly: Strategies for improving outcomes for Indigenous students. In M. Keeffe and S. Carrington (eds.). *Schools and Diversity.* Frenchs Forest, NSW.: Pearson Education Australia, 2007: 74 – 89.

Sleeter, C. *Professional Development for Culturally Responsive*

Relationship Based Pedagogy. New York: Peter Lang Publishing, 2011.

Smith, L. T. *Decolonizing Methodologies: Research and Indigenous Peoples.* London: Zed Books, 2003.

Somekh, B. *Pedagogy and Learning with ICT: Researching the Art of Innovation.* London: Routledge, 2007.

—— Factors affecting teachers' pedagogical adoption of ICT. In J. Voogt and G. Knezek (eds.). *International Handbook of Information Technology in Primary and Secondary Education* (Vol. 1). New York: Springer, 2009: 449–460.

Teese, R. *From Opportunity to Outcomes: The Changing Role of Public Schooling in Australia and National Funding Arrangements.* Commissioned report by the Centre for Research on Education Systems. Melbourne, VIC.: University of Melbourne, 2011.

Thomas, J., J. Barraket, C. Wilson, S. Ewing, T. MacDonald, J. Tucker and E. Rennie. *Measuring Australia's digital divide: The Australian Digital Inclusion Index.* Melbourne, VIC.: RMIT University, 2017.

Villegas, A. M. and T. Lucas. *Educating Culturally Responsive Teachers: A Coherent Approach.* Albany, NY: SUNY Press, 2002.

White, S., Z. Ma Rhea, P. Anderson and B. Atkinson (eds.). *A Unit Outline and Content for Professional Learning Units to Support Teachers in Meeting Focus Areas 1.4 and 2.4.* Melbourne, VIC.: Australian Institute for Teaching and School Leadership, 2013.

Worby, G., L.-I. Rigney and S. U. Tur. Where the salt and fresh water meet: Reconciliation and change in education. In G. Worby and L.-I. Rigney (eds.). *Sharing Spaces: Indigenous and Non-Indigenous Responses to Story, Country and Rights*. Perth, WA: API Network, Australian Research Institute, Curtin University of Technolog, 2006: 418–447.

Yunkaporta, T. and S. McGinty. Reclaiming Aboriginal knowledge at the cultural interface. *Australian Educational Researcher*, 2009, 36 (2): 55–72.

Author bio

Dr Lester-Irabinna Rigney, BEd, MEd, PhD (Flinders), MACE, is Professor of Aboriginal Education at University of South Australia. One of Australia's most respected Aboriginal educationalists, Professor Rigney is a descendant of the Narungga, Kaurna and Ngarrindjeri peoples of South Australia. He is an expert on Aboriginal Minority Education. He is Research Fellow at Kings College, London and Professor of Education at the Centre for Research in Education at University of South Australia. He is best known for his theorisation of *Indigenist Research Epistemologies* and *Aboriginal Education* putting him at the forefront for schooling and language rights from 1990s to the 2000s. According to Rigney's three principles of Indigenist epistemology – schools, teachers and researchers must build community partnerships and embed Aboriginal cultures as driving force for transformative, culturally responsive education. Many teachers and policy writers have been inspired by Rigney's writings that promote the idea that culturally responsive schooling is built from the experiences and abilities students bring to class. Professor Rigney has worked across the Pacific on Indigenous Education.

澳大利亚语言政策的发展变迁及其动机分析

刘晓波　战　菊

　　澳大利亚与中国一样，是一个典型的多语国家。如何管理多样的语言，实现多样性与统一性的和谐，中澳两国都做出了有益的尝试。澳大利亚对语言政策的重视和取得的成就值得我国研究和借鉴。近年来，语言规划与语言政策的理论研究也非常重视动机的研究，本文尝试梳理澳大利亚语言政策的发展变迁并探究其背后的动因，期望能为语言政策和语言规划的动机研究提供一种视角与思路。首先需要说明的是，语言规划与语言政策的定义一直在变化发展，本文在分析澳大利亚语言政策背后的动机的时候，把语言规划和语言政策的主体限定在国家层面上。

一、澳大利亚语言政策的发展变迁

　　澳大利亚在历史上就是一个多民族、多语言的国家。在大批欧洲殖民者到来之前，澳大利亚大约有30万人讲着大约

250种不同的语言。英国殖民地的建立及后来的"淘金热"吸引了大批欧洲、亚洲的淘金者，为这块土地带来了更多不同种类的文化和语言。如何管理众多的语言，是每一个包括澳大利亚在内的多语国家都需要面临和解决的问题。澳大利亚在其并不漫长的国家历史中，出于不同的动机和目的对其多种语言采取过不同的管理形式，其语言规划和语言政策的发展变迁经历了四个阶段。

（一）放任语言政策阶段（20世纪以前）

在1788年英国政府在澳洲建立殖民地之前，土著人就在这里繁衍生息，每个部落都有自己的语言，邻近的部落彼此可以互通彼此的语言。1788年之后，英国政府决定在澳洲建立犯人流放殖民地，大批英国人来到澳大利亚，他们对土著赶尽杀绝，直接导致土著语言的消亡与减少。19世纪后半叶，澳大利亚多地发现金矿，吸引了大批从亚洲、欧洲、美洲来的淘金者涌入澳洲，并带来了他们各自的语言，从而改变了澳大利亚移民的单一来源，使澳大利亚的语言景观呈现出显著的多样性。使用最广泛的语言除了英语之外，还有德语、法语、汉语等，那时，墨尔本和阿德莱德的商业交易几乎都用德语，许多报纸也用双语刊发，多种双语学校遍布澳洲。虽然非英裔移民来源广泛，但是与英裔移民相比，人口数量还是相对较少。在1891年，所有非英裔移民约占全澳总人口的5%，英语是事实上的通用语，移民语言的使用范围比较小，影响不是很大。因为人们当时对语言及其功能还缺乏认识，语言问题的重要性尚未显现出来，所以在这一时期，英国政府对澳大利亚多样的移民语言没有采取任何措施，未做任何干预。此外，澳大利亚当时处于殖民时期，各殖民地情况也不相同,没有形成一个统一的责任政府,政治管理比较松散,这也是采取放任管理的因素之一(Clyne 2005: 1-2)。

(二)同化语言政策阶段(20世纪初到20世纪60年代末)

1901年澳大利亚建国,在民族主义思想的影响下,澳大利亚英语成为民族的象征,成为民族认同的重要标记。占人口主体的英裔澳大利亚人为建立自由独立的"澳大利亚英国人"的国家,开始限制非欧洲移民进入澳大利亚,并对有色人种采取同化政策,这就是澳大利亚历史上臭名昭著的白澳政策。同化政策主要有二:一是希望血缘上有色人种和白色人种混血,使有色人种同化直至消失;二是语言文化上的同化,要求土著居民和其他移民放弃他们自己的语言和文化,从而丧失原有的族群特征,最后融入主流社会。1901年,澳大利亚联邦国会通过的《限制移民法案》中始创了"语言听写测验",其目的就是限制排斥有色人种入境。澳大利亚政府要求为所有非英裔的成年移民开展 AMEP(Adult Migrant English Program,成人移民英语培训项目),该项目至今仍在运行,同时要求这些移民家庭的家长在家监督儿童讲英语。第一次世界大战的爆发,使英语之外的所有语言都受到怀疑,尤其是德语,以至于在英裔澳大利亚人眼里,在任何公共场合使用英语之外的其他语言都是一种非澳大利亚行为。"二战"期间,澳大利亚政府不仅取消了大量的双语学校,在新闻媒体领域也大力推行语言同化,规定英语之外的其他语言的广播电视节目不得超过全部播出时间的2.5%。澳大利亚政府对土著居民的同化最为惨绝人寰,土著居民不仅没有选举权,而且人口统计也不把他们包括在内。土著居民被赶进专门的保留区，接受各种所谓现代文明的教化，当然包括学习使用英语。政府甚至违背土著孩子母亲和家庭的意愿，将土著孩子强行带走送到教会、寄养家庭或慈善机构，接受"正统、文明"的主流教育，这些人被称为"被偷走的一代"。这些土著孩子与家庭的隔绝导致他们无法习得他们的母语（Smolicz and Secome 2003：3-25）。

（三）多元语言政策时期（20世纪70年代初到90年代初）

第二次世界大战后，澳大利亚的战后经济重建遇到人口瓶颈，英国由于自己亦需要大量劳动力，所以没有移民可供输出，在"不增加人口就是自取灭亡"的危急关头，澳大利亚只好将目光转向东欧、南欧和亚洲国家，从1947年开始长期大规模地招收外来移民。到20世纪60年代末，已有100多个国家的200多万人移入澳大利亚定居，使澳大利亚的人口结构发生了重大变化，具有不列颠血统的人口在总人口中的比例逐渐下降。大量非英国移民的到来也带来了他们自己的传统文化、语言和生活方式，而且新移民为澳大利亚的经济建设做出了重要贡献，他们的社会地位逐渐获得认可，这自然延伸到语言和文化意识的群体认同。澳大利亚又开始了长期的关于自己文化和身份的讨论。为了实现不同族群间的平等和多元文化认同，在澳大利亚政府、少数族群社区和语言专业团体的共同努力下，澳大利亚改变了英语是唯一语言的事实，接受了多语多文化的现实，并制定了历史上第一部明确的官方语言政策《国家语言政策》（以下简称《政策》），宣布成立负责推广《政策》的澳大利亚语言与多元文化教育咨询委员会。《政策》对语言地位进行了规划：确认英语为澳大利亚的国语，承认土著语言是澳大利亚的本土语言，承认移民语言为澳大利亚的社区语言及它们被接受、被尊重的权利。政府开始拨款实施各种英语、土著语言和社区语言项目，如：为新移民提供以英语为第二语言/外语（English as a Second Language，ESL）项目；澳大利亚第二语言项目，资助州地区及私立学校的非英语语言教学；成年人读写行动项目；亚洲研究计划，为学校开发教材，为高校建立研究和教学中心；跨文化培训项目，包括跨文化态度培养课程和社区语言课程；国家土著语言项目，帮助土著语言的保持，包括双语教育、文学创作、语言保持和语言识别（Lo Bianco 1987：71-72）。为移民和土著人提供语言翻译服务、语言学习服务、语言保持服务、语言测试服务、语言广播电视服务。此外，澳大利亚特有的电话翻译服务（Translating and Interpreting Service，TIS），澳大利亚翻译资格认可局（National Accreditation Authority of Translators and Interpreters，NAATI），以及除了新闻、体育和部分纪录片用英语播送外其余节目均用澳洲各民族语言配英文字幕播送的多元文化电视台 SBS，均是在这期间建立的。

（四）优先化语言政策时期（20世纪90年代初至今）

进入20世纪90年代，在西方经济理性主义思潮和澳大利亚的亚洲转向的影响下，澳大利亚的语言政策发生了转向。英语学习，尤其是英语读写能力受到高度重视，同时亚洲语言的学习在政策上得到了进一步强化。1990年，澳大利亚发布了名为《澳大利亚的语言：20世纪90年代澳大利亚读写能力语言政策讨论》的绿皮书，在一定程度上背弃了文化多元政策，招致批评。1991年，联邦政府颁布了《澳大利亚的语言：澳大利亚语言与读写能力政策》，将英语的读写能力放在首位。1992年颁布的《澳大利亚国家学校亚洲语言与研究战略》将学习亚洲语言提到国家经济发展的战略高度,并根据澳大利亚与亚洲各个国家贸易额的统计数据选择了汉语、日语、印尼语和韩语这四门亚洲语言,于1994年实施为期10年的语言和文化项目。1997年《国家读写能力规划》出台,2009年陆克文政府启动《国家学校亚洲语言与研究计划》,同样是为了支持四种亚洲语言的学习(王辉2010)。

二、语言规划与与语言政策的动机研究

语言生活是人类生活的重要组成部分,人类有意识的影响语言发展变化的历史也很悠久,所以现代研究根据历史上的语言规划基本认定语言是可以被规划的。语言政策与语言规划这两个术语经常在一起使用,有的学者认为二者之间有区别,如认为语言规划表示那些由个人或集体从事的非官方活动,而语言政策是指官方的行为,或者语言规划是政府或者社会团体为了解决交际中出现的问题而有计划、有组织地对语言文字进行的各种工作和活动的统称,它是语言政策的具体体现。而有学者认为,语言规划是有意识的工程化的语言改变,语言政策是规划者为了达到预订的目标而制定并实施的特定策略。另外也有很多学者对二者不予区分。事实上,关于语言规划和语言政策的定义一直处于变迁之中,很多学者都从不同角度对这两个术语予以了定义和解释,具体措辞和角度不尽相同,他们对语言规划的主体、对象、目标/目的等做了不同的阐释。Cooper(1989:89)给出了一个分析语言规划的框架,他认为可以从以下8个方面分析:语言规划的主体、语言规划的客体、语言规划的对象、语言规划的背

景、语言规划的动机/目的、语言规划的方式和手段、语言规划的决策过程、语言规划的效果。本文关注的就是语言规划与语言政策的动机。事实上，在不同学者定义语言规划和语言政策时，也分别提到了动机这一要素。Haugen 在 1959 年定义语言规划、语言政策时，就提到其"旨在指导非同质言语社区中的书面和口头语言应用"。Weinstein 则提到"为了解决交际问题"。胡壮麟认为语言规划旨在发现和解决交际问题。Grin 认为解决语言问题是语言政策和语言规划的首要目标，所有语言问题的共同核心是多样性，因此，语言政策的根本使命是对多样性的管理。Mühlhäusler 认为语言规划旨在保持人类交际系统最大多样性的活动。所以语言规划和语言政策的动机一直在学者的讨论范围之内，只不过措辞不同，角度不同。实际上，无论是保持语言的多样性还是解决源自语言多样性的交际问题，都不是语言规划的全部出发点，因为语言政策作为社会政策的一部分，着眼的不单单是语言问题。因为语言不仅仅是交际的工具，它也是文化的容器和身份的象征，语言政策制定者在制定语言政策的时候往往会根据当时的国情权衡各种政治、经济、文化、语言等因素，出于不同的动机制定不同的语言政策。

中国语言规划学界对语言规划的动机研究以不同的名称分别进行论述。如就语言规划的目标，薄守生、赖慧玲（2009）认为语言规划的目标有四个取向，即语言同化、语言多样化、本国语化和语言国际化，并特别提到，语言规划的目标可以是多重的，并且多重目标之间是可以并且往往是存在先后之分的。他们还总结了语言规划的任务：①促进国家政通人和；②服务于国家团结统一；③致力于国家繁荣昌盛;④保障人民安居乐业,实现平等外交。语言规划的任务,会随着国情国力的发展而变化,因此需要把语言规划的任务纳入国家每一个时期的情景叙事中来考察,而不是机械地对语言规划做出任务规定。姚亚平(2006:70)在《中国语言规划研究》中归纳了三个语言规划的任务:一是提高全社会的语言交往效率;二是提高语言的社会凝聚力,对于国家和民族来说,语言是实现民族团结、国家统一、社会凝聚的基本条件之一;三是提高本国语言的国际影响力。

丹尼斯·艾格(Ager 2001)对深藏于语言规划和语言政策背后的动机进行了深入、细致的研究与分析。艾格把动机分为七类:身份或认同、意识形态、形象、危机感、不平等、融合、工具等。此外,他加入了政策制定者的语言态度和规划的目标两个考察维度,并以个案分析的方式分别阐释了这七种动机。艾格认为,认同,尤其是国家民族认同,是很多国家制定语言政策有意识地改变人们的语言行为的动机。因为语言是国家民族、族群、社会认同的重要标识,当一个国家或民族想区别于别的国家和民族时,语言成为首选。艾格以法国为例,充分阐释了语言在实现法国民族认同中所发挥的重要作用,以及法国为了实现民族认同所采取的语言政策。法国的民族国家理念"一种语言、一种文化、一种政治实体"为当时世界上许多国家所接受和采纳。许多国家像法国一样,在发展自己的区别特征时首先选择语言政策。为了实现国家民族认同,许多国家在早期都不约而同地采取了语言同化政策。艾格以英国为例,阐释了标准英语教育政策背后国家领导层面的意识形态因素的推动作用。这里的意识形态主要是指以撒切尔夫人为首的保守党对语言和语言教育的看法和态度，他们认为学校教育就应该教标准英语，按照传统方式学习、背诵语法。尽管语言学者和语言教学工作者积极阐释、抗争，但是在政治斗争中，语言和文化都不得不退却，所以英国语言学者米尔洛伊夫妇总结说，语言问题发展成社会问题，并最终成为政治问题。这里的语言意识形态专指执政者对语言的看法和态度，是政治意识形态在语言领域的扩散和延伸。艾格将形象动机定义为认同动机的外在反映，由于语言对身份的塑造起着不可或缺的作用，其对身份的外显——形象的塑造自然也至关重要。战后德国和日本的海外语言推广的动机就是想树立、推广、宣传正面的国家形象。危机感是很多国家采取语言纯化政策的直接动机，法国就是最好的例子。法国为了抗衡外来语言尤其是英语对法语的影响，甚至建立了术语委员会并对词汇进行审查。危机感也包括对少数族群的警惕。解决社会中的权利、性别和族群不平等问题，也通常通过制定语言政策的形式进行。美国的女权运动引发了美国英语词汇表达的中性化，欧洲区域或少数民族语言宪章也旨在解决社会不平等问题。除了对从上至下的国家层面的语言政策进行探讨，艾格对个人语言行为规划的动机也进行了探讨与分析，认为融入主流文化和工具动机是个人语言行为选择背后的主要因素。

艾格更尝试对语言规划和语言政策的动机进行量化测量，并形成了一个比较完整的分析语言行为的框架（Ager 2001：1 - 124）。

虽然各位学者的用词不太一致，对语言规划动机探讨的深度、广度和角度都不太相同，但是都在一定程度上揭示了语言规划动机的性质和范畴。语言规划的动机不是单一的，而是一个涉及心理和社会等诸多因素的复杂的多维结构。不仅在国家主体层面上有规划动机,在集体和个人层面上也都存在着语言规划,当然其背后也都有着多维的规划层面。下文利用诸位学者提到的语言规划动机对澳大利亚的语言政策进行动机分析。

三、澳大利亚语言政策的发展变迁及其动因分析

在澳大利亚放任语言政策阶段,由于当时处于殖民时期,没有一个统一的责任政府,英国政府对澳大利亚多样的移民语言没有采取任何措施,未做任何干预。虽然人们当时对语言及其功能还缺乏认识,语言问题的重要性尚未显现出来,但是移民和土著族群集体和个人出于交际的便利,选择使用或者学习自己母语以外的语言来进行商业和社会生活的沟通,交际动机或者工具动机就是当时人们支配语言行为的动机。

在同化语言政策时期,民族国家认同的动机和危机感动机成为同化语言政策的推动因素。19世纪70年代,澳大利亚形成了一批具有民族意识的知识分子,他们想摆脱母国英国的控制,摆脱等级森严、腐朽的英国社会,提出了在澳大利亚建立独立统一的民主共和国的政治纲领。语言是民族认同的象征,是民族认同的基础,因为语言用最简单的方式区别"我们"和"别人",使用某种语言通常表明对使用该语言的民族的认同,而某种语言的通行与使用又可以增强民族认同感,而国民的国家认同感对国家的强盛至关重要。什么样的人是澳大利亚人?在澳大利亚民族主义思想的影响下,澳大利亚英语成为民族的文化象征,讲澳大利亚英语的人才是澳大利亚人。所以,为了促进国民对国家的认同,实行英

语单语同化政策在当时成为不二的选择。在移民准入上设置语言障碍，排斥有色人种，对移民加大英语教学力度与密度，期望他们快速融入主流社会。两次世界大战的爆发使英裔澳大利亚人对其他少数族群产生怀疑和警惕，危机感继而引发了更严厉、更苛刻的语言同化政策：取消双语教学；禁止在公共场合讲英语以外的其他语言；严格限制报刊、广播、电视等媒体上非英语语言的使用。

在多元语言政策时期，多种动机在发挥影响。在著名的《政策》中确定各个语言的地位时，首先承认澳大利亚英语的国语地位，英语在澳大利亚具有凝聚力和统一性，能促进对国家和文化的认同和忠诚。澳大利亚英语是澳大利亚独特文化的表达方式，是民族认同的组成要素。英语是澳大利亚不同语言背景的人的通用语，是联邦、州及地区议会制定、颁布和解释澳大利亚法律所公开正式使用的语言。《政策》亦承认土著语言和移民语言为澳大利亚语言，承认这些语言应该被接受和尊重。对澳大利亚多元文化的民族国家认同是多元语言认同的动因，而为实现全体国民的交际沟通，采取了 English for all（所有人都要学英语）的政策原则。《政策》也非常强调全民的双语能力：对非英语使用者而言，双语就是保持母语的同时学习英语；对英语使用者而言，双语意味着学习英语之外的第二语言。《政策》在第二语言学习上提出了四个社会目标：丰富（enrichment）、经济（economics）、平等（equality）、对外（external），即丰富文化知识、增进族群包容、开发语言经济价值、服务对外贸易、促进社会公平公正、加强国际关系、提升国家安全。这些都是澳大利亚大力开展第二语言学习的动机。

在优先化语言政策时期,尽管支持非英语语言的学习,但动机发生了变化,跨文化和多元文化的目的不复存在,取而代之的是经济原因和洲际认同的改变。事实上早在1987年12月,政府部门的官员在一次新闻发布会上就将提高经济竞争力作为国家语言政策的主要依据。从1992年就开始实施的国家亚洲语言战略将国家当时有限的资源用到亚洲语言的学习项目上,以促进澳大利亚与亚洲国家的国际贸易,提高澳大利亚的经济实力。语言政策成为一种可以用来获得经济竞争优势、促进经济发展的工具。

通过以上的论述我们可以看出:在澳大利亚不同发展阶段的语言政策的背后,都有着多种动机在发挥作用,如认同、语言交际、平等、经济、国家安全、国际关系、智力开发等;而且这些动机在每一个阶段并不是都存在或均衡存在的,因为任何语言政策的背后的动机都不是单一的,而是一个复杂的多维结构。在这个复杂的结构中,不同的动机处于不同的层次,甚至可能相互矛盾,因为社会就是一个复杂的系统。

四、对语言规划和语言政策动机研究的一点思考

学界对语言规划动机的研究刚刚起步,艾格的《语言规划和语言政策的动机研究》算得上目前的集大成之作,他提出了语言规划的七种动机,但是并不全面。如刘海涛就认为艾格没有将最重要的一种动机包括进去,事实上许多东方国家的语言规划、实践已经证明了提高语言交际效率也是人们进行语言规划的一种动机(刘海涛 2007)。国家安全在近几年也成为推动语言政策的重要因素,美国在"9·11"恐怖袭击事件以后,中央情报局等一些机构一直哀叹缺乏阿拉伯

语和其他外语的专家，尤其是在翻译涉及国家安全信息方面的专家，所以先后启动了"关键语言"项目和"国家安全语言倡议"计划（潘海英、张凌坤 2011）。所以国家安全也是当代很多国家语言规划的重要动机。

我们可以对每一个国家语言政策背后的动因进行分析，继而总结语言规划和语言政策动机的种类、层次、系统，并进而研究语言政策动机、措施、效果之间的关系。我们也应该认识到每一个国家语言规划和语言政策的动机都不是静止不动的，都是动态变化的。

李宇明（2012）把语言生活划分为宏观、中观、微观三个层级，要在语言生活的不同的层级上考察语言政策和语言管理。同样，对语言政策动机的研究也应该放在不同的层级上考虑。对个人而言，选择或放弃哪一种语言或许和认同关系不大，完全是利益驱动，或者说是为了更好的生活，或者说是按艾格所采用的术语——工具动机。在语言生活的不同层面上，语言选择和改变语言行为的动机及其层次性或许差异很大，这都值得我们在未来进行研究探讨。

我们非常赞同艾格把态度因素作为另外的维度加入对动机的考察中，但同时也觉得其对动机量化测量的框架仍须完善，尤其是如何确定态度因素中各因素的强度问题值得推敲。

*本文原载于《东北师大学报（哲学社会科学版）》2013 年第 6 期。收入本文集时略有删改。

参考文献

Ager, D. *Motivation in Language Planning and Language Policy*.

Clevedon: Multilingual Matters Ltd., 2001.

Clyne, M. *Australia's Language Potential*. Sydney: University of New South Wales Press, 2005.

Cooper, R. L. *Language Planning and Social Change*. Cambridge: Cambridge University Press, 1989.

Lo Bianco, J. *National Policy on Language*. Canberra: Australian Goverment Publishing Service, 1987.

Smolicz, J. J. and M. J. Secome. Assimilation or pluralism? Changing policies for monority languages education in Australia. *Language Policy*, 2003 (2): 3 - 25.

薄守生, 赖慧玲. 当代中国语言规划研究: 侧重于区域学的视角 [M]. 北京: 中国社会科学出版社, 2009.

李宇明. 论语言生活的层级 [J]. 语言教学与研究, 2012 (5): 1 - 10.

刘海涛. 语言规划和语言政策: 从定义变迁看学科发展 [C] //教育部语用所社会语言学与媒体语言研究室. 语言规划的理论与实践. 北京: 语文出版社, 2006: 55 - 60.

刘海涛. 语言规划的动机分析 [J]. 北华大学学报 (社会科学版), 2007 (4): 63 - 68.

王辉. 近20年澳大利亚外语教育政策演变的启示 [J]. 北华大学学报 (社会科学版), 2010 (6): 28 - 32.

潘海英, 张凌坤. 美国语言政策的国家利益观透析 [J]. 东北师大学报 (哲学社会科学版), 2011 (5): 97 - 100.

姚亚平. 中国语言规划研究 [M]. 北京: 商务印书馆, 2006.

作者简介

刘晓波,女,吉林长春人,吉林大学文学院语言学与应用语言学在读博士研究生,现任吉林大学副教授、硕士研究生导师。中国社会语言学会会员。主要从事语言教学、语言政策研究。曾于2011—2012年在澳大利亚墨尔本莫纳什大学(Monash University)访学。

战菊,女,吉林长春人,现任吉林大学公共外语教育学院教授、博士研究生导师(文学院),教育部大学外语教学指导委员会委员(2013年至今),全国外语教师教育与发展专业委员会副主任(2013年至今),中国社会语言学学会理事(2006年至今)。《语言政策与语言教育》编审委员会委员,吉林大学高校外语教育基地主任,吉林大学外国语言学及应用语言学和英语翻译方向学术带头人。主要研究方向:应用语言学(二语写作、教师发展、课程设置),社会语言学(语言教育、语言态度、语言政策和语言规划)。在国内外学术期刊发表论文30多篇。曾主持省部级研究项目若干,一项国家社科项目在研中。曾为《中国应用语言学》(Chinese Journal of Applied Linguistics)主编二语写作专辑(2012年第3期)。

中南半岛四国的语言生态与语言政策的历时演变

王晋军　黄兴亚

一、引　言

　　我国正在实施和推进的"一带一路"倡议,其实质是借鉴"丝绸之路"的历史符号,致力于亚欧非大陆及附近海洋的互联互通,以共商、共建、共享为发展理念,共同打造政治互信、经济融合、文化包容的利益共同体。而深入了解"一带一路"沿线国家的语言对促进民心相通及"一带一路"倡议的实施都有着重要意义。本文主要探讨"一带一路"沿线东南亚国家中的中南半岛四国在主要历史时期语言生态及语言政策的变迁,从而加深对中南半岛四国语言国情的了解和认识,以期对我国的语言政策制定及实施有一定的启示。

二、中南半岛四国简介

　　中南半岛(Indo-China Peninsula),亚洲南部三大半岛之一,旧称印度支那半岛,又称中印半岛。中南半岛包括越南、老挝、柬埔寨、缅甸、泰国及马来西亚西部。从 19 世纪中叶至 20 世纪中叶,中南半岛除泰国外(泰国古称暹罗,在 1896 年与英国和法国签订了条约,成为英属和法属印度支那的缓冲国,因此没有沦为殖民地),其余五个国家先后遭到英国、法国殖民者的侵略,并长期受到西方殖民者的统治。其中老挝、柬埔寨、越南被法国统治,被称为"法属印度支那";缅甸、马来西亚被英国统治。因越南、老挝、柬埔寨、缅甸四国在历史阶段的相似性,本文主要探讨这四个国家的语言生态及语言政策的历时演变。

越南,全称越南社会主义共和国(the Socialist Republic of Vietnam),位于东南亚中南半岛东部,北与中国广西、云南接壤,西与老挝、柬埔寨交界,东面和南面临南海,海岸线长 3260 多公里,国土狭长,国土面积约 32.96 万平方公里。越南是个多民族国家,全国共有 54 个民族。京族又称越族,为主体民族,其人口占了越南总人口的 86%(2020 年 5 月)。越南经历了 1000 多年的中国封建朝代郡县时期,900 多年的中国封建朝代藩属时期,其名称几经更换。汉代被称为交趾、交州;唐、五代被称为安南都护府、大瞿越,宋代改为大越。1802 年,清政府同意把安南改名为越南。19 世纪中叶后,越南逐渐沦为法国殖民地。1945 年八月革命以后,胡志明宣布成立越南民主共和国,1976 年统一后改名为越南社会主义共和国。1986 年开始施行革新开放,1995 年越南加入东盟,成为第七个加入东盟的成员国。

缅甸联邦共和国(the Republic of the Union of Myanmar)位于亚洲东南部、中南半岛西部,东北与中国毗邻,西北与印度、孟加拉国相接,东南与老挝、泰国交界,西南濒临孟加拉湾和缅甸海;国土面积为约为67.66万平方公里,是中南半岛上面积最大、东南亚面积第二大的国家。缅甸总人口为5458万(2020年)。缅甸是一个典型的佛教国家,全国85%以上的人口信仰佛教;同时它也是个多宗教信仰的国家,除了绝大多数人信仰佛教外,还有5%的人口信仰基督教,8%的人口信仰伊斯兰教,0.5%的人信仰印度教。缅甸是个多民族、多语言的国家,全国共有135个民族,缅族作为主体民族约占总人口的65%。各少数民族均有自己的语言,其中克钦族、克伦族、掸族和孟族等民族有文字。缅语是全国通用语、官方语言和公立学校的教学语言。

老挝人民民主共和国(the Lao People's Democratic Republic),简称老挝,是中南半岛上的唯一一个内陆国家。它地处中南半岛的北部,北面与我国的云南省接壤,东面与越南为邻,西面和西南面分别与缅甸和泰国交界,南面与柬埔寨相接。国土面积为23.68万平方公里,人口为706万(2018年)。老挝素有"中南半岛屋脊"之称,以山地和高原居多,低山、丘陵次之,平原低谷较少。老挝共有50个民族,分属老泰语族系、孟-高棉语族系、苗-瑶语族系、汉-藏语族系,统称为老挝民族。通用语及官方语言为老挝语。老挝是一个典型的佛教国家,历史上曾尊佛教为国教,老挝的政治、语言、文学、传统习俗等无不打上佛教文化的印记。

柬埔寨王国(the Kingdom of Cambodia)位于中南半岛南部,是中国的近邻,东部和东南部同越南接壤,北部与老挝交界,西部和西北部与泰国毗邻,西南濒临暹罗湾。国土面积约为 18 万平方公里，海岸线长约 460 公里。全国人口约为 1600 万，其中农村人口占 80% 左右。境内有 20 多个民族，高棉族是主体民族，占总人口的 80%。高棉语为通用语言，与英语、法语同为官方语言。佛教为国教，93% 以上的居民信奉佛教，占族信奉伊斯兰教，少数城市居民信奉天主教。柬埔寨是个有着 2000 多年历史的文明古国，历经了扶南、真腊时期，其中最强盛时期（9—14 世纪）的吴哥王朝，创造了举世闻名的吴哥文明。近代以来，柬埔寨遭受法国殖民统治达 90 年之久，1953 年 11 月柬埔寨宣布完全独立。之后又经历了战争和动荡。1991 年《巴黎和平协定》签署后，柬埔寨才走上了和平、独立发展的道路。1999 年 4 月 30 日，柬埔寨加入东盟。①

三、生态语言学与语言政策

语言研究的生态观由来已久，可以追溯到 19 世纪德国语言学家洪堡特（Humboldt），他认为所有的语言都是有机体（姚小平 1995）。同时期的德国语言学家施莱歇尔（Schleiche）在《达尔文理论与语言学》一文中论述了语言发展的规律与生物进化具有一脉相承的特点（施莱歇尔 2008）。美国语言学家爱德华·萨丕尔（Edward Sapir）的《语言与环境》一文深入探讨了语言与说话者的自然环境与社会环境之间的关系（Sapir，引自 Fill & Mühlhäusler 2001）。

而把语言与环境之间的关系研究确立为一门学科却是近 30 年来的事。学界通常认为 1972 年美国语言学家艾纳·豪

---

① 以上国家信息来自中国外交部网站。

根（Einar Haugen）提出的一个比喻"语言生态"（language ecology），即用生态中动物、植物与环境的关系来比喻语言与其周围环境发生的相互作用（Haugen 1972），开启了语言生态学的研究，这也就是很多学者所认同的豪根模式。有些学者使用生态语言学来取代语言生态学。不少学者把语言生态学和生态语言学两者等同，如菲尔（Fill）（2000）、菲尔和缪尔豪斯勒（Fill & Mühlhäusler）（2001）、李国正（1991，1992）、范俊军（2005）、冯广艺（2013）等。一些学者如黄国文、陈旸（2016）认为语言生态学反映的是豪根模式，而生态语言学反映的韩礼德（Halliday）模式，两者同属一个学科，只是侧重点不同而已。韩礼德模式侧重于生态话语批评或话语的生态批评，而豪根模式关注语言的多样性、濒危语言的保护，"研究语言生态与语言政策、语言生态系统中的语言接触、语言生活、语言态度、语言应用等问题"（王晋军、刘娟娟 2017：149）。豪根把语言生态定义为"特定语言与环境之间的相互作用关系"（Haugen 1972：325）。他进而把语言所处的环境分为三个维度，即语言所处的社会环境（social environment of language）、语言所处的自然环境（natural environment of language）以及语言所处的心理环境（psychological environment of language）（Haugen 1972）。社会环境是指语言作为交际媒介与社会发生的相互关系，它主要由语言数量、人口、民族、宗教、经济、政治因素等构成；自然环境是指对语言使用者产生影响的地理分布、动物及植物状况、气候等；心理环境主要涉及双语或多语者的语言选择，它包括人们的语言态度以及人们对语言的选择等。豪根认为，语言生态是由学习、使用和传播语言的人所决定的

（Haugen 1972）。可以说，任何一个维度的变化都会对语言生态产生影响。

语言生态学与语言政策紧密相关，因为"语言生态学的基本理念决定了语言生态与语言政策息息相关"（王晋军、刘娟娟 2017：149）。一个国家语言政策的制定一般是在该国的语言生态出现某种特殊的状态时，国家或政府所采取的有针对性的相应措施。就语言生态与语言政策的关系，许多学者都进行了探讨。Mühlhäusler（2000）认为，语言政策的制定与实施都要考虑语言生态。博纳德·斯波斯基（2011）指出，探讨语言生态对语言政策的影响及作用是语言政策研究的一个基本内容和特点。冯广艺（2013）认为，语言政策的制定应该考虑语言生态的实情。

总之，语言政策可以调适一个国家的语言生态环境，但语言政策可能也会对一个国家的语言生态带来损害，并对政局稳定、国家安全产生威胁。而关键的一点是语言政策的制定是否能结合语言生态的实情，更好地解决一国在语言使用中存在的问题，从而保持语言生态的可持续发展和语言多样性。

四、中南半岛四国不同历史时期的语言生态和语言政策

中南半岛四国都经历了相同的历史时期，即都经历了前殖民期、殖民时期、民族独立时期和加入东盟后四个主要历史时期，在这些重要的历史时期各国的语言生态及语言政策都呈现出各自的特点，有共性，也有个性。

（一）前殖民期

中南半岛四国在前殖民期都大力发展民族语言，使民族

语言逐渐确立，并为大众所接受。越南使用文字的变化经历了复杂而又漫长的历史过程，这在许多国家中都非常少见。越南的语言文字使用经历了三个时期：使用汉字时期，使用喃字（Chu Nom）时期，使用拉丁语即国语字（Chu Quoc Ngu）时期（见表1）。

表1　越南主要历史时期的语言文字

历史时期	使用语言	文字系统
8—9世纪	越语、汉语	汉字
10—12世纪	越语、汉语	汉字
13—16世纪	越语、汉语	喃字、汉字
17—19世纪	越语、汉语	喃字、汉字、国语字
法国殖民时期（1861—1945年）	越语、汉语、法语	喃字、汉字、国语字、法语
1945年至今	越语	国语字

（参照 Nguyen Tai Can 1999：7）

1945年八月革命胜利后，国语字获得了正式的地位，成为越南民主共和国的唯一正式文字（兰强等 2012）。之后在1948年，新颁布的越南宪法第18条规定，越南公民必须能读写越南国语字。

老挝语的文字起源于公元1世纪中叶古印度语言的婆罗米字母和梵文天城体字母，后来又受到孟—高棉文字的影响。老挝语在其早期的形成和发展阶段，都受到了很多外来语的影响，如古高棉语、梵语和巴利语。澜沧王国期间（1353—1707年）由于法昂王从柬埔寨引入小乘佛教，翻译佛教经典，古高棉语词汇逐渐应用到老挝人的日常生活与交往中，从而成为老挝语词汇。巴利文和巴利语是小乘佛教传播教义的载体，随着小乘佛教的广泛传播，大量的梵语和巴利语词汇也开始融入老挝语中。1829—1893年，老挝再度受到暹罗入侵和统治，老挝人被迫学习泰语，泰语词汇逐渐融入老挝语中。

柬埔寨历史上深受"印度化"的影响，早期的"印度化"出现在扶南王朝，同时也带来了印度的文字。柬埔寨人吸收印度文化的过程持续了1000多年（Mebbett 1977：1-14）。公元14世纪以前，梵文在柬埔寨一直占据着统治地位。15世纪初，巴利文取代梵语成为柬埔寨的官方语言。安赞王统治时期（1516—1566年），柬埔寨国力有所增强，在这一时期，高棉语成为官方语言，而梵语和巴利语则降为了辅助语言。16世纪末直到19世纪，柬埔寨受到越南和暹罗的两面进攻，从而使高棉语吸收了一些泰语和越南语词汇。

缅甸在蒲甘王朝初期使用大量的孟文，而缅文是在孟文的基础上发展而来的。为了将缅文规范化，蒲甘时期先后开展了两次正字运动（刘书琳、邹长虹 2015）。12世纪后，缅文成为了缅甸最重要的文字。13世纪时缅语发展相对稳定，并确立了中部语音的强势地位，为日后中部语音发展成为标准语音打下了基础（钟智翔 2004：79-91）。东吁王朝时期和贡榜王朝时期随着正字运动的开展，出版了不少正字法的书籍，如《文字要津》《温纳拨达纳正字法》《智者特征正字法》等（李佳 2009）。

(二) 殖民时期

四个国家在19世纪先后遭受了英国和法国的殖民统治。

在英法殖民统治期间，中南半岛四国的语言政策都体现出以殖民统治者为主体和以殖民统治者语言独尊的特征。殖民地国家都确立了以宗主国语言为唯一法定官方语言的法规，而各国的民族语言都受到压制，备受冷落。

1893年老挝沦为法国的殖民地后，法国殖民当局规定，所有学校课程必须用法语教学，学生的课本也基本上是照搬法国的。法国殖民当局还规定法语是唯一合法的文字。19世纪中叶法国占领了越南，从1917年开始在越南推行法式教育制度，开办小学、中学和大学，迫使学生学习法语，维护法国的殖民统治。在法国殖民期间，法语是越南唯一的官方语言。1885年的第三次英缅战争之后，缅甸成为英属印度的一个省，缅甸完全沦为英国殖民地。在英国的殖民统治时期，英语被规定为官方语言和全国通用语。柬埔寨沦为法属殖民地期间，法殖民当局强制推行法语教育，并把法语作为其官方语言，高棉语的使用和发展在这一时期受到了极大的限制。

（三）民族独立时期

民族独立时期四个国家语言政策的重要内容就是去殖民化，取消殖民者语言作为官方语言的地位，优先发展民族语言，并确立民族语言的官方语言地位，从而提升民族和国家意识。

柬埔寨1953年独立以后，高棉语取代了法语作为学校教育用语。由于法语在长达90年的殖民统治中所产生的影响，它仍然作为政府的工作语言一直延续到红色高棉时期。1954年越南取得反法战争的胜利，法国殖民统治就此终结，法语不再作为越南的官方语言。在北越，越南语成为各教育阶段的唯一语言（Gayle 1994）。1961年，越南语最终成为唯一的可以用于教育的官方语言。相对而言，南越的语言政策形成得相对较慢，直到1968年，南越西贡政府才将越南语推广到各教育阶段。1948年缅甸宣告独立，成立缅甸联邦，吴努政权就以宪法形式确立缅语为官方语言，把缅语作为各级公立学校的教学语言，在全国推广缅语，以提升缅语地位，提高其普及率和使用率。1975年老挝成立人民民主共和国后，由于法语的深远影响，法语仍然是老挝的工作语言和教学语言。1975年12月第一届老挝全国人民代表大会做出决议，将老龙族老语确定为老挝人民民主共和国的通用语即官方标准老挝语（杜敦信、赵和曼1988），学校要求使用标准老挝语教学（郑淑花，2004），这是老挝历史上第一次出台独立的语言政策。

（四）加入东盟后

在20世纪末期随着东南亚国家联盟（简称"东盟"）的成立，四个国家先后加入该组织，以谋求在地区事务中发挥越来越大的作用，同时促进区域经济与贸易的发展。随着四个国家先后加入东盟，其语言政策也在发生变化，同时也对四国的语言生态产生了影响。

首先，由于东盟在地区事务和国际事务中发挥着越来越重要的作用，四个国家中英语的地位不断凸显。《东南亚国家联盟宪章》规定英语为东盟唯一的工作语言和官方语言，这对东南亚国家的语言政策有很大的影响。缅甸于1997年加入东盟后，缅甸政府的高级官员开始接受英语培训，有的还参加了新加坡的培训项目，以便更好地掌握东盟的工作语言——英语。柬埔寨1999年加入东盟后，商界的就业机会不断增加，柬埔寨与国际援助机构的频繁交流扩大了英语的使用范围，也加速了柬埔寨对英语的选择。老挝于 1997 年加入东盟后，老挝外交部的国际关系培训中心就开始对涉及东盟事务的官员进行高层次的特殊用途英语培训。越南在 1995 年 7 月加入东盟后，越南政府就制定了一系列的语言政策来突出英语作为第一外语的重要地位。而且这四个国家都把英语作为第一外语在各教学层次进行推广和普及。

其次，进入 21 世纪，四国不仅重视英语，而且推行了多元化的语言政策。进入新世纪，四个国家除了大力推广英语外，还不断扩大包括汉语、法语及其他语种的教育，从而使四国的语言政策呈现多元化的特点。

随着中国国力和影响力的不断增强，东南亚国家兴起了"汉语热"。中国政府在四个国家设立了孔子学院、孔子学堂等来推广汉语和中华文化，华语教学的规模逐年扩大，华语已成为东南亚国家继英语之后的主要外语。如柬埔寨的中文教育已经形成了一套完整的教学和管理体系，包括统一教材、统一师资调配和统一学制等。柬埔寨多元化的语言政策为华语教育提供了不断发展的空间。越南教育部门除了把英语定为必修课外，还重视其他语种的学习，如越南在一些具备条件的地区开设了汉语、俄语、法语、日语、德语作为第二语言课程，而且第二语言的教学从 6 年级开始一直持续到 12 年级（王晋军 2015）。

五、中南半岛四国语言生态及语言政策的共性与个性

通过对中南半岛四国语言生态与语言政策历时演变的分析，我们发现中南半岛四国在语言政策及语言生态上呈现出很多共性，当然也存在着一些差异。

(一) 四国语言生态的共性

四国语言生态共性主要体现在地理、民族、历史、经济、政治、语言等多方面。

1. 地理环境相似

中南半岛四国地处中南半岛,有三个国家与中国接壤,即越南、老挝和缅甸。各国境内地形较为复杂,河流、山脉纵横。这四个国家地理上的相似性和相邻关系,在一定程度上对其民族尤其是跨境民族及其语言产生了影响。

2. 民族和语言多样性极其显著

中南半岛四国地理上相互为邻,地形复杂而多样,境内多高山、丘陵及河流,这些地理特征在很大程度上影响了民族的形成和分布。其民族构成具有一些共同的特点,即:民族众多,各国都有其主体民族;民族杂居,不少民族跨界而居;民族关系复杂;各民族经济发展不均衡;等等。

3. 经济的相似性

中南半岛四国中,有三个国家被联合国列为世界上最不发达的国家(柬埔寨、老挝和缅甸)。这四个国家既是发展中国家又是低收入国家(祁广谋、钟智翔 2013)。

4. 长期被殖民的历史

这四个国家先后遭受英国、法国殖民者的侵略,并长期受到西方殖民者的统治。"老挝成为法国殖民地达 61 年,柬埔寨沦为法国殖民地达 90 年,越南遭受法国殖民统治达 91 年,缅甸成为英国的殖民地达 106 年。"(王晋军 2015:11)"二战"结束后,曾经的殖民地纷纷宣布独立,从而摆脱殖民统治的影响。进入 20 世纪,这四个国家先后加入东盟。这些重要的历史节点都对四国的语言使用、语言政策产生了较大的影响。

(二) 四国语言政策的相似性

四国的语言政策也呈现出一些共性,表现在以下四个方面。

(1) 在殖民前期各国都经历了民族语言形成和发展的时期,使得民族语言被国民逐渐接受。

(2) 殖民地时期各国被迫接受宗主国的语言为官方语言。

(3) 民族独立时期,各国都摈弃前殖民者的语言,并确立了民族语言为官方语言和通用语言。

(4) 加入东盟后,中南半岛四国在英语全球化的影响下,大力推广英语,英语成为各国的主要外语;进入21世纪,四国的语言政策呈现出多元化的态势,汉语及其他外语的教育及教学也在不断发展。

(三) 四国语言生态和语言政策的差异

由于中南半岛四国在社会、政治、经济、文化等方面的差异,其语言生态及语言政策也呈现出一些差异。

1. 由于四国国情的差异,民族独立后各国在确立民族语言的方式上存在着差异

柬埔寨1953年独立以后,由于法语的长期影响,柬政府一直沿用法语到红色高棉时期。老挝的情况也较为相近,在1975年1月成立老挝人民民主共和国近一年后,才确定了标准老挝语作为通用语和官方语言的地位。1954年越南取得独立后,北越和南越由于多重原因,在确定越南语作为官方语言上存在差异。

2. 对待少数民族语言上的差异

由于经济实力和民族矛盾的多重原因,四国在对待少数

民族语言的问题上差异较大。越南由于经济状况好于其余三个国家，其对少数民族语言的重视程度高于缅甸、老挝、柬埔寨三个国家，而其余三国由于积贫积弱，对少数民族语言则听之任之。

3. 在英语推广上的差异

在英语全球化的过程中，虽然越来越多的年轻人倾向于选择英语，但是由于老挝、柬埔寨、缅甸三国基础教育落后，国力贫穷，能够接受英语教育的人还只是少数。相比之下，越南的境况则大不相同。如越南教育部门将英语开设为必修课，在重视英语教育的同时也鼓励其他语种的教学和学习。

六、结　语

本文试图从中南半岛四国语言生态和语言政策的历时演变来阐释语言生态与语言政策的密切联系。对四国语言政策与语言生态的分析，也促使我们就语言政策与语言生态间的关系进行深入思考，同时也可为我国语言政策的制定和实施提供一些借鉴。通过分析，我们可以做出如下几点判断：一个国家没有主权独立和领土完整就不可能保证语言生态维持正常的状态；一个国家的语言生态是制定语言政策的基本依据；一国的政治、经济因素在语言政策的制定过程中有着较为重要的作用；语言政策的实施能够调适和影响一个国家的语言生态；语言的心理环境不可避免地受到了全球化的影响，语言资本论在很大程度上引导了语言使用者做出语言选择。

＊本文为国家语言文字工作委员会"十二五"科研规划重点项目"中国和东盟国家的民族语言政策对比研究"

(ZDI125-27)以及国家社会科学基金西部项目"中国和东盟国家的国家语言能力对比研究"(15XYY008)的阶段性成果。

参考文献

Fill, A. Language and ecology: Ecolinguistics perspectives for 2000 beyond. In AILA Organizing Committee (ed.). *Selected Papers from AILA 1999 Tokyo*. Tokyo: Waseda University Press, 2000.

Fill, A. and P. Mühlhäusler (eds.). *The Ecolinguistics Reader: Language, Ecology and Environment*. London and New York: Continuum, 2001.

Gayle, J. K. English teaching boom in Vietnam: An American perspective. Paper presented at the TESOL Convention, Baltimore, MD., 1994.

Haugen, E. *The Ecology of Language: Essays by Einar Haugen*. Stanford: Stanford University Press, 1972.

Mebbett, L. W. The Indianization of Southeast Asia. *Journal of Southeast Asian Studies (JSEAS)*, 1977, 8 (1): 1-14.

Mühlhäusler, P. Language planning and language ecology. *Current Issues in Language Planning*, 2000, 1 (3): 306-367.

Nguyen, Tai Can. 12 centuries of history of the Vietnamese language: Essay on the delimination of periods. *Vietnamese Studies*, 1999 (3): 53-61.

杜敦信,赵和曼. 越南老挝柬埔寨手册[M]. 北京:时事出版社,1988.

范俊军. 生态语言学研究述评［J］. 外语教学与研究，2005，37（2）：110-115.

冯广艺. 语言生态学引论［M］. 北京：人民出版社，2013.

黄国文，陈旸. 菲尔生态语言学研究述评［J］. 鄱阳湖学刊，2016（4）：19-24.

兰强，徐方宇，李华杰. 越南概论［M］. 广州：世界图书出版广东有限公司，2012.

李佳. 缅甸的语言政策和语言教育［J］. 东南亚南亚研究，2009（2）：75-80.

李国正. 生态汉语学［M］. 长春：吉林教育出版社，1991.

李国正. 语言新论［J］. 厦门大学学报（哲学社会科学版），1992（2）：121-127.

刘书琳，邹长虹. 中国与缅甸语言政策、语言规划的对比研究及启示［J］. 广西师范学院学报（哲学社会科学版），2015（6）：167-171.

祁广谋，钟智翔. 东南亚概论［M］. 广州：世界图书出版广东有限公司，2013.

施莱歇尔. 达尔文理论与语言学：致耶拿大学动物学教授、动物学博物馆馆长恩斯特·海克尔先生［J］. 姚小平，译. 方言，2008（4）：373-383.

斯波斯基. 语言政策：社会语言学中的重要论题［M］. 张治国，译. 北京：商务印书馆，2011.

王晋军. 中国和东盟国家外语政策对比研究［M］. 昆明：云南大学出版社，2015.

王晋军，刘娟娟. 语言生态视域下的双语教育政策研究［J］. 英语研究，2017（2）：147-156.

姚小平. 洪堡特：人文研究和语言研究［M］. 北京：外语教学与研究出版社, 1995.

郑淑花. 从殖民地语言政策到民族独立的语言政策：老挝语言政策研究［J］. 广西教育学院学报, 2004 (6)：135–137.

钟智翔. 论缅语历史分期问题［M］//东方语言文化论丛：第3辑. 广州：广东经济出版社, 2004：79–91.

作者简介

王晋军，博士，广州大学外国语学院教授，云南大学博士研究生导师。研究方向：功能语言学、社会语言学、生态语言学。

黄兴亚，博士，云南中医药大学国际教育学院副教授。研究方向：社会语言学、生态语言学。

澳门社会的语言状况与语言政策

张桂菊

自从1999年12月20日澳门回归祖国以来,澳门的政治、经济、文化、教育等各领域发生了巨大的变化。本文拟对澳门的语言状况进行回顾,并对语言政策对变化中的语言状况做出应然的回应等加以探讨。本文将研究的时间范围限制在1999年12月到2009年之间,即澳门回归祖国后的第一个十年。

一、澳门的语言状况

(一)"葡语独尊"与"个人双语"

葡萄牙人1553年登陆澳门,改变了澳门开埠之前的单语社会,澳门此后逐渐形成了汉语和葡萄牙语(以下简称"葡语")等双语和多语社会。随着1840年鸦片战争的失败,葡语在澳门获得了官方语言的合法地位。当时实行的语言政策有三个特征:一是在官立及政府资助的中小学中推销葡语

语言的可持续性

——将葡语作为教学语言或开设葡语课程；二是在招聘政府公职人员时，要求应聘者"必须懂得阅读及讲葡语"；三是要求所有餐馆、会所或场所的招牌、海报、通告都必须用葡语书写。这些语言政策在一定程度上起到了推广葡语的作用。总之，回归前澳葡政府推行的是语言霸权主义，采取"葡语独尊"的立场，坚持葡文教育政策，仅关心少数官立葡文学校的发展，为只占澳门人口4%的葡萄牙后裔提供相对较好的教育条件和支持。对基础教育中的语言教学，特别是占澳门绝大多数私立学校中的语言教学，长期"扮演着不闻不问，不负责任的角色"（刘羡冰1994）。

1987年3月16日中葡政府签署《中华人民共和国政府和葡萄牙共和国政府关于澳门问题的联合声明》，该声明第二条第五款规定："澳门特别行政区政府机关、立法机关和法院，除使用中文外，还可使用葡文。"1991年第455/91号法令出台并规定：中文在澳门具有与葡文相等之官方地位及法律效力。1993年3月31日中华人民共和国主席令第3号公布，自1999年12月20日起实施《中华人民共和国澳门特别行政区基本法》，该法案第一章第九条规定：澳门特别行政区的行政机关、立法机关和司法机关，除使用中文外，还可使用葡文，葡文也是正式语文。至此，中文作为官方语言在澳门的法律地位得以确立。但是，由于历史原因，中文作为官方语言比葡语已经晚了150多年，中文在行政、司法、立法部门的官方地位与葡文相差甚远。再加上过渡期澳葡政府执行的是"个人双语"的语言政策，他们花费大量公帑派公务员到北京学习普通话，到里斯本学习葡语。由于短期的语言培训难以达到标本兼治的目的，公务员大多会说几句葡语或普通话,但两种官方语言的水平都难以满足行政、立法及司法的要求。而澳门基础教育中的语文课仍旧以粤语教授,普通话被视为弱势官方语言而游离于语文课之外,政府给予学校的教学自主权使普通话的推广受到了一定程度的影响。

(二) 澳门日常用语的状况

澳门的人口和语言状况不但能为社会语言学研究人员提供生动的第一手材料,而且还是制定澳门语言规划的依据和出发点。语言政策决策者要回应澳门的双语和多语问题,制定澳门的语言教育政策,不可忽略澳门的人口和语言状况,所以,对澳门统计暨普查局公布的1991年、1996年、2001年及2006年人口普查数据与语言问题相关的资料(见表1、表2)进行整理、分析,有助于厘清回归前后澳门语言的发展状况及其语言政策的实施情况(值得注意的是,为了讨论方便,本节把粤语、普通话和其他中国方言均视作独立的"常用语言",虽然从语言学、语言政策的角度来看,它们都是"汉语",属于同一种语言的不同变体)。

表1 1991—2006年人口普查家中日常使用语言 (3岁及以上居住人口)

日常使用语言	人数			
	1991年	1996年	2001年	2006年
总数	337277	397488	424203	492291
粤语	289297	346082	372697	421699
普通话	4016	4955	6660	15937
其他中国方言	32217	30848	32125	32218
葡语	6132	7352	2813	3036

（续上表）

日常使用语言	人数			
	1991 年	1996 年	2001 年	2006 年
英语	1777	3189	2792	7290
其他	3838	5062	7116	11111

表2 2001—2006 年人口普查有关语言能力的数据

日常使用语言	人数		
	1996 年	2001 年	2006 年
总数	397488	424203	492291
其他一种语言/方言	108882	129793	182701
粤语	15191	12755	13057
普通话	37134	58625	101166
福建话	—	5771	6383
其他中国方言	25740	19446	23024
葡语	4336	3418	2838
英语	21889	25390	29135
其他语言（日语、法语、泰语等）	4592	4388	7098
两种其他语言/方言	32087	50017	74362
普通话及英语	6254	16926	31161
普通话及福建话	—	4025	7475
葡语及英语	2900	2793	2083
粤语及普通话	—	10436	22063

(续上表)

日常使用语言	人数		
	1996 年	2001 年	2006 年
普通话及其他中国方言	—	7961	1342
其他两种语言/方言	20742	7876	10238
三种其他语言/方言	4325	7577	8708
普通话、葡语及英语	927	2120	2228
普通话、其他中国方言及英语	—	1100	1247
其他三种语言/方言	3318	4357	5233
不懂其他语言/方言	251616	236816	226520

注：由于回归前后统计分类不同，故对1996年的统计数据加以说明：(1) 可使用两种其他语言/方言中，讲粤语及葡语者为188人，讲粤语及英语者为1542人，讲普通话及英语者为477人，此项共计32087人；(2) 讲普通话、其他中国方言及葡语者为80人；(3) 讲四种及以上语言的人数为578人（回归后未统计此项）。

1. 回归前日常用语的状况

1991年澳门居住人口为401,873人，3岁及以上的居住人口中：85.8%以粤语为家中常用语言，而普通话及其他中国方言分别占1.2%及9.6%；以葡语为家中常用语言的居住人口占1.8%；以英语及其他语言为家中常用语言的分别占0.5%及1.1%。

1996年澳门居住人口为414,128人，3岁及以上的居住人口中：87.1%以粤语为家中常用语言，而普通话及其他中国方言分别占1.2%及7.8%；以葡语为家中常用语言的居住人口占 1.8%；以英语及其他语言为家中常用语言的分别占 0.8% 及 1.3%。除家中常用语言外，有 36.6% 的居住人口可流利使用另一种或多种语言与人沟通。当中以懂普通话的比例最高，占上述人口 30.5%；其次是英语，占 22%。按常用语言及其他可使用语言合计，发现 3 岁及以上居住人口中，90.9% 懂粤语，12.4% 能使用普通话，而懂英语及葡语的则分别占 8.8% 及 3.9%。

2. 回归后日常用语的状况

2001 年澳门居住人口为 435,235 人，其中 3 岁及以上的居住人口为 424,203 人。3 岁及以上的居住人口中，87.9% 在家中使用的常用语言为粤语，而普通话及其他中国方言分别占 1.6% 及 7.6%；以葡语为家中常用语言的居住人口占总体的 0.7%；以英语及其他语言为家中常用语言的分别占 0.7% 及 1.7%。除家中常用语言外，30.6% 的居住人口可操另一种语言，当中以普通话所占比例最大，为 45.2%。此外，11.8% 的居住人口可操另两种语言，而可操另三种或以上语言的则占 1.8%。与 1996 年中期的人口统计比较，可操另一种、两种以至三种或以上语言的居住人口所占比例分别上升了 3.2%、3.7% 及 0.6%。

2006 年澳门居住人口为 502,113 人，3 岁及以上的居住人口中：85.7% 以粤语为家中常用语言，而普通话及其他中国方言分别占 3.2% 及 6.7%；以葡语为家中常用语言的居住人口占 0.6%；以英语及其他语言为家中常用语言的分别占 1.5% 及 2.3%。除家中常用语言外，有 54.0% 的居住人口可流利使用另一种或多种语言与人沟通。当中以懂普通话的比例最高，占上述人口 65.3%；其次是英语，占 27.9%。按常用语言及其他可使用语言合计，发现 3 岁及以上居住人口中，91.9%懂粤语，38.5%能使用普通话，而懂英语及葡语的则分别占 16.6%及 2.4%。

3. 澳门回归前后日常语言使用对比

澳门的多元文化造就了公民对不同语言和文化持"平等宽容、知其所异、敬其所异"的态度。从表 2 可以看出，回归前的澳葡政府比较重视葡语，1996 年人口普查语言能力中"可使用三种其他语言/方言"一项没有统计普通话、其他中国方言与英语组合的情况，仅统计了普通话、其他中国方言与葡语组合的情况。同时，从表 3 中可知，使用两种及以上语言人数持续增加，这体现出回归后澳门语言政策的成功之处。例如，可使用一种其他语言/方言的居民，从 1996 年的 27.4%增加到 2001 年的 30.6%及 2006 年的 37.1%，2001 年、2006 年依次比 1996 年增加了 3.2%、9.7%；可使用两种其他语言/方言的比例，从 1996 年的 8.1%增加到 2001 年的 11.8%及 2006 年的 15.1%，2001 年、2006 年依次比 1996 年增加了 3.7%、7.0%；可使用三种其他语言/方言的比例，1996 年是 1.1%，2001 年及 2006 年均为 1.8%，比 1996 年多了 0.7%；但是，不懂其他语言/方言的人数反而有大幅下降，从 1996 年的 63.4%降至 2001 年的 55.8%及 2006 年的 46.0%，2001 年、2006 年依次比 1996 年减少了 7.6%、17.4%。由此可见，澳门政府没有剥夺葡萄牙语言和文化这种有生命力的遗产的发展权利，而是采取相对科学、合理的语言政策，推动澳门成为一个日渐茁壮成长的"小宇宙"（Martins 2009），多种语言和谐共处，多种文化互相交融、共同发展。

表3　澳门回归前后使用语言种类一览表

种类	1996年		2001年		2006年	
	人数	占比（%）	人数	占比（%）	人数	占比（%）
一种语言	251616	63.4	236816	55.8	226520	46.0
两种语言	108882	27.4	129793	30.6	182701	37.1
三种语言	32087	8.1	50017	11.8	74362	15.1
四种语言	4325	1.1	7577	1.8	8708	1.8

二、对中葡英三语现状的解读

澳门社会的人口、语言状况在回归后有明显改变，不仅人口总数增加了，而且居民的语言成分也发生了变化。如放宽内地人来澳门定居的限制使操普通话的人数有所增多；葡萄牙官员的离去和对原来拥有双重国籍的人实行自由选择国籍的政策使操葡语人数明显下降；受全球化的影响，作为国际通用语言的英语的使用者日益增加。

（一）中文官方语言地位的确立与提高

澳门是个中、葡、英三种语言同时使用的"三语区"。以前，葡萄牙语是唯一的官方语言，在政府、司法、公务中通用。自澳门政府公报刊登葡萄牙外交部关于中文官方地位法令之日（即1992年1月1日）起，中文也成了官方语言，澳门开始实行双语制。

无论在澳门回归前还是回归后，中文"始终是澳门地区使用最普遍、作用也最大的语文"（程祥徽 2003），发挥着

“描述、表达和社交”（理查兹 1993）三大功能的中心语言作用（陈恩泉 2005）。1991 年中文使用者占当时澳门人口总数的 96. 6 % ，1996 年为 96. 1%，2001 年中文使用者占当时的 97%，2006 年为 95. 6%。这说明中文在绝大多数澳门人心中始终占据绝对优势，人们把讲中文视为对中华民族的归属以及对中国文化的认同。澳门使用普通话的人口的快速增长说明澳门人把讲普通话作为身份的一种认同，这也是国家在经济、文化等领域强盛后，其政治力量不断强大的一种体现，语言的政治性已经渗透到澳门个人和地区认同上。我们从澳门一名小学生写的一篇作文的字里行间，可以感受到一个澳门儿童对中国文字的骄傲、对中国传统文化的深切认同（如图 1 所示）。

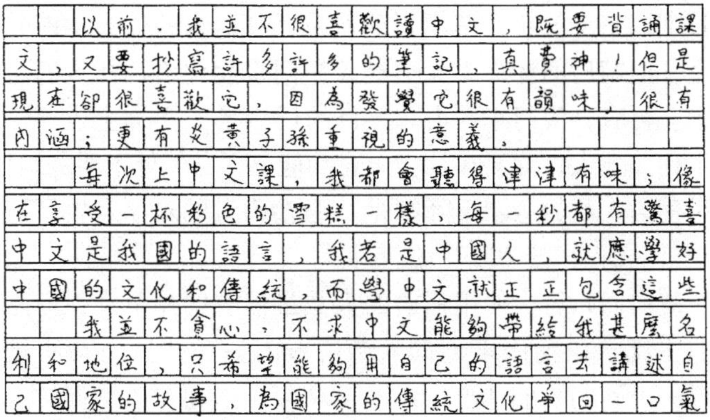
以前，我並不很喜歡讀中文，既要背誦課文，又要抄寫許多許多的筆記，真費神！但是現在卻很喜歡它，因為發覺它很有韻味，很有內涵；更有炎黃子孫重視的意義。
每次上中文課，我都會聽得津津有味；像在享受一杯彩色的雪糕一樣，每一秒都有驚喜中文是我國的語言，我若是中國人，就應學好中國的文化和傳統，而學中文就正正包含這些
我並不貪心，不求中文能夠帶給我甚麼名利和地位，只希望能夠用自己的語言去講述自己國家的故事，為國家的傳統文化爭回一口氣

图 1　一名澳门小学生写的作文

资料来源：2001 年 11 月《澳门基础教育学科能力检定性评核研究报告》

(二) 葡语政治地位与语言使用的预期与现实

语言是社会交际的工具，语言使用的变化取决于社会对这种语言的实际需求；此外，作为一种与众不同的、有价值的、能决定生活中各种机会的文化资本，语言还可以发挥其独特的作用。澳门回归后，葡语仍然是官方语言之一，但中葡两种官方语言在澳门过渡期不能平等相处的窘境有了较大的改观，"独尊葡语"成为历史。澳门回归前，1991年及1996年以葡语为家庭用语的人数没有发生任何变化，均占当时人口的1.8%；澳门回归后，葡语的使用人口明显下降，2001年及2006年分别降至0.7%和0.6%。回归前的葡语作为唯一的官方语言在行政、立法、司法部门的独特地位，使其处于强势的政治地位，是人们谋生的一种工具。由于葡语长期以来并没有在澳门得到普及，其语言的社会功能并不健全，回归后的葡文更无力涵盖澳门多元化语言社区的全部范围。再者，澳门华人占总人口的近96%，再加上讲粤语的土生葡萄牙人，葡语在社会语言功能方面必然处于弱势地位，而讲葡语人数的急剧下降则是"政治力量的对比发生了巨变的结果"（程祥徽 2003）的真实写照。

澳门回归后，使用葡语的人数虽然有明显下降，但是报读非主流学校葡语培训的人数并没有减少，反而有所增加（如图2所示）。自1999年至2007年，参加葡语培训的人数多达23,558人次，参加中文（普通话及粤语）培训的人数是22,500人次，参加英文培训的人数达13,328人次。从整体上看，参加葡语培训的人数最多，特别是从2003/2004学年开始，参加葡语培训的人数明显增长。这种现象说明澳门政府需要精通葡语的公务人员，社会个体看到了学习葡语对提升经济和社会地位的作用，澳门政府隐性的语言政策——将葡语作为连接葡语文化国家的细节——起到了一定的作用。另一方面，说明澳门政府实践"一国两制""五十年不变"的基本国策取得了成效。

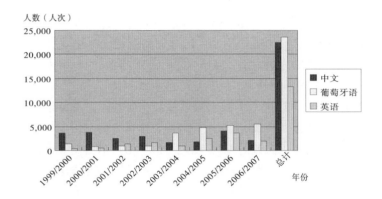

图2 1999/2000学年至2006/2007学年"语言培训"人数统计数据

注：根据澳门教育暨青年局《教育数字概览》整理而成

http://www.dsej.gov.mo/~webdsej/www/inter_dsej_page.php?layout=3col&con=grp_db/statisti.htm, 2009-1-30.

（三）英语经济地位的凸显与超越

英语虽然不是澳门的官方语言，但回归后使用英语的人数却在急剧增长。澳门回归前，1991年使用英语者占当时人口的0.5%，1996年使用英语者占当时人口的0.8%，而澳门回归后的2001年和2006年，使用英语者分别占总人口的0.7%和1.5%。虽然2001年葡语与英语的使用人数不相上下，或者说"打成平局了"（程祥徽 2003），但 2006 年使用葡语的人数占澳门总人口的 0.6%，讲英语的人数已经超过讲葡语的人数，占总人口的 0.9%。而且这只是对讲单语人数的分析结果。如果从英语和葡语与其他不同语种组合的双语数据分析，如中英、菲英、泰英，中葡、菲葡、泰葡等，使用英语的人数更为可观。2001 年及 2006 年人口普查数据中有关可使用一种其他语言（日常用语除外）的双语人数的统计数据更能说明英语的地位已远远超越葡语：2001 年与葡语组成双语的人数只有 3,418 人，与英语组成的双语人数却有 25,390 人，即英语双语人数是葡语双语人数的 7.4 倍；2006 年与葡语组成双语的人数已降至 2,838 人，与英语组成的双语人数上升至 29,135 人，即与英语组合的双语人数是与葡语组合的双语人数的 10.3 倍之多。葡语可以占据官方语言的优势政治地位，但取代不了英语作为国际通用语在经济贸易、金融机构及高等教育等领域中的经济、文化地位。使用英语人数的不断上升说明英语已经具备了在本土和国际背景下的影响地位、排他的权利以及形成知识的重要手段。

三、对澳门语言政策的思考

一种语言的活力取决于三个因素：①制度上的支持；②经济力量；③人口（黄宣范 1995）。反思澳门回归十年来的中英葡等语言的发展状况，可以说得益于澳门人口的多元化与多元经济的快速发展，最重要的是澳门政府在语言政策上对澳门的双语或多语问题的应然回应。回归后的澳门语言现状与学者们的预测基本上是吻合的，即葡语政治地位的式微导致讲葡语的人数下降；中文官方语言地位的上升，得益于普通话的推广及语言认同感；操粤语之外的其他中国方言的人数减少，是弱势语言被强势语言同化的结果。

（一）促进语言教学多元化，提升葡语社会功能地位

澳门有位议员曾抱怨澳门政府"在语言教育方面推展不足"，时任澳门社会文化司司长崔世安回应说，政府一直都在官校及私校推展葡语教育，目前在非高等教育范畴内开展的语言教育包括中文（粤语及普通话）、葡语及英语。澳门缺乏大型的语言测试中心，所以很难确定语言教育水平，但政府会鼓励学校请更多以英语为母语的教师教授英语（《澳门日报》，2008-11-28）。从这则新闻中可以看出，澳门语言教育政策鼓励多种语言教学，如非高等教育范畴学生一般接受多种语言训练，包括中文（粤语及普通话）、葡语及英语。但正是澳门语言政策中隐性的一面容易让人置疑。实际上，与其"不得不"对葡语采取"容忍多元语言主义政策"，即希望它能自己保持现状，既不主动扭转葡语官方语言优越的政治地位，也不采取积极策略推动葡语社会语言功能的发挥，还不如"为何不"采取"提倡多元语言主义政策"，在中文学校开设葡语课，在葡语学校开设中文课，在葡国本土人和土生葡人中实施中葡双语教育政策，全方位提高葡语的社会功能地位。

未来澳门语言政策目标不但要把葡语作为一种单纯的文化资产加以保存，而且也可寄希望于葡语能够化解政治冲突，提升澳门经济发展速度。语言政策的制定者不可小觑葡语文化、经济资源的价值，不能忽略在国际全球化背景下更要凸显澳门多元化、本土化对提升其国际地位的强大作用。当然，澳门语言政策的隐性价值也同样不可忽略，从目前语言发展

的状况来看，它不失为一种成功的语言政策。当社会环境尚未成熟，人们对某种语言的认同度还不够时，政策决策者不能利用政策权利强硬推广，只能等待时机成熟，方可顺理成章地实施某种语言政策。

（二）厘清双语概念，培养双语和多语人才

澳门是一个双语社会，回归后"双语"的概念如何界定，众人看法不一，澳门政府也没有相应明确的语言政策，即未详细规定中文使用的场合和提供的服务。有学者指出：在澳门整个社会范围内，存在着汉语和葡语两种官方语言，不是指澳门人或澳门政府的公务员个个都会说汉、葡两种语言，个个都必须掌握汉、葡两种语文（程祥徽 2001）。当然，政府公务人员最好能掌握这两种官方语言，以便提高政府在执政、司法和立法中的工作效率，但目前公务人员中存在中文素质不能满足有效、高效执政的需要的问题。政府要将语言政策与澳门的社会、政治与经济利益相结合，找出双语人才培养效率不高的关键所在；政府还要明白精通中文或葡文的优秀人才的培养，不能仅限于依靠花费大量公帑派公务员到北京或里斯本学习中文或葡语，或在高校或培训机构进修，短期培训只能在简单的听说技能方面使人有所提高，很难提高其真正的读写能力。

众所周知，双语或多语的掌握，一是要在社会环境中自幼习得（如家庭），二是要接受正规教育（以外语或第二语言的形式学习掌握）。要加强中文在澳门官方语言中的地位，改变中文仅是法令的、象征仪式性的官方地位，使之真正像葡语那样成为政府机关的工作语言。政府必须依靠基础教育，加大政府财政投入力度，提供完善的教学设备，让学生在听说读写译等方面达到双语的标准要求，为未来的双语或多语精英人才的培养打好基础。双语人才不仅仅是指中葡或葡中，还包括任何不同组合的双语。此外，语言的复兴还要靠语言基础建设的支撑才能达成目标，政府还要增强中英等多语言学习和使用的环境建设，诸如多语言的电视和广播、报纸、杂志和期刊等。

（三）加强母语教学，善用儿童"语言关键期"

"三文"（中文、葡文、英文）和"四语"（粤语、葡语、英语、普通话）是澳门文化和社会生活中的独特现象，也是长期困扰澳门非高等教育的难题。无论是从澳门的社会发展来看，还是从人力资源理论的视角看，语言都是一笔巨大的财富，是人们用来增加产品潜在价值的资源的一部分，双语或多语会给个人带来多方面的益处，包括更大范围或更多地得到社会承认等经济和非经济方面的益处。双语或多语对澳门旅游、博彩、艺术、生产企业等的发展有很大的促进作用，对促进澳门社会和谐、增强澳门活力及建构多元文化价值，均有不可估量的影响。

从教育学和语言教育理论的视角看，语言精英应该从小开始培养，这样可以节约教育成本，更可以节约政府为后期培训所付出的大量公帑。但是，学生要在有限的时间内掌握双语或多语的确要承受不小的压力。不能把握好双语或多语教学的时机，语言师资素质欠佳或教学方法不当都可能会伤害到学生的自尊、自信，使学生产生厌学情绪，学习成绩下降，最后导致辍学。所以，澳门语言教育政策必须对此做出应然的回应。

加强母语教学是儿童智力开发，建立自信、自尊的最好路径，也是儿童保持其母语语言及文化的最佳策略。语言教育政策的决策者要依据科学的语言教育理论，适时调整澳门非高等教育中双语或多语的语言教学政策，把握好儿童学习第二语言的最佳时机，解决非高等教育中的语言教育问题。根据语言学的观点，儿童的课堂第二语言可在母语习得基本完成之后开始，因为"每一个正常的人，在童年晚些时候，也就是在10岁之内，就获得了一种语言，即他的母语，包括基本词汇、语法和发音"（Robins 2000）。鉴于"语言关键期假说"，儿童在9～10岁是学习第二语言的较好时间，他们的模仿能力和记忆力较强，情感屏障也较低，如果在语言师资力量有所保障的前提下，可以在小学4年级开设第二语言教学，增加培养儿童的第二语言的口语教学，使儿童在语言关键期得到最好的发展；到了中学可以增加第二语言的教学时数，或者可以加开第三语言作为选修课程。

（四）把语言资源转化为文化资源和经济资源

澳门是个被人称为语言拼盘、语言博物馆或语言花园的语言多样化城市。依据 Ruiz 提出的影响语言规划的三种取向，即把语言当作问题、把语言当作权利及把语言当作资源（Ruiz 1990），分析澳门的语言政策问题：首先，规划语言学家认为语言多样化是一个"问题"，因此要制定语言规划，解决这个"问题"；其次，现实生活中的个体，因为某一语言（普通话或英语或葡语）的匮乏构成了他们参与社会、经济和政治生活的障碍，所以他们要直面语言"问题"，通过掌握其基本技能，将语言问题转化为语言资源，提升他们在全球化经济中的竞争能力；最后，语言政策制定者在破解语言问题的同时，要认识到政府有责任保护澳门居民选择语言的基本权利，不剥夺葡语和葡语文化这种有生命力的遗产在澳门发展的权利。将澳门多元语言作为资源，把语言资源转变为经济资源、文化资源。

今后澳门语言教育政策值得考虑的是如何在非高等教育中，科学合理地利用澳门丰富的语言资源优势和多种语言的学习环境，让适龄儿童得到有效的"双语教学"，例如，能否让讲两种不同语言（母语）的儿童编入同一个教学班，教师运用双语进行语言或学科教学。在这种教学环境中，教师可以转换两种语言进行授课，学生可以在学习过程中转化两种语言进行语言或学科知识的学习；课余时间学生还可以通过交往等活动学习同伴的母语，达到学习第二外语的目的。当然，考核仍然可以让学生自主选择母语或第二语言，直到学生完全有信心使用第二语言进行其他学科的考核。这种语言教学模式在花费较少的情况下，同伴之间可以创设较为自然的第二语言环境。

四、结 语

随着全球化的到来，澳门已经成为国际化的组成部分，英语的重要地位也越来越不可否定。作为全球通用语言，英语对个人经济、前途有着不可估量的作用，比起中文，澳门人更普遍认同英语在国际上占据的主要地位。这种对英语至上主义的认同，源于语言的实用性和经济价值，这种"磁性认同效应"也是影响语言政策制定的重要且不可忽略的因素，这种语言资源的充分利用，小至影响个人、家庭，大至影响国家、社会。政府在制定、执行及评估语言教育政策时，显然不能忽略语言实用主义的价值观的统领作用。除此之外，还要考虑澳门人的历史情结、权利关系及族群意识等各种影响因素。正如 Kaplan 所言:"英语虽然是世界通用语言,但是只用英语和世界各国打交道还是不够的。"(Kaplan 1994)

在 21 世纪新的国际政治、经济、文化的情势之下,语言的失衡及其所受到的正面挑战,为澳门政府微调语言政策提供了一个契机。正视多元语言所能带来的优势,如生活在多元语言环境下的个体心胸较为开阔,对其他文化有较高的接受程度。多元语言环境还有助于提高学习其他语言的能力,在多元语言环境下培养出的学生更具宏观的世界观,在未来的全球化竞争中更具优势。积极对待多元语言环境的消极因素,科学地考量各种语言内外部的供给与需求,制定出合理的语言教育政策。

本文原载于《语言文字应用》2010 年第 3 期。收入本文集时略有删改。

参考文献

Kaplan, R. B. Language policy and planning in New Zealand. *Annual Review of Applied Linguistic*, 1994.

Robins, R. H. *General Linguistics*. Beijing: Foreign Language Teaching and Research Press, 2000.

Ruiz, R. Empowerment, voice, and language. Paper presented at the Annual Meeting of the American Educational Research Association, Boston, MA., April, 1990. In C. Sleeter (ed.). *Empowerment Through Multicultural Education*. Albany:

SUNY Press, 1990.

陈恩泉. 澳门回归后葡文的地位与语言架构 [J]. 学术研究, 2005 (12): 95-98.

程祥徽. 澳门中文公文的回归之路 [J]. 语言文字应用, 2001 (1): 82-86.

程祥徽. 新世纪的澳门语言策略 [J]. 语言文字应用, 2003 (1): 19-26.

黄宣范. 语言、社会与族群意识: 台湾语言社会学的研究 [M]. 台北: 文鹤出版有限公司, 1994.

理查兹. 朗曼语言学词典 [M]. 刘润清, 等译. 太原: 山西教育出版社, 1993.

刘羡冰. 澳门教育改革的路向 [C] //古鼎仪, 马庆堂. 澳门教育: 抉择与自由. 澳门: 澳门基金会, 1994.

政府鼓励多语言基本教育 [N]. 澳门日报, 2008-11-28.

Martins, R. "小宇宙"澳门是葡萄牙/巴西与中国之间的技术桥梁, 第七届 AULP 会议上发言, 2009. http://www.library.gov.mo/macreturn/DATA/A40-615/index.htm 2009-1-28

作者简介

张桂菊, 博士, 广东外语外贸大学南国商学院教授。研究方向: 社会语言学、语言教育、语言政策。

从被动到主动的双语使用者
——青少年语言态度、身份认同转变的跟踪研究

梁斯华

一、引论：影响青少年双语能力和语言态度的因素

语言学家普遍认为，双语和多语社会中青少年的语言态度、语言能力及语言实践是影响相关语言可持续发展的关键因素（Baker 2006），而家庭被认为是实现语言维持的关键领域（Spolsky 2012）。在近年来逐渐兴起的家庭语言政策（Family Language Policy，简称 FLP）研究领域中，儿童早期的双语能力发展是主要的研究对象（Schwartz 2010；Spolsky 2012；King & Fogle 2013）。De Houwer（1999）指出，过去的研究主要关注那些能够实际使用两种语言与人交流的孩子，对于被动式的双语使用者（passive bilingual）了解甚少。同样在双语环境中成长，他们为何没有成为主动的双语使用者（active bilingual）？在他们语言社会化的过程中有哪些因素可

能导致了这样的结果？De Houwer 认为，父母的语言信念和语言态度在其中起着关键的作用。这里所说的语言信念是特指父母对自身在孩子语言发展过程中所起作用的看法，即自己能否控制或影响孩子的语言发展轨迹和结果，分为"有影响派"（impact belief）和"无影响派"（no impact belief）两种。父母的语言态度则包括父母对特定语言、语言环境、语言使用方式以及双语现象的总体态度。两者的排列组合会影响父母在家庭语言实践中采取的策略以及对家庭外语言环境的应对，从而影响孩子的双语习得结果。例如，对语言态度积极但是持"无影响派"观点或者选择不干预政策的父母，其子女成长为主动双语使用者的可能性较低。

"父母一人一语"（One-Parent-One-Language，简称 OPOL）可能是最广为人知，也是被研究最多的双语家庭语言政策（De Houwer 2007），也许是因为一般父母认为语言选择就是家庭语言规划中最主要的因素。实际上，语言选择只是父母语言输入的其中一个方面，研究中发现，家庭中的双语互动策略（Lanza 1992，2004）、语文实践（Ren & Hu 2013）、语言输入的数量与质量等（King & Logan-Terry 2008）都对儿童的双语能力有重要影响。父母对这些方面不了解可能会产生南辕北辙的状况——一心想培养具备双语能力的后代却最终导致了语言的转用与流失（Kulick 1997；Gafaranga 2010）。

在 Spolsky（2009）的"家庭语言政策"三分模型中，（语言）意识形态是一个重要的组成部分。实证研究中也发现，来自家庭外部的因素往往也通过意识形态的中介作用影响着 FLP 和儿童语言态度与实践，如社会政治意识形态

（Canagarajah 2008），本地语言的国际地位（Curdt-Christiansen 2016），传统思想的影响（如儒家思想对教育的强调，参见 Curdt-Christiansen 2009），对语言的刻板印象（Fogle 2013），社会网络与朋辈影响（Li 1994；Caldas 2006），等。

这些外部的因素在 FLP 研究中多数是作为背景知识或者论据存在的，与 FLP 交叉的语言态度研究更直接地关注这些家庭以外的因素，其中又以后殖民语境中的语言态度研究为代表。在后殖民主义时期，许多国家和地区面临着国家或民族（再）建构的政治和意识形态任务，语言规划、语言态度和语言身份认同的"管理"是这个任务中不可或缺的一环（Gupta 1994；Giles 1998；Korth 2005；Dyers & Abongdia 2010）。而在少数族裔语言（Coady 2001；Siegel 2006；McEwan-Fujita 2010）和移民、离散群体（Lotherington 2003；Wiley 2009）的语境中，语言的维持与复兴则是重要的研究话题。以香港为例，众多学者关注回归前后香港人的语言使用、语言态度与身份认同的变化（Bruche-Schulz 1997；Axler, et al. 1998；Lai 2001，2005；Poon 2004），由香港大学主持的年度身份认同调查也总是备受关注（香港大学 2018）。黎美玲（2001，2012）对回归后香港学生对普通话、粤语和英语的语言态度进行了数次问卷调查。她对照 2009 年与 2001 年的调查结果，发现香港学生对普通话的语言态度变得更积极，普通话带来的经济机遇是促使语言态度转变的重要因素。而根据香港大学的年度身份调查研究，在 18～29 岁的年龄组别中，在过去的十年间认为自己是香港人的比例从 46.2% 飙升到 70.9%，认为自己是中国人的比例则从 29%

下降到 2.9%（梁斯华，待刊稿），这与香港近年来的社会运动和年轻人中本土主义思想的抬头应有关系。

在中国内地的语境中，对年轻人的双语双言能力以及语言态度的研究往往以多方言、城市化、国内移民和普通话推广为背景，而 20 世纪以后，地方方言的传承与流失逐渐成为城市语言调查的研究热点（唐叶 2006；孙晓先等 2007；郭媛媛 2012；俞玮奇 2012；Liang 2014）。俞玮奇及其研究团队一直关注长江三角洲地区的城市语言文字状况（俞玮奇 2011；俞玮奇、杨璟琰 2016）。他们的最新研究调查了 2515 名上海市本地学生的语言使用和语言能力状况（俞玮奇、杨璟琰 2016），并与过去十五年中在上海地区进行的多次语言使用和语言态度问卷调查的结果进行比较，发现上海本地学生以普通话为第一语言的人口比例明显上升，普通话已经成为大部分人最经常使用和说得最流利的语言。相对而言，尽管大部分上海本地学生仍能不同程度地使用上海方言，但他们的方言能力并未随着年龄的增长而提高。作者以较有力的数据说明了在过去十五年中，上海本地学生的语言使用习惯与语言能力发生了明显的变化，上海方言能力呈明显下降的趋势。文章提出，应该改变传统的单语单言的意识，重视家庭语言规划，才能保护和传承上海方言。

在香港和上海进行的跟踪问卷调查研究帮助我们了解在多语社会变迁过程中，青少年的语言态度和语言使用能力如何发生历时性的变化。但受问卷调查的方法论所限，我们只能得知不同时间点的状态，并与社会学的因素进行相关性分析，却无法了解具体的变化机制，也不能了解这些变化在日常生活中是如何产生与发展的，以及微观的言语行为如何形成更宏观的变化。单凭问卷调查的结果，我们仍然无法回答文章开头 De Houwer 提出的问题：为何有些孩子没有发展出主动的双语能力？有哪些因素在其中产生了影响？只有真正深入的历时性研究才有可能让我们窥见"黑盒子"中的一些秘密，但这种历时性的跟踪研究费时费力，受到客观条件的诸多限制，在学界中并不多见（例如 Heath 1983；Goodz 1994；Zentella 1997；Caldas 2006；Heath 2012）。

  本文的写作目的就是通过对青少年语言态度和双语能力发展的历时性跟踪研究，在一定程度上填补以上的研究空缺。本文案例的主人公是一名在广州土生土长但传统上被定义为二代移民的男性（文中化名为李雷），数据分别来自长达一年的民族志参与式观察、两次跟踪回访（分别为 2015 年和 2018 年）和部分社交媒体上的互动，从 2009 年到 2018 年，时间跨度为九年。研究开始时，李雷是 10 岁的小学五年级学生，2018 年时高中毕业，在香港修读副学士学位。以语言使用者为中心，结合家庭语言政策、语言态度和语言意识形态的理论，跟踪李雷语言社会化和在时空中移动的轨迹，通过不同时间、场景下对他的深入观察与访谈，探究在他成长的过程中，有哪些因素对他的双语能力（或说言语库，参见 Busch 2012）及语言态度的变化产生影响。李雷这个案例比较特殊，他小时候一直以普通话为主要沟通语言，粤语只具备一定的被动接收能力，很少在生活中积极使用粤语，但是以去香港学习为界，他的语言态度和语言使用习惯产生了明显的变化。现在，当他在香港生活时，他是一名普通话、粤语的双语使用者，积极学习并在生活中使用粤语。李雷从被动的双语者到主动的双语者的变化为我们的探索性研究提供了丰富的材料。另外，过去对双语能力习得的研究大多关注婴幼儿，家庭语言政策的研究则大多从父母的角度出发，对孩子的主观能动性研究只是刚刚开展（Luykx 2003；Zhu 2008；Fogle and King 2013），对成年后发展出主动双语能力的语言使用者的研究更是少之又少（如 Doyle 2013；Fogle 2013）。李雷的案例研究也有助于我们填补这方面的研究空白。

二、研究背景与研究方法

（一）广州市的社会语言学背景介绍

案例的主人公李雷1999年出生于中国华南地区最重要的历史、文化、经济中心城市广州市，粤方言中最具影响力的地方变体广府话（英语文献中常被称为 Cantonese）是当地的强势方言，与国家通用语普通话形成相互竞争的局面。20世纪90年代借着广东省经济的快速发展与香港流行文化的影响，曾出现"粤语北上"的局面（詹伯慧1993），粤语中的许多词汇进入普通话，成为日常用语。与此同时，大规模的来自省内和国内其他地区的移民涌入广州，使得广州的人口结构和社会语言状况发生巨大变化。但是在90年代，大批移民的迁入没有马上带来普通话的迅速普及（《中共广东省委广东省人民政府关于大力推广普通话的决定》1992），早期移民反而大部分通过自学，都能够以粤语在日常生活、工作中与人交流。2000年以后，随着《中华人民共和国国家通用语言文字法》的颁布，普通话在广州的普及程度不断提高，相较之下，粤语在广州市公共领域的使用范围（包括学校、电视媒体、商店等）则不断萎缩。许多像本案例主人公一样在 2000 年前后出生的二代移民受到语言环境变化的影响，并不像他们的父母一样熟练掌握粤语，有的只会听，有的连听都不会。

必须指出的是，由于社会经济结构和原生社区网络的差异，广州市内各个地区的语言环境差异是很大的（Liang 2013）。李雷家在广州市新城区天河区，是金融商贸的中心区域，有大批高薪职位和商业机会，吸引了大批来自全国各地的移民，是广州市最受欢迎的移民输入区之一。2000 年到 2010 年间，天河区的人口增长了 158%（廖学明等 2001），2016 年年末，45.36% 的天河区常住人口为非户籍人口，即官方意义上的"移民"（广州市统计局 2017），而算上已经成功入户的一代移民与二代移民，天河区真正的移民人数比例远大于官方数字。例如，李雷小学时所在的班级就有 80% 以上的同学是二代移民，但他们都具有广州市户口。与 20 世纪 90 年代不同的是，粤语能力此时已经不再是在广州生存的必备技能，而在天河区普通话往往成为公共领域与陌生人沟通时的第一选择，因此天河区有时被人们戏称为"普通话区"。

（二）研究方法

本研究以语言民族志为主要研究方法。语言民族志源于美国语言人类学的理论和方法，将人类学中的经典研究方法，即强调浸入式参与观察的民族志和语言学的学科理论结合起来，如以 Gumperz 和 Hymes 为代表的交际民族志（1964）、语言社会化的理论（Duff 2010）、互动语言学的分析框架（Goffman 1974）、语言的社会指向性理论（Silverstein 2003）等。Ben Rampton 以及 Angela Creese 等学者（Rampton 2007；

Creese 2008；Maybin and Tusting 2011）将语言人类学中的主要研究方法提取出来，把语言民族志作为一种独立的研究方法，便于其他学科的学者使用。这种研究方法强调对交际行为的语境进行批判性的分析，关注意识形态假设、话语的历史链条、交际中的社会关系等，也强调对微观的话语进行详细深入的分析，把言语互动的过程看作建构社会意义的实践，而不仅仅是观点的平铺直叙。

语言民族志研究涉及的参与者一般比较少，目的不在于得出具有统计学意义的可简单重现的普遍性结论，而是通过尽可能详细的"深描"（thick description），以具有反思性、反身性（reflexive）的描述方式，为后续的研究提供比较和累积的基础（Rampton 2006；Flick 2009）。本文选择了李雷这个较为特殊的案例，不是因为他的案例具有普遍性，而是因为他的丰富经历能够给本文以及后继的探索性研究提供更多珍贵的信息。

本文的数据涉及三次调查期间的数据，时间跨度九年。2009年到2010年，作者隔周到李雷所在的A校B班级进行语言民族志的调查，调查期间，每天参与他们的课堂和班级活动，有时也在教师办公室观察老师们工作的方式，课间、午休或者放学后找同学们聊天或者进行正式的录音访问，也安排了焦点小组讨论和围绕语言的活动。民族志的调查持续了一整个学年。2015年时对部分主要参与者进行了面对面的回访，2018年时是第二次回访。

其余时间，作者主要通过社交媒体与参与者保持联系并进行偶尔的互动，例如，对李雷的第二次回访就是根据社交媒体获取的线索安排的。2018年的回访就在微信上进行，为了方便李雷查阅回答，作者使用文字留言，李雷用语音回答了作者的问题，正好也可创造机会听李雷说粤语，评估他目前的粤语水平。

（三）参与者的概况

李雷的父母在20世纪90年代从陕西来到广州居住和工作，李雷出生和成长于广州，是传统意义上的二代移民。李雷家在天河区的A小区，小学时，他与他的父母、奶奶以及保姆住在一起。姐姐在佛山工作，偶尔回家，据他所说，姐姐的粤语说得很好。他的父母在与日本相关的企业工作，平日都很忙，几次家访都没见到，只见到他的奶奶和保姆。他的奶奶完全不会说普通话，只会说陕西话，负责照顾她的保姆换过几个，也都来自陕西。保姆与奶奶用陕西话交流，与李雷则以说普通话为主，偶尔说几句陕西话。父母在家时相互之间说陕西话，与李雷则说普通话。普通话是李雷的第一语言，也是他运用最纯熟的语言。李雷说他基本能够听懂陕西话，但是除了"你、我、他"这样简单的词语之外，他就只会用陕西话来骂人了。

2009—2010年时，李雷是A小区内的公立学校A校的一名五年级小学生。2015年时，李雷和他的大部分小学同学一样在A校对应的天河区一家公立中学读初中。2018年时，由于高考成绩不理想，李雷没有在国内升学，而是到了香港修读副学士学位，性质与内地的大专学位较为接近。正是由于他在广州和香港这两个紧密联系又相互区别的粤语文化地区迁移的经历，使他的语言态度、语言使用习惯乃至身份认同都发生了显著的变化。

三、数据分析

（一）在广州：家庭语言政策与学校语言环境

FLP 研究者（Spolsky 2009；Schwartz 2010）总结了几种不同的为孩子创造有利双语习得环境的家庭语言管理策略。

（1）控制家庭语言环境，例如选择特定语言的童谣、早教节目，提出家庭内部语言使用的规则等。

（2）在家庭中增加说目标语言的成员，如来自乡下的亲戚或佣人。

（3）让孩子与其他使用目标语言的同伴玩耍，选择居住在目标语使用者聚集的地区。比如，广州市老城区有较多粤语使用者，白云区、萝岗区（现为黄埔区）有客家人聚居的区域，或者有的家长会将孩子送回老家或者参加特定的夏令营。

（4）改变家庭外的语言环境，如建立语言学习机构，通过建议、投诉等方式影响政府、机关、企业或其他机构的语言选择等。

在作者对李雷所在班级的调查中，大部分家庭采取的是前三种策略中的一种或几种，有的父母更是有目的性地使用这些策略，有些则像李雷父母一样实践无意识的规划（unplanned language planning）（Spolsky 2009）。李雷的父母主要采取的是第二种策略，让李雷与只会说陕西话的奶奶同住，并配给一名会说陕西话的保姆，长辈之间在家也主要以陕西话进行交流，创造了用陕西话沟通的语言环境。尽管李雷说曾有来访的亲戚认为"陕西人必须会说陕西话"，他的父母也曾要求他学习陕西话，但父母践行的还是比较放任（laisser faire）的管理方式，并不积极干预李雷的语言使用习惯，属于第一节提到的"无影响派"（De Houwer 1999）。李雷上初中之后，他奶奶回老家去了，之后家里便没再请保姆，李雷父母后来在家里也很少说陕西话了，普通话成为家里的主要语言。

作者问李雷知不知道为什么父母没教他说陕西话时，他如是回答：

她觉得普通话通用呗，然后就教普通话。一般家庭都是这样，先教普通话。

（摘录1：首次访问李雷，2009-11-25）

李雷认为他家的家庭语言的选择主要是基于实用，对"陕西人""必须"学会的陕西话并没有硬性要求。类似的实用主义原则也多次出现在其他以普通话为第一方言的二代移民参与者的话语中。李雷的生活经验让他认为，"一般家庭"都是先教孩子普通话，再考虑其他方言，"很多人都一出生就学那个普通话"——这是一种再"正常"不过的做法，是大多数人的生活方式，自己的经历没有任何"异常"之处。这是明显的语言意识形态的合理化过程（rationalisation）。这个过程显得如此"自然"，以至于李雷完全没有意识到。李雷表述出来的语言意识形态其实是他与父母在实践家庭语言规划的过程中共同建构的产物，已经融合到他的日常经验与对这种经验的合理化理解中。因此，当作者回应，自己小时候是先学粤语之后再学普通话，李雷显然感到有些意外。

作者问李雷最喜欢的语言是什么时，他说他最喜欢说的是普通话。他解释，这种偏好不是因为觉得普通话更好听或者更高级，而是因为这是他最熟悉、最常用的语言：

> 李雷：不是喜不喜欢，而是经常用普通话嘛。中国假如有十个人，肯定有八个半都是用普通话的。
> 作者：你说用普通话的意思是说他们会说普通话还是他们……
> 李雷：经常用普通话。
> （摘录2：首次访问李雷，2009-11-25）

李雷从自己的成长经历出发，得出中国大部分人（85%以上）最经常使用的语言是普通话的结论，这与前一段摘录中他认为一般人都是先学普通话的逻辑是一致的。可见对于社会生活经验不多的小学生而言，家庭中的语言实践，包括家庭语言选择、教育理念、语言态度等，对他们该阶段的语言使用和语言观念有重要影响。

（二）在广州：对语言环境的认知和语言态度

小学的时候，李雷感觉自己的广州话还可以，他觉得比起陕西话，广州话还更好学、更好记，因为每天在A小区散步的时候，或者是在天河区逛街的时候，都能听到很多人在讲广州话，只是在学校里面就很少。据他所说，他的广州话主要是在幼儿园时学的。那时，他在市郊一所幼儿园上学，据他回忆，同学当中有说广州话的，因此他也学会了一些，让他印象深刻的是，对方用粤语说"对不起"，他听了两天才听明白。但他小学一年级转学进入A校后，学校里便几乎是全普通话的语言环境。小学班里有个叫阿熙的男生（也是焦点小组的成员）与李雷比较要好，李雷有时便向他学些广州话。在田野调查期间,作者数次听到李雷说广州话,都是一些用来骂人的短语短句。作者问他有没有想过提高自己的陕西话或者广州话,他这样回答:

李雷:提高白话,要。陕西话不用,因为现在很少讲。
作者:那白话呢?
李雷:白话就得提高点。
作者:为什么?
李雷:毕竟在广州生活嘛。
作者:你觉得这能派上什么样的用场?白话,对你来说。
李雷:在广州来说,白话交流的确很有用。广州很多人都会说白话,有些人普通话都不会说。
作者:你遇到过不会说普通话的人吗?
李雷:遇到过。
作者:在哪里啊?
李雷:【粤语】的士咯。
作者:【普通话】就是司机不会说?
李雷:Yeah.
作者:会听吧?
李雷:上次跟他说"华侨医院",他说【粤语】"你讲咩?"【普通话】"华侨医院!"【粤语】"你讲咩啊?"【普通话】我姐就说华侨医院那个白话他才开。

(摘录3:首次访问李雷,2009–11–25)

李雷说的"白话"是广东省内人们对粤语的习惯称呼。小学时,他认为学习粤语的主要动力是实用和交流,并举了不会说普通话的出租车司机的例子。在举例时，他在普通话和粤语之间切换很自然。由于他认为学习粤语是为了消除沟通障碍，与身份、文化没有直接的关系，所以当普通话充分普及而没有沟通障碍时，这种学习动力便不复存在了，在后面的访问中他也提到这点。

在2015年的回访中，作者问他有没有执行自己五年前提高粤语的计划，他认为自己的听力方面是进步了，因为生活中有机会可以接触到。李雷对周围人讲粤语并不排斥，语言态度方面是开放和合作的，但他不会主动告诉别人他会粤语，也不会主动与他人用粤语交流。在学校的语言环境方面，他说，初中、高中的语言环境与小学时并无二致，都是大部分同学使用普通话，粤语很少用到，尽管（他认为）班上大部分都是广东人。这些同学不但不会主动跟他说粤语，还会在他参与对话时，主动进行语码转换，用普通话交流。

李雷：反正，他们说白话的话，我有时候会（说两句）……他们可能就，条件反射，直接就跟我用普通话说了。

作者：那现在没有人跟你讲白话吗？

李雷：对，都是讲普通话。

作者：那你岂不是会退化？

（两人笑）

李雷：可是我觉得语言这种东西你会的话还是会，有些是，它在你生活中如果有应用，就像，中文你不管多久不用，但是你还会记得它是怎么说的。英文你可能，你在国内，十年不用，你可能真的就忘记了。

>作者：所以，白话已经进入到那个虽然你很久不用但是你还是会的那种……
>
>李雷：（打断）因为我在广州待了十多年嘛。
>
> （摘录4：第一次回访李雷，2015-03-28）

李雷提到的"条件反射"般优先使用普通话交流的现象在广州很常见，也是经常在方言保护者当中引起争议的现象。在日常交流中，在对方不太熟悉粤语的情况下，例如会听不会说，会说但是说得不顺畅的情况下，人们通常认为以普通话作为沟通语言是一种礼节（etiquette）和尊重（McEwan-Fujita 2010）。但是这种互动策略也会从客观上剥夺了对方接触和使用粤语的机会，在微观环境中推动语言转用的发生（Gafaranga 2010）。我们通常很难观察到微观互动策略的差异对长期语言使用习惯的影响，但李雷从广州迁移到香港的经历，使他经历了宏观语言环境与微观互动策略的双重改变，也为我们提供了珍贵的机会观察他的语言使用习惯如何随之发生显著的变化。

（三）在香港：自我语言能力评价和语言习惯的转变

从上文可以看到，在第一次回访时，李雷对自己的粤语能力仍是有一定信心的，认为自己的粤语能力是稳定的，也是"够用"的，只是没有机会去用。到了第二次回访时，他刚刚在香港完成了一个学期的学习，对自己粤语能力的看法却产生了翻天覆地的变化。

>然后这帮（在学生组织里认识的）香港人呢，就他们知道我们是 *mainland* 的嘛，所以一开始用普通话跟我们说。而

且我刚来的时候其实，粤语是非常差的，所以用普通话跟他们聊，这样子。

(摘录5：第二次回访李雷，2018-02-05)

在这一次回访中，李雷的话语中增加了不少普通话和英语之间的混用，以单个单词为主，如摘录5中的"mainland"和摘录6中的"local""group"等，都是香港学校语境中常见的英语表达，看得出香港的校园生活对他的语言使用习惯的影响。

李雷到了香港之后，才发现自己的粤语原来是"非常差"的，与他之前的自我评价相去甚远。这种"非常差"的主观感受主要来自强烈的语言环境冲击。他在广州生活了18年，使用普通话可以满足他的大部分需求，粤语只是可有可无。但是到香港以后，他发现粤语成为一种不可或缺的生存技能，是融入香港生活的必需品。此时，他才觉得自己的粤语是不够用的，一开始只敢说普通话。但是这种状况没有持续很久，他的香港同学不会总是条件反射地跟他说普通话，而是非常积极地教他说粤语。

有很多 *local* 的同学，就无论是我们 *group* 里面的，还是那个学生组织里面的那些 *local*，就很愿意教我粤语这样子。然后，我也就跟他们学啊，他们跟我学普通话，我跟他们学粤语这样，互相进步，所以慢慢地也够胆去讲了。然后现在平常去吃饭啊，出去买东西啊，或者说有什么问题啊，我都先尝试用广东话去问。

(摘录6：第二次回访李雷，2018-02-05)

在香港时，本地的朋友教他粤语，他教朋友们普通话，大家是相互平等的"互相进步"的关系。作者问他，在香港人人都说粤语会不会让他有被歧视或者"排外"的感觉。他说不能说是"排外"，是刚开始感觉比较难融入。但是由于他积极参加学生组织，也有一定的粤语基础，加上开朗外向的个性，让他比其他一些"陆生"更迅速地适应了新的语言环境，发展自己的普通话粤语双语能力。来到一个新的文化、新的社区，参与（participation）与融入（integration）是相互促进、相辅相成的，积极参与的共同实践越多，建构的身份认同感便越强（Eckert 2006）。

在采访的末尾，作者提到下次见面会不会用粤语一起聊天，李雷立刻转换语码用粤语与作者聊了一段，虽然仍有口音，却也相当流利。其实在第一次回访时，作者也提出了同样的要求，当时李雷并没有积极回应，只在对话中有需要时插入粤语的片言只语。从两次对比来看，李雷使用粤语的意愿和能力确实都有了很大的变化。

随之发生变化的，还有他对广州语言环境的看法。

你知道在广州，尤其是在天河，现在粤语的普及是越来越差了。你很少能听到有人在街上说粤语，或者说是……就怎么说，可能说广州本地人呢，很多还是会说粤语的，因为天河，或者说全广州，外地来的越来越多，所以我觉得粤语在广东，在广州就消失得很厉害。之前在广州这么多年都没有机会去学……

（摘录7：第二次回访李雷，2018-02-05）

在广州上学时,李雷觉得在小区散步、在天河逛街都有很多机会听到别人说粤语,只是学校里不说,到香港读书后,却觉得"很少听到"了。第一次和第二次回访的时间间隔不到三年,广州的语言环境并没有发生太大的变化,变化的是李雷的心态与视角。个人对语言环境的描述是从自己的生活经验、生活习惯出发的主观觉知(perception)。对习惯使用粤语的人来说,在公共场所经常听到普通话,使用公共服务时优先选用普通话,或者先使用粤语不成功转而再使用普通话,这样的体验会让人觉得"到处都是普通话,很少人会说粤语";对李雷来说,过去在广州生活习惯于使用普通话,如果能够偶尔听到一些粤语便觉得粤语还是普遍存在的,遇上一个出租车司机似乎不会听普通话,便觉得广州还是很多人不会说普通话。到了香港之后,他才发现生活中处处都要用到粤语,用粤语比用普通话更便利,对比之下,用普通话畅通无阻的广州,尤其是天河区,便显得是"粤语普及越来越差"了。

(四)从广州到香港:身份认同的转变

在2009—2010年田野调查时,作者问过李雷他是哪里人。初次见面,他告诉作者他是陕西渭南人,也就是跟他的爸爸一样。在后来的互动与焦点小组讨论中,一些与他语言和移民背景相似的同学公开或私下里主张自己的广州人身份时,他也一直主张自己陕西人的身份。

在2018年的回访中,李雷的叙述里出现了更多的关于语言与身份认同的讨论,显示出较强的语言意识和明确的语言态度。这种变化似乎与他学习粤语是息息相关的。在谈到广州语言环境时(摘录7),他说到广州市尤其天河区的外来人口很多,然后提起身份的问题。

>……之前在广州这么多年都没有机会去学（广州话），因为我也是个外来人，我也是外地过来的。
>
>（摘录8：第二次回访李雷，2018-02-05）

这是作者第一次听到李雷描述自己是"外来人"，从前他虽然不说自己是广州人，却也从没说过自己是外来人或者外地人。他自称"是外地过来的"，一方面可能是在广州生活时被贴过这样的标签，因为他这样家庭背景的小孩，通常不会被认为是"本地人"，另一方面，这体现了一种地方归属感的缺失。他介绍自己时会告诉别人自己是"广州来的"不会说是"陕西来的"，但只代表他学习、生活的城市，是一种不带归属感，"非身份"的介绍方式。作者向他追问为何不觉得自己是广州人时，以下是李雷的回答。

>其实我不敢说自己是一个广州人，因为我觉得如果你说你是哪里人呢，有两个很必要的元素，一个是你会说这里的语言，因为语言承载着文化，第二个是你了解这里的文化，你做的事情是和这个文化有关的。我觉得这两点我都没有做得很好。
>
>所以我现在学广东话呢……我觉得很大一个原因，是因为我想成为一个广东人、广州人，这样子。
>
>因为我觉得这个原因是，呃，我是外地过来的，但是我从小又在这里长大，但是又没有学粤语。所以说，我没有继承到老家的文化，也没有继承到广州的文化，所以我有时候觉得自己哪里人都不是。
>
>（摘录9：第二次回访李雷，2018-02-05）

从摘录的第一段可以看出，如果说从前李雷不觉得自己是广州人，那么现在他觉得自己没有资格自称广州人。他说这个资格有两个方面，包括通晓本地方言与了解本地文化，而归根到底还是要通晓本地方言——粤语。这种语言与文化的关系，地方身份认同与地方语言能力之间的捆绑，他在广州时也有所接触。读小学时，亲戚曾对他说"陕西人应该会说陕西话"，但父母没有坚持，他似乎也没有认真考虑过这句话的意义。在摘录9中却可以看出，在香港时，李雷对此有了比较深入的思考。第三段中连续的两个"但是"表明李雷看到了自己身上的语言与身份之间的矛盾，他认为方言能力的缺失使得他在"寻根"时失去线索，成为一个找不到归属感的人。他说自己既没有继承"老家"的文化，又没有继承广州的文化，因此"有时候觉得自己哪里人都不是"。这里面的"哪里人"代表的就是一种地方的归属感。

李雷认为学习粤语可以帮助自己找到"广州人"的身份认同。他认为，能够熟练掌握一个地方的方言，是了解地方文化、找到地方归属感的必由之路。为何在香港生活的短短几个月会改变他在广州生活十几年的想法呢？他多次提到，在香港，粤语第一次成了他"赖以生存的方式"，这与粤语在他的广州生活中"可有可无"的状况形成强烈对比。在香港得到充分的机会学习粤语，他重新发现了自己成为一个广东人或广州人的可能，而这种可能性又给了他更充足的动力去学好粤语。学习机会的增加、语言能力的提高和身份认同感的加强形成相辅相成的互动关系。

另一方面，在2018年的采访中，李雷提到能够用粤语与当地人沟通会给他一种"价值满足感"。他说那是一种类似于成就感的感觉，甚至将之与英语能力和雅思成绩相比。

因为觉得自己，在这门语言上进步了。就像，如果我，就像我的雅思，如果说我有一天能跟外国人沟通毫无压力，我觉得这也是值得自己骄傲的一件事情。或者说，我可以说，我的雅思可以拿到7，拿到8这样子，我觉得也是让自己很有价值感和满足感的事情。

（摘录10：第二次回访李雷，2018-02-05）

英语是一种国际通用语言，英语读写能力是一种被学校承认的"合法读写能力"（legitimate literacy）（Gee 2008），雅思考试是一种在世界上被广为接受的标准化考试。李雷将这些与粤语能力相提并论，说"都"是值得他骄傲和能带给他价值感、满足感的事情，可见他对粤语的高度推崇。粤语读写能力的半官方地位来自粤语在香港的半官方地位，李雷对粤语高度推崇的根本原因是粤语在香港的社会声望远高于其在广州的社会声望。在这种语境下，对李雷来说，粤语不但具有亲和力，更是一种能提供珍贵的社会资本的高声望语言。因此，虽然他依然说陕西是他的老家，但是到了香港读书之后，他第一次有强烈的意愿去成为一个会说粤语的广州人。

四、讨论及结语

根据前文的分析，我们发现李雷的语言使用习惯和身份认同的变化明显以他离开广州去香港读书为分水岭。

在广州时，李雷父母虽然也在有意无意间采取了一些语言管理的策略，但并不刻意引导李雷的语言选择；在实践方面，李雷父母包容李雷的语言选择，以普通话与之交流，而他们自己在家中交流的语言也逐渐从以陕西话为主变为以普通话为主。

李雷所在的中小学里，普通话是校园语言，身边的同学、朋友通过语码转换等双语互动策略主动包容他的语言偏好，在其他的公共领域，使用普通话也能畅通无阻，会说粤语不过是锦上添花。因此，尽管可以听懂大部分粤语，李雷却很少在生活中主动使用粤语，既没有必要也没有其他方面的驱动力。他的双语能力主要表现为被动的双语能力，对他人使用粤语持积极开放的态度。这种积极的态度和被动双语能力为他学习粤语、快速融入大学生活与香港社会奠定了基础。

到香港后，他发现生活中处处要用到粤语，如果不会粤语就无法融入校园团体，无法真正理解本地人的生活，甚至无法很好地完成课程作业，因此粤语成为一种必要的生存技能。他的"广州人"身份认同与他粤语能力的提高有着交互促进（reciprocal）的关系。随着语言能力的上升和使用频率的提高，"广州人"的身份认同也变得更明确，而随着身份认同的加强，学习语言的动力也变得更加充足。李雷到香港读书后，对粤语的语言态度也发生了明显的变化。广州和香港虽然同为传统的粤语城市，但是由于历史、经济、文化、政治等多重原因，语言状况有很大的区别，表现为语言使用、社会地位，以及粤语能力被赋予的价值（valorization）。粤语在香港的高社会地位使李雷很向往这种语言，并萌生了学会粤语，成为广州人的想法。

李雷的案例中，从广州到香港的移动经历是个重要的转折。在以往的语言态度研究中,空间与地方往往以宏观社会因素的角色出现,是研究的背景而不是中心。但是在语言学其他分支的研究中,对于空间的符号学意义,空间与语言之间不可分割的关系其实已经有了深入的研究(Blommaert 2013;Gorter 2006;Shohamy & Gorter 2009)。空间不是中立的,而总是带着历史、经济、文化、社会形态的意义(梁斯华 2016)。语言与空间的关系密不可分,人们对一种语言的认知、态度及其语言身份的认同都与其所处空间有着紧密的联系。随着人在空间的移动,他的言语库也随之移动,语言库中的各种语言能力要根据新的语言环境被重新赋予价值。有些在原来的语境中具有高社会地位、高价值的语言能力,在新的环境可能不被认可,反之亦然(Dong & Blommaert 2009;Fogle 2013)。

本文通过一个跨越九年的纵向语言民族志个案分析,主要利用2009年、2015年、2018年三次采访的数据进行对比分析,系统地回顾了李雷的家庭语言环境,在家庭以外的语言社会化经验以及他的语言态度、语言能力和身份认同发生的变化。李雷从一个被动的双语使用者变成主动的双语使用者,从广州到香港的移动经验是一个重要的转折。随着空间移动的经验而来的是多语使用者语言库中各种语言的重新"洗牌",重新被赋予社会地位和社会价值,从而带来了语言使用习惯、语言态度和身份认同方面的变化。社会语言环境的变化对李雷双语能力的变化产生了关键的影响,而从李雷的叙述中,我们还可看到他的主观能动性在他的双语能力成长中也扮演了重要的角色。由于本文是个案分析,研究结果不具有普遍性。但我们从李雷的案例中可看到,个人双语、多语能力最初的构成或许与家庭语言政策有关,但其可持续发展与家庭以外的社会语言环境,如学校语言、社会上默认的语言互动准则、各种语言在社会中的地位和价值都是分不开的。保护语言的多样化,促进语言的可持续发展,需要家庭、学校、社会各个语域的协同合作。

参考文献

Axler, M., A. Yang and T. Stevens. Current language attitudes of Hong Kong Chinese adolescents and young adults. In M. C. Pennington (ed.). *Language in Hong Kong at Century's End.* Hong Kong: Hong Kong University Press, 1998: 329–338.

Baker, C. *Foundations of Bilingual Education and Bilingualism.* Bristol, Buffalo and Toronto: Multilingual Matters, 2006.

Bruche-Schulz, G. "Fuzzy" Chinese: The status of Cantonese in Hong Kong. *Journal of Pragmatics*, 1997 (27): 295–314.

Busch, B. The linguistic repertoire revisited. *Applied Linguistics*, 2012, 33 (5): 503–523.

Caldas, S. J. *Raising Bilingual-Biliterate Children in Monolingual Cultures.* London: Multilingual Matters, 2006.

Canagarajah, A. S. Language shift and the family: Questions from the Sri Lankan Tamil diaspora. *Journal of Sociolinguistics*, 2008, 12 (2): 143–176.

Coady, M. R. Attitudes toward bilingualism in Ireland. *Bilingual Research Journal*, 2001, 25 (1&2): 1–20.

Creese, A. Linguistic ethnography. In K. A. King and N. H. Hornberger (eds.). *Encyclopedia of Language and Education.* New York: Springer, 2008: 229 – 241.

Curdt-Christiansen, X. L. Invisible and visible language planning: Ideological factors in the family language policy of Chinese immigrant families in Quebec. *Language Policy*, 2009, 8 (4): 351 – 375.

—— Conflicting language ideologies and contradictory language practices in Singaporean multilingual families. *Journal of Multilingual and Multicultural Development*, 2016, 37 (7): 694 – 709.

De Houwer, A. Environmental factors in early bilingual development: The role of parental beliefs and attitudes. In G. Extra and L. Verhoeven (eds.). *Bilingualism and Migration.* Berlin and New York: Mouton de Gruyter, 1999: 75 – 95.

—— Parental language input patterns and children's bilingual use. *Applied psycholinguistics*, 2007, 28 (3): 411 – 424.

Doyle, C. To make the root stronger: Language policies and experiences of successful multilingual intermarried families with adolescent children in Tallinn. In Mila Schwartz and Anna Verschic (eds.). *Successful Family Language Policy*, Dordrecht: Springer, 2013: 145 – 175.

Duff, P. Language socialization. In N. H. Hornberger and S. McKay (eds.). *Sociolinguistics and Language Education.* Bristol, Buffalo and Toronto: Multilingual Matters, 2010:

427-452.

Dyers, C. and J. -F. Abongdia. An exploration of the relationship between language attitudes and ideologies in a study of francophone students of English in Cameroon. *Journal of Multilingual and Multicultural Development*, 2010, 31 (2): 119-134.

Eckert, P. Communities of practice. In B. Keith (ed.). *Encyclopedia of Language and Linguistics*. Oxford: Elsevier, 2006: 683-685.

Flick, U. *An Introduction to Qualitative Research*. London and Thousand Oaks: SAGE, 2009.

Fogle, L. W. Family language policy from the children's point of view: Bilingualism in place and time. In M. Schwarz and A. Verschic (eds.). *Successful Family Language Policy: Parents, Children and Educators in Interaction*. New York and London: Springer, 2013: 177-200.

Fogle, L. W. and K. A. King. Child agency and language policy in transnational families. *Issues in Applied Linguistics*, 2013 (19).

Gafaranga, J. Medium request: Talking language shift into being. *Language in Society*, 2010, 39 (2): 241.

Giles, H. Language attitudes and language cognitions: Future prospects for Hong Kong. In M. C. Pennington (ed.). *Language in Hong Kong at Century's End*. Hong Kong: Hong Kong University Press, 1998: 425-436.

Goffman, E. *Frame Analysis: An Essay on the Organization of Experience*. New York: Harper & Row, 1974.

Goodz, N. S. Interactions between parents and children in

bilingual families. In F. Genesee (ed.). *Educating Second Language Children*. Cambridge: Cambridge University Press, 1994: 61 -81.

Gumperz, J. J. and D. Hymes. *The Ethnography of Communication*. New York: Blackwell, 1964.

Gupta, A. F. *The Step-tongue: Children's English in Singapore*. Bristol, Buffalo and Toronto: Multilingual Matters, 1994.

Heath, S. B. *Ways with Words: Language Life and Work in Communities and Classrooms*. Cambridge: Cambridge University Press, 1983.

── *Words at Work and Play: Three Decades in Family and Community Life*. Cambridge: Cambridge University Press, 2012.

King, K. A. and A. Logan-Terry. Additive bilingualism through family language policy: Strategies, identities and interactional outcomes. *Calidoscopio*, 2008, 6 (1): 5 -19.

King, K. A. and L. W. Fogle. Family language policy and bilingual parenting. *Language Teaching*, 2013, 46 (2): 172 -194.

Korth, B. *Language Attitudes Towards Kyrgyz and Russian: Discourse, education and policy in post-Soviet Kyrgyzstan*. Switzerland: Peter Lang, 2005.

Kulick, D. *Language Shift and Cultural Reproduction: Socialization, Self and Syncretism in a Papua New Guinean Village*. Cambridge: Cambridge University Press, 1997.

Lai, M. -L. Hong Kong students' attitude towards Cantonese, Putonghua and English after the change of sovereignty. *Journal* of *Multilingual and Multicultural Development*, 2001, 22 (2): 112-133.

—Language attitudes of the first postcolonial generation in Hong Kong secondary schools. *Language in Society*, 2005, 34 (3): 363-388.

—Tracking language attitudes in postcolonial Hong Kong: An interplay of localization, mainlandization and internationalization. *Multilingua: Journal of Cross-Cultural and Interlanguage Communication*, 2012, 31: 1-29.

Lanza, E. Can bilingual two-year-olds code-switch? *Journal of Child Language*, 1992, 19 (3): 633-658.

— *Language Mixing in Infant Bilingualism: A Sociolinguistic Perspective*. Oxford: Oxford University Press, 2004 (on demand).

Li, Wei. *Three Generations, Two Languages, One Family: Language Choice and Language Shift in a Chinese Community in Britain*. Bristol, Buffalo and Toronto: Multilingual Matters, 1994.

Liang, S. Construction of language attitudes in multilingual China: Linguistic ethnographies of two primary schools in Guangzhou. Doctor of Philosophy. Cambridge: University of Cambridge, 2013.

— Problematizing monolingual identities and competence in Guangzhou in the era of multilingualism and superdiversity. In E. Esch and M. Solly (eds.). *Language Education and the Challenges of Globalisation: Sociolinguistic Issues*. Cambridge:

Cambridge Scholars Publishing: 2014: 67 -92.

Lotherington, H. Multiliteracies in Springvale: Negotiating language, culture and identity in suburban Melbourne. In R. Bayley and S. R. Schecter (eds.). *Language Socialization in Bilingual and Multilingual Societies*. Bristol, Buffalo and Toronto: Multilingual Matters, 2003: 200 -217.

Luykx, A. Weaving languages together: Family language policy and gender socialization in bilingual Aymara households. In R. Bayley and S. R. Schecter (eds.). *Language Socialization in Bilingual and Multilingual Societies*. Bristol, Buffalo and Toronto: Multilingual Matters, 2003: 25 -43.

Maybin, J. and K. Tusting. Linguistic ethnography. In J. Simpson (ed.). *The Routledge Handbook of Applied Linguistics*. London and New York: Routledge, 2011: 515 -528.

McEwan-Fujita, E. Ideology, affect, and socialization in language shift and revitalization: The experiences of adults learning gaelic in the western isles of Scotland. *Language in Society*, 2010, 39 (1): 27.

Poon, A. Y. K. Language policy of Hong Kong: Its impact on language education and language use in post-handover Hong Kong. *Journal of Taiwan Normal University*, 2004, 49 (1): 53 -74.

Rampton, B. *Language in Late Modernity: Interaction in an Urban School*. Cambridge and New York: Cambridge University Press, 2006.

—— Neo-Hymesian linguistic ethnography in the United Kingdom.

Journal of Sociolinguistics, 2007, 11 (5): 584 -607.

Ren, L. and G. Hu. Prolepsis, syncretism, and synergy in early language and literacy practices: A case study of family language policy in Singapore. *Language Policy*, 2013, 12 (1): 63 -82.

Schwartz, M. Family language policy: Core issues of an emerging field. *Applied Linguistics Review*, 2010 (1): 171 -192.

Siegel, J. Language ideologies and the education of speakers of marginalized language varieties: Adopting a critical awareness approach. *Linguistics and Education*, 2006, 17 (2): 157 -174.

Silverstein, M. Indexical order and the dialectics of sociolinguistic life. *Language and Communication*, 2003, 23 (3): 193 -229.

Spolsky, B. *Language Management.* Cambridge: Cambridge University Press, 2009.

——Family language policy: the critical domain. *Journal of Multilingual and Multicultural Development*, 2012, 33 (1): 3 -11.

Wiley, T. G. Chinese "dialect" speakers as heritage language learners: A case study. In D. Brinton, O. Kagan and S. Bauckus (eds.). *Heritage Language Education: A New Field Emerging.* London and New York: Routledge, 2009: 91 - 106.

Zentella, A. C. *Growing Up Bilingual: Puerto Rican Children in New York.* Malden, MA.: Blackwell, 1997.

Zhu, H. Duelling languages, duelling values: Codeswitching in bilingual intergenerational conflict talk in diasporic families. *Journal of Pragmatics*, 2008, 40 (10): 1799 -1816.

广州市统计局,国家统计局广州调查队. 广州统计年鉴

2017. 北京：中国统计出版社，2017.
郭媛媛. 南京市城区中学生语言状况调查研究［D］. 南京：南京大学，2012.
梁斯华. 母语作为一种意识形态［J］. 语言学研究［待发］.
廖雪明，吴永佳，郑纪军. 广州公布二号人口公报：凸显城市化进程［N］. 新快报，2001-04-23.
孙晓先，蒋冰冰，王颐嘉，等. 上海市学生普通话和上海话使用情况调查［J］. 长江学术，2007（3）：1-10.
香港大学. 市民的身份认同［EB/OL］. 7 July，2018，https：//www.hkupop.hku.hk/chinese/popexpress/ethnic/.
俞玮奇. 市场领域的语言生活状况：在南京、苏州和常州农贸市场的非介入式观察［J］. 语言文字应用，2011a（4）：25-34.
俞玮奇. 苏州市外来人口第二代的语言转用考察［J］. 语言教学与研究，2011b（1）：82-88.
俞玮奇. 城市青少年语言使用与语言认同的年龄变化：南京市中小学生语言生活状况调查［J］. 语言文字应用，2012（3）：90-98.
俞玮奇，杨璟琰. 近十五年来上海青少年方言使用与能力的变化态势及影响因素［J］. 语言文字应用，2016（4）：26-34.
詹伯慧. 普通话"南下"与粤方言"北上"［J］. 学术研究，1993（4）：67-72.

作者简介

梁斯华,剑桥大学博士,现任中山大学国际翻译学院研究员。
　研究方向:社会语言学。

生态语言学研究综观

何 伟 高 然

一、引 言

生态语言学发展至今已有近 50 年的历史,背景各异的学者秉持着对语言和生态环境问题的共同关注,将不同的语言学理论框架、研究方法与生态学的原理和方法结合起来,尝试通过对语言之间关系的研究以及对语言系统及语言使用方面的研究,来解决语言象征环境、自然环境、社会文化环境、认知心理环境中的生态问题。这种多学科间的融合使生态语言学具备了交叉性和开放性的特点,也为其学科内涵的定义、研究范畴的界定造成一定困难。与其他语言学派相比,生态语言学还存在一些新兴学科所面临的共同问题。例如,研究对象不尽明确,研究方法尚不系统,研究范围边界不清,等。本文通过梳理生态语言学的缘起、发展历程和研究现状,明晰其现存问题,以期为其发展指明方向。

二、生态语言学的缘起

随着经济社会不断进步，科学技术不断发展，在人类生活得到较大改善、生活水平逐渐提升的同时，人口压力、气候变暖、环境恶化、资源短缺等全球性问题也日益显著。由此，研究生物与其有机及无机环境之间相互作用关系的科学——生态学（Ecology）（Haeckel 1866）——便应运而生。随着其研究的不断深入以及人们生态意识的不断提高，生态学观点及视角开始广泛应用于自然科学及人文社会科学，"生态"这一概念也已从最初的生物生态、环境生态延展到语言生态、人口生态、社会生态、政治生态、经济生态等。可以说，任何与环境（包括生物环境及非生物环境）发生相互作用的活动都与"生态"二字密切相关。而语言活动作为人类社会生活中最重要的活动之一，同样也在生态系统中扮演着举足轻重的角色。

早在19世纪初期，普通语言学奠基人、德国哲学家和语言学家Wilhelm von Humboldt在进行"总体语言研究"时，从哲学角度出发关注语言本质、语言内在形式及语言类型等问题，将"探究人类语言结构的差异"作为普通语言学所承担的重要任务之一（Humboldt 1836，转引自姚小平 1999）。他认为：人类语言的多样性是人类精神的内在需要，语言的特性差异实际上反映了民族思维方式和活动感知方式的不同（Humboldt 1829，转引自姚小平 2001b）；语言像人一样会经历产生和死亡的自然进程，但消亡的语言并非失去"生命"，而是通过混合产生了新的语言（Humboldt 1836，转引自姚小平 1999）。由于Humboldt更多关注语言差异对人类认知层面及精神发展造成的影响，将语言的消亡看作一种必然过程，因此并未产生对濒危语言的保护意识。一个多世纪后，受 Humboldt 语言和文化具有多样性的观点的影响，美国语言学家和人类学家 Edward Sapir（1912）对多种语言和文化进行进一步研究，超越语言在结构、语音系统以及词义等层级的描述，对语言与环境之间关系的建立进行了初步尝试。值得注意的是，Sapir 所提及的环境（environment）不只停留于其生态意义（ecological meaning），而是更强调物理和社会环境（physical and social surroundings）。他认为，词汇是最能反映说话者环境特征的语言因素，它不仅能反映说话者所处环境的地形特征、文化背景的复杂性，还能反映为地形和文化所影响的人们的兴趣倾向。无论是 Humboldt 关于人类语言的哲学思想，还是 Sapir 对建立语言与环境关系的初步尝试，一百多年来，人们都在思考语言多样性以及语言与环境之间关系的问题，为语言学家进行语言生态研究并积极探索语言在解决环境问题中所发挥的有效作用奠定了思想基础。

20 世纪 70 年代，Einar Haugen（1972）在奥地利（Burg Wartenstein, Austria）举办的一次学术会议上做了题为 On the Ecology of Languages 的学术报告，用动物、植物与其生存环境的关系来类比语言与其周围环境之间发生的相互作用，并用 "ecology of language" 一词，也称 "language ecology"，来表示语言生态，即对语言与多语社团（multilingual community）间的相互作用关系进行的一种新型生态学研究。1972 年，Haugen 将这一术语收录进其论文集 *The Ecology of Language: Essays by Einar Haugen*，并进一步将 "language ecology" 定义为 "任意一种语言与其环境之间相互作用的研究"（Haugen 1972：325），这里的"语言环境"指语言实际被使用、被解码的社会环境。Haugen（1972）认为，语言生态的一部分是心理的，表现在双语者和多语者思想中语言与语言的相互作用关系；一部分是社会的，指语言与社会的相互作用关系。然而，Haugen 并不是第一位将生态概念与语言现象联系在一起的学者（Fill 1993；Steffensen 2007；Eliasson 2015）。在此之前，美国语言学家和人类学家 Carl Voegelin 等人（Voegelin and Voegelin 1964；Voegelin, et al. 1967）曾使用"linguistic ecology"一词表达"语言生态"概念，认为语言生态是"从独立存在的单一语言转向相互联系的多种语言的研究"（Voegelin and Voegelin 1964：2），强调对一个特定地区中所有语言的全面关注，如 Voegelin, et al.（1967）对美国西南部多种语言之间的复杂关系进行研究，Peter Mühlhäusler（1995）对殖民化、西化与现代化影响下的澳大利亚和太平洋地区的语言与生物的多样性进行考察等。

1985 年，法国语言学家 Claude Hagège 从达尔文生物进化论的角度研究语言的多样性、语言的演变与进化以及语言的退化与消亡等问题，并发现 19 世纪的许多语言学者被生命科学激发的强劲思潮所吸引，开始将生物学研究的模型和术语运用到人文科学上（转引自张祖建 2012）。Hagège 在《语言人：论语言学对人文科学的贡献》一书中提出"écolinguistique"（ecolinguistic）一词，其"专门研究经过文化加工的'天然'参照物怎样进入语言，例如方向、地理特点、人类的栖居方式或宇宙因素等"，即探索自然现象与语言、文化之间的关系，之后被翻译为"环境语言学"（张祖建 2012：261）。这也是学界最早使用"ecolinguistic"这一术语来表示与语言和自然相关的研究。

值得注意的是,Hagège 认为,人们在用语言谈论世界的同时,也对世界加以再造。这一观点与系统功能语言学家 M. A. K. Halliday(1990)所提出的"语言建构论"(language constructionism)不谋而合。在 1990 年的国际应用语言学大会上,Halliday 针对语言系统与生态因素发表了以《意义表达的新方式:对应用语言学的挑战》(New Ways of Meaning: The Challenge to Applied Linguistics)为题的主旨报告,对语言系统之于某些生态现象的不合理表述进行了批评,关注语言学研究在解决生态问题中所发挥的重要作用。他将语言对世界的影响描述为"系统与事件之间的辩证法"(Halliday 2001:186),认为语言并不是被动地反映现实,"语言主动建构现实"(Halliday 2001:196),强调增长主义、种族灭绝、环境污染、性别歧视、阶级歧视等不只是生物学家和物理学家的问题,同样也是语言学家应该关注的问题。同时期在国内,李国正(1987,1991)将语言置于自然生态系统中进行考察研究,开始运用生态学原理研究汉语问题,在了解多层次、多功能的语言基础上,引入生态系统的基本原则,继而提出"生态语言系统"概念(李国正 1991:35),将语言系统的生态环境分为外生态环境系统和内生态环境系统,将汉语分为五种不同的生态类型,并提出了生态汉语学的研究方法,如系统分析法、实验法等。这一时期还出现了一些以"语言生态学"或"生态语言学"为题的著述,如此一来,生态语言学的学科理论框架便逐渐丰富起来(范俊军 2005)。

此外,德国学者(Mackey 1980;Finke 1983;Fill 1987;

Tramp 1990；Mühlhäusler 1992，1995）将此类生物生态学与语言学的概念、原理相结合的研究称为"ecological linguistics"。国内许多学者（范俊军 2005；韩军 2013）将"生态语言学"（ecolinguistics 或 ecological linguistics）与"语言生态学"（language ecology 或 ecology of language）这两个概念等同起来，认为它们指代同一门学科（黄国文 2016）。我们认为，"生态语言学（ecolinguistics）"一词更能体现该类研究是一个具有超学科属性的、统一的学科。

三、生态语言学的发展历程及研究现状

生态语言学兴起至今的发展历程可主要分为两个阶段：第一个阶段是 1970—2001 年，以 Haugen 首次提出"语言生态"为起始点，至 Alwin Fill 和 Mühlhäusler 为推动学界进行更深层次的研究，系统回顾了 30 年来不同领域的生态语言学的思想，主编《生态语言学读本：语言、生态与环境》（*The Ecolinguistics Reader: Language, Ecology and Environment*）（2001）为节点；第二个阶段是 21 世纪以来至今，随着经济社会的飞速发展，科学技术的进步，许多新兴科学的出现为生态语言学的发展注入了新的生命力，加之生态语言学过去 30 年在各个领域的探索奠定了些许基础，不少语言学家也开始思考更深层次乃至哲学思想在生态语言学研究中所起的作用，因此这一时期的生态语言学研究呈现出继往开来的特点。

（一）生态语言学的发展历程

"生态语言学始于一个隐喻。"（王晋军 2007：54）Haugen（1970，1972）提出的"语言生态"概念开创了语言学与生态学研究相结合的新模式。20 世纪 80 年代，基于

Haugen 的语言生态隐喻思想,许多学者开始将生物生态学的概念和原理以不同的方式用于心理语言学和社会语言学现象研究(Fill 1998),少数民族濒危语言逐渐成为语言学家关注的热点问题,尤其表现在有关太平洋地区少数民族语言以及语言帝国主义问题的研究中。例如,William Mackey(1980)将 Haugen "语言的生态学" 发展为 "语言转用(language shift)的生态学",并提出语言学家区分语言形式和语言行为的做法是值得商榷的,因为语言和语言使用都与社会活动有着不可分割的关系。Norman Dension(1982)通过研究欧洲语言多样性及近年来它们的生态变化进一步证实了生态隐喻思想的适用性,明确提出语言生态离不开语言经济(language economy)(Weinrich 1990),以及 "语言种类的保护是否应与濒危自然物种的保护并驾齐驱" 的问题(Dension 2001:77)。此外,Dension 还指出语言生态隐喻思想具有一定局限性:自然生态是有生物居住的,因此它们显然是有界的(bounded)自然种类;但语言的边界并不明确,且互通性很强,这就给语言的生态研究造成了不确定性。

Haugen 的语言生态隐喻思想奠定了生态语言学的第一种主流研究范式,主要涉及生态学、社会学、心理学、语言学以及哲学等学科领域,被称为 "豪根模式" "隐喻模式" 或 "语言的生态学"(Fill 2001;范俊军 2005;韩军 2013)。在此研究范式之下,许多语言学家从语言与环境的关系入手进行了更深层次的研究,包括对语言生态现象的原因剖析,例如通过研究少数民族语言,阐述为何有些语言的生存受到威胁,而另一些语言却得以幸存(Krier 1996)。Bastardas-Boada(2003,2013)还通过关注 "语言可持续性"(linguistic sustainability）强调生物多样性与语言多样性之间的联系。有的学者侧重对语言环境、语言生态系统的理论建构，如 Harald Haarmann（1980，1986）建立了生态语言学变量，其中包括种族人口统计、种族社会、种族文化以及其他方面的各种因子，共同构成了一种语言的"环境"。Peter Finke（1983，1996）用生态系统（ecosystem）的概念转指语言世界系统（language world system）和文化系统，将生物生态和语言进行比较，指出我们使用语言的方式就如同我们对待自然的方式：人类对自然环境的破坏造成了对生命创造力的威胁，对语言的不合理使用造成了语言的濒危和消亡。Wilhelm Trampe（1990）继承了这一观点，指出语言的生态系统由语言、语言使用以及与之相互作用的环境构成。近年来，还有生态语言学家将语言与政治联系起来，认为政治活动也是一种象征性的语言生态环境（symbolic ecology of language）（Steffensen and Fill 2014）。他们（Skuttnabb-Kangas and Phillipson 2008：11）关注语言人权（linguistic human rights）和语言权利（language rights），认为个人和团体有权利使用他们自己的语言说话和接受教育，语言像个人或团体一样具有"法律人格"（legal personality），同样也享有相应的权利。

20世纪90年代，生态环境的恶化进一步推动了语言与生态的研究，语言学家开始探索语言在生态环境问题中所起的作用，尝试将语言作为环境问题解决方式中的一种。Halliday首先关注到语言以及语言学在环境问题中发挥的作用，强调语言与增长主义（growthism）、等级主义（classism）和物种主义（speciesism）之间的关系，劝告语言学家不要忽视自己的研究对象（即语言）在日益恶化的环境问题中所担当的角色。Halliday认为,语言不仅能反映世界,还能够建构世界,同时帮助人们认识世界。因此,人们对世界的许多不合理认知都来自语言系统(或语法),主要表现在以下四个方面。

(1) 欧洲通用语种(Standard Average European,以下简称SAE)将"物"分为两个类别,可数与不可数。在表达与自然资源相关的物时,所选择的词都是无界的(unbounded)、不可数的,如air、water、soil、coal、iron、oil等,语言使用者只有通过"量化"的方式才能将其表达为"有界",如a barrel of oil、a seam of coal等。当全球资源短缺的问题逐渐显现,人们开始意识到地球上的资源大多都是不可再生的、有限的,而并不是语言系统所描述的那样。

(2) 在选择表达事物性质的等级词时,人们大多选择"高程度词"(positive pole)。例如,在提问时使用"How long/tall/far is it?"(它有多长/高/远?),而不使用"How short/near is it?"(它有多短/矮/近?)。并且,数量的等级表达通常与性质的等级表达相一致,如"bigger and better"。这表明,"越'多'越'好'"的增长主义(growthism)已经内化为人们的认知,因此在发展经济的过程中无节制地追求经济增长,忽视了由此带来的环境问题。

(3) 在及物性系统中,过程参与者的类别可根据其是否有发起该过程的潜质来判断,即他们有多大可能性去发起这个动作或造成这个事件的发生。例如,"人"通常是主动的施事,而非生命体通常是被动的受事。只有在"灾难语境"中,非生命体才可能作为施事隐喻出现,如"*The earthquake destroyed the city*"。由此可见,语言系统使我们很难意识到非生命体（自然）能够作为事件的主动参与者，继而忽视了潜在的环境破坏因素。

（4）在代词系统中，有意识的用 he/she 表示，无意识的用 it 表示。而且，无意识的事物可以作为信息的来源，但不能反映思想（idea），不能与 think、believe、know 等表达认知心理过程的动词连用。这种人类特权地位造成了"我们"与其他创造物之间的割裂，使我们很难接受地球是一个与我们有着共同命运的生命体。

由此可见，人类不仅将语言作为中介来反映和表达对世界的认知，同时也通过语言来构建世界。这种"人类头脑中对世界的认知"被 Stibbe（2015）称为"故事"（story）：不同生存背景下的人类对世界的认知不同，由此而形成的生态理念和对生态环境的方式也就不同。自然资源的无限性和人类享有特权地位的思想意识已经内化在语言系统中，这对人类形成良好的生态理念以及环境问题的解决产生了阻碍作用。

Halliday 对语言在环境问题中作用的思考为生态语言学提供了新的研究路径，被称为"韩礼德模式""非隐喻模式""环境的语言学"（environmental linguistics）（Fill 2001；范俊军 2005；韩军 2013）。主要涉及生态学、语言学、经济学、环境科学、宗教研究、心理学、哲学以及其他多种领域，重点关注语言对生态所产生的作用，这种作用可能是积极的、和谐的，也可能是消极的、破坏性的。对能产生积极、有益作用的语言需要鼓励和提倡，而对产生破坏性作用的语言则需要抵制和改进。

基于韩礼德模式，语言学家开始对语言和语言实践（即语言系统和语篇）的生态特征和非生态特征进行批评性分析。主要包括以下三种研究路径：

（1）运用批评话语分析的理论框架，对有关环境的文本进行分析，例如，通过对文本中主动、被动、作格结构的分析（Gerbig 1993）或对施事、受事的分析（Alexander 1996），可以看出不同利益群体在描述环境问题时的侧重点和规避点。Andrew Goatly（1996：55）还指出，删除施事或受事可以通过名词化（nominalization）的方式来实现，以此来弱化人们对受影响对象的关注（Fill 1998）。

（2）从生态角度对语言系统进行批评性分析。除Halliday（1990）对语言系统的批判之外，Trampe（1991）通过对比工业化农业和传统农耕农业中的语言现象，对工业化农业语言中表现的"人类中心主义"（anthropocentrism）和"重商主义"（commercialism）进行批判，认为语言反映世界不能只从人类视角出发，还要关注自然对人类及其商业活动的作用。Goatly（1996）认为，欧洲通用语种中分化的语言系统不符合现今世界整体化的生态思想，主要表现在：及物性分析将现实世界划分为施事、受事和环境成分，不适用于表现当代科学理论或盖亚理论（Gaia theory）；参与者角色中对施事和受事的划分表现了一种错误的单向因果关系，不符合当代科学理论"多向的""互为因果的"特点；将施事、受事参与者角色与环境成分分化，由状语表达的环境成分通常被边缘化，暗示"环境"既没有能动性，也不会受到影响（Goatly 1996）。因此，Goatly 提出"协和语法"（consonant grammar），也称"绿色语法"（green grammar），即用作格分析法激活在及物性分析中被边缘化的自然环境，使其成为动作过程的参与者（Goatly 2007），从而引起人们对自然环境的重视。

（3）从生态角度对社会热点话题文章或环保类话题广告中的非生态特征进行批评性分析。例如，Fill（2000）通过分析 *Times* 和 *Newsweek* 中有关环境问题的广告发现，广告中使用越多的"绿色"语言，实际大众对生态环境问题的关注度越低，从而揭示了广告语篇背后虚伪的环保意识；Mary Kahn（2001）在描写动物实验的科学语篇中发现，全文仅在致谢部分使用代词"I""We"以及主动语态，正文均使用被动语态，这种语言使用习惯表明人们在潜意识中并没有将动物作为与人平等的生物对待。

在以上三种研究路径中，第一种和第三种属于生态批评话语分析，第二种属于批评生态语言学（critical ecolinguistics）的研究内容。生态批评话语分析与批评生态语言学的不同之处在于，生态批评话语分析侧重于具体语言的使用，通过批判话语或文本中的词法、句法和语用，揭示话语背后所隐含的意识形态，这种意识形态表现在生态语言学中就是生态意识；而批评生态语言学侧重于对语言系统（language system）中非生态特征的批判（Fill 1998；Fill and Mühlhäusler 2001；范俊军 2005；王晋军 2007），如名词的可数与不可数之分、代词的用法以及语法系统的描写等。Stibbe（2015）提出批评生态语言学（critical ecolinguistics）这一概念，从批评性角度研究人类"赖以生存的话语"，通过改变语言系统的模式和语言使用方法，使其更加适合生态系统的和谐发展。

相比而言，"豪根模式"关注的是语言生态本身，"语言"与"生物"具有相似的发展历程，在生态系统中起到等同的作用；而"韩礼德模式"则注重语言对生态环境所能造成的影响，对话语和行为的生态特征和非生态特征进行分析。虽然侧重点各有不同，但二者并不排斥，关系互补（Fill 1998），在促进不同生态系统的良性发展中做出了各自的贡献。

（二）生态语言学的研究现状

自生态语言学兴起以来，经过国内外学界的共同努力，以生态语言学命名的学会组织、学术网站、学术期刊以及论文集大量涌现，国际学术会议定期召开，国内外高校也开始逐步推进生态语言学专业的本科、硕士研究生、博士研究生等多种层次人才的培养。

以生态语言学命名的学会组织逐渐遍及全球。1990 年，丹麦学者 Jørgen Døør 和 Jørgen Christian Bang 在丹麦创立了一个生态、语言和意识形态研究小组，自 2012 年起，这一小组更名为"人类互动中心"（Centre for Human Interactivity），从认知科学和人文科学的视角研究人们的认知如何塑造事件以及人类行为的结果对生态产生的影响，其组织者也在积极思考如何将"生态语言学"作为组织名称的一部分。1996 年，国际应用语言学协会成立生态语言学分会。21 世纪以来，生态语言学的倡导者专门成立了国际应用语言学会语言与生态科学委员会。2004 年，Stibbe 初步构建国际生态语言学学会的组织框架，至 2017 年 1 月正式成立，目前拥有 1000 多名成员。此外，目前较为活跃的巴西"生态语言学团队"拥有 220 名成员，已出版 12 本生态语言学书籍及多篇期刊文章、博硕士论文。在国内，中国生态语言学研究会于 2017 年 4 月成立，2019 年正式改为中国英汉语比较研究会生态语言学专业委员会，每年召开生态语言学战略发展研讨会及国际生态语言学会议，并组织生态语言学研修班。

与此同时，有关生态语言学研究的三个网站也相继建立并完善，包括语言与生态研究中心网站（http：//www-gewi.uni-graz.at/ecoling/）、生态语言学网站（http：//www.ecoling.net/），以及国际生态语言学学会网站（ecolInguistics-association.org），国内外学者可以在网站中查找有关生态语言学的参考书单、生态语言学发展的最新动态，还可以进行生态语言学的在线课程学习。目前国内外以生态语言学为主要研究内容的期刊杂志较少，有 Stibbe 和 Fill 共同主编的一个在线网络期刊《语言与生态》（*Language and Ecology*），致力于探索与生态相和谐的语篇，以及一本葡萄牙语期刊《生态语言学：巴西生态语言学学刊》。然而，国内外不少期刊都致力于通过专刊或专栏的方式进一步推广生态语言学的研究成果，如 Routledge 出版的《世界语言学刊》（*Journal of World Languages*），以及国内多种期刊。此外，有两本论文集收录了自 20 世纪 70 年代以来至今的有关生态语言学研究的文章，内容齐全，涉及生态语言学的多种研究方法，一是《生态语言学读本：语言、生态与环境》（*The Ecolinguistics Reader：Language, Ecology and Environment*）（Fill and Mühlhausler 2001），二是《劳特利奇生态语言学手册》（*The Routledge Handbook of Ecolinguistics*）（Fill and Penz 2018a）。

进入 21 世纪以来，生态语言学研究主要呈现出以下三个特点：①研究地域逐渐扩大。生态语言学研究始于欧美国家，扩展到澳大利亚、巴西、中国、尼日利亚等多个国家和地区，逐渐演变为一种全球性质的意识形态和活动（Fill and Penz 2018b）。②研究范式趋于融合。生态语言学目前拥有两个主要研究范式——Haugen 隐喻范式和 Halliday 非隐喻范式，而 Steffensen 和 Fill（2014）提出，生态语言学研究没有必要区分隐喻和非隐喻范式，两个范式可以通过自然化的生态语言观融合在一起，以解决人类生态问题。③理论基础及研究方法趋于多元化。生态语言学自兴起以来就借鉴了多种理论基础，不同学科背景的语言学家为其提供了不同的研究路径。由于生态语言学以解决生态问题为出发点和落脚点，因此其借鉴的语言学理论是功能取向的，例如系统功能语言学、认知语言学、社会语言学等。研究方法的多元化表现在研究的实际手段从定性研究发展到定性与定量研究相结合，以及利用现代科学技术进行语言搜集和记录。

21 世纪的生态语言学具有更大的包容性和开放性，通过积极融合多种学科及研究领域，进一步发展了两大研究范式："隐喻模式"下发展了官场生态话语分析等，"非隐喻模式"下发展了"哲学模式"（philosophical model）（Fill and Penz 2017）、"文化外交模式"（何伟、魏榕 2017a，2017b，2018a）以及生态话语分析（辛志英、黄国文 2013；黄国文、赵蕊华 2017；何伟、张瑞杰 2017；何伟、魏榕 2018b）等，研究方法从定性研究逐渐转向定性与定量研究相结合（Chen 2016；连佳欣、吴白音那 2018）。此外，Steffensen 和 Fill（2014）还关注到，语言生态环境的界限十分模糊，根据不同学者对语言生态环境的不同解释，目前学界研究可分为四类：①语言存在于象征性环境（symbolic ecology）中，即研究多种语言或符号系统在同一地理区域中或同一社会制度下的共存关系；②语言存在于自然环境（natural ecology）中，即研究语言与生物或生态系统（如气候、地形、动物等）的关系；③语言存在于社会文化环境（sociocultural ecology）中，即研究语言与塑造言语社团或说话者环境的社会和文化因素的关系；④语言存在于认知环境（cognitive ecology）中，即研究语言是如何通过生物有机体和环境之间的动态关系来实现的。Steffensen 和 Fill（2014）认为，语言的生态环境应涵盖以上四种类型，并提倡在此基础上建构一个"统一的生态语言科学"（unified ecological language science），即不区分"隐喻模式"和"非隐喻模式"的研究范式，将语言与自然看作统一融合的整体，并通过将价值观与意义融入生态结构来延展人类生态环境，从而也称为"延展性生态假设"（Extended Ecology Hypothesis）。

基于"隐喻模式"下的研究大多关注语言的生存发展状态，语言多样性及其与生物多样性的关系（范俊军 2007；张东辉 2009；文兰芳 2016），语言世界系统（Language World Systems），语言的生存、发展及消亡，濒危语言的保护（徐世璇 2002；徐世璇、廖乔婧 2003；范俊军 2006；范俊军等 2006），以及语言进化等热点问题。还有学者（祝克懿 2013；祝克懿、殷祯岑 2014；殷祯岑、祝克懿 2015）采用"隐喻模式"对官场话语进行生态性分析，从生态语言学的视角分析官场话语的内涵、特征及特殊运作机制，并从生物环境、社会环境及精神环境三个方面勾勒出官场话语的生态位体系，为人们较为准确地理解官场话语提供了有效策略，同时也为生态语言学与话语分析的结合提供了有益参考。

基于"非隐喻模式"的研究大多关注对语言中生态性的

分析。基于 Stibbe（2015）的研究将话语分为三类：有益性话语（beneficial discourse）、模糊性话语（ambivalent discourse）和破坏性话语（destructive discourse）。话语分析的目的是推广有益性话语，改善模糊性话语，抵制破坏性话语，从而构建有益的、和谐的生态系统。在此基础上，生态语言学界主要发展了两种生态话语分析模式，即生态批评话语分析与生态积极话语分析（或和谐话语分析）。Goatly（2007）将生态批评话语分析分为传统的批评话语分析与替代性批评话语分析（alternative critical discourse analysis），后者更聚焦生态与环境，关注言语社团中的所有人，比前者具有更积极的态度；他还进一步提出了侧重文学批评研究的"生态文体学"（ecostylistics），运用语言学理论分析文学话语中对自然或人与自然关系的表征，对其中的不合理表征进行批判，进而建构人与自然和谐平等的关系表征体系（Goatly 2018）。Richard Alexander（2018）还将批评话语分析与语料库语言学相结合，通过分析大型跨国商业机构关于环境问题的语篇，揭示他们话语中的非生态因素以及对环境产生的消极影响。Stibbe 对批评话语分析和积极话语分析的生态语言学模式都进行了探索。他（Stibbe 2014，2018a）认为，生态语言学家在用传统批评话语分析框架进行话语分析时对话语的语境进行了扩展：不仅考虑到人与人之间的关系，还关注到人与所有生物赖以生存的更大的生态系统之间的关系；不仅考虑到社会层面的不合理现象，还考虑到生态层面的不和谐之音。此时人与自然环境的关系就如同压迫者（oppressor）和受压迫者（oppressed）之间的关系。之后，Stibbe（2018b）提出，生态语言学界不应只对语言进行消极的批评（negative critique），还应关注话语中对生态持积极态度的研究，提倡盲目增长不如稳定发展、征服自然不如尊重自然等积极有益的生态理念，将 James Martin（2004）积极话语分析（Positive Discourse Analysis）的理论运用到生态语言学研究中，同时为传统话语和地方话语（如自然写作话语和诗歌）分析奠定了理论基础。从生态语言学视角来看，批评话语分析与积极话语分析的动机不同：前者旨在揭露隐藏在语言背后不公平、不可持续的破坏性现象，这种现象不仅存在于生态环境保护中，还存在于政治、经济、社会、人际交往等各种生态系统中，从而引导人们抵制破坏性话语；后者旨在倡导并鼓励对生态系统有益的话语和行为，从而引导人们推广有益性话语。在此之前还有许多学者进行过生态积极话语分析，如 Goatly（2000）对比诗歌和新闻报道两种文体关于自然的语言表征，Alexander（2003）对环保运动者的演讲进行积极话语分析，以判断其中生态特征的表征。

生态语言学视角下的话语分析经历了从对生态话语的分析（analysis of ecological discourse）到对任何话语的生态分析（ecological analysis of discourse）的发展过程（Alexander and Stibbe 2014）。何伟、魏榕（2018a）以及何伟（2018）指出，尽管批评话语分析、积极话语分析和多模态话语分析模式可以应用于话语的生态性分析，然而，生态话语分析应自成体系，应被界定为一种新的话语分析范式。与其他话语分析范式相比，生态话语分析有着宏大的目标与明确的价值观导向（何伟、魏榕 2018b），其研究对象既可以是与环境相关的话语（赵蕊华 2016；郑红莲、王馥芳 2018），也可以是对其他任何话语的生态取向的分析，如诗歌话语（黄国文

2018)、小说话语（尹静媛 2016）、广告性话语（戴桂玉、仇娟 2012；何伟、耿芳 2018）、政治话语（常军芳、丛迎旭 2018）以及媒体话语（杨阳 2018；袁颖 2018）等。换言之，生态话语分析的范围既包括"人与自然"类型的话题，使语言学家逐渐意识到自身所承担的社会责任，为环境保护提供了新的研究视角；还涵盖"人与社会"类型的话题，尤其为国际关系研究提供了新的研究范式（何伟、魏榕 2017a，2017b，2018a），并最终促进国际社会生态系统的良性发展。

在"非隐喻模式"内部，许多学者还尝试将自己研究的学科领域与生态语言学结合起来，从而进行理论框架的建构。例如，辛志英、黄国文（2013）以及黄国文（2017）将具有普适性的系统功能语言学与生态语言学联系起来，尝试在系统功能语言学视域下建构生态话语分析模式。此后，生态话语分析模式（何伟、张瑞杰 2017）、国际生态话语及物性分析模式（何伟、魏榕 2017a）、生态语言学视角下的人际系统和意义系统（张瑞杰、何伟 2018）等相继构建起来，为生态语言学的应用研究提供了坚实的理论基础。

值得注意的是，生态哲学观对人们的生态理念、生态话语与行为有着指导作用，是语言影响思维和行动的内在机制（deeper mechanism）。因此，无论是隐喻模式还是非隐喻模式的生态语言学研究，都需要在生态哲学观的指导下进行。针对各种生态系统，学界有不同的生态哲学观表述。比如针对国际社会生态系统的"和平观"（Mowat 1935），针对农业生态的"天人合一"生态观（张壬午等 1996），针对自然—社会生态的"可持续发展观"（Baker 2006），针对语言象征生态系统的"语言生态伦理观"（潘世松 2014），针对人与自然关系的"生活"（Living）哲学观（Stibbe 2015），针对中国语境下政治、经济、文化等活动系统的"和谐"生态观（黄国文 2017），针对人与自然关系的"和谐生态场所观"（何伟、张瑞杰 2017），等。这些观点的提出都是为了特定生态系统的良性发展，而生态系统的良性发展应有基本的共性。因此，本文认为，生态哲学观的表述应会逐渐统一。何伟、魏榕（2018b）针对国际生态系统提出的"多元和谐，交互共生"具有高度概括性，可以作为一个具有普遍指导意义的生态哲学观。

此外，从 Stibbe（2015）用"我们赖以生存的故事"（The Stories We Live By）来表示人类对世界的认知来看，生态语言学与认知语言学之间也存在可相互借鉴之处（王馥芳 2017）：认知语言学能够为生态语言学提供理论分析工具，从而夯实生态语言学的理论基础；而生态语言学也在一定程度上丰富了认知语言学的意义构建研究。

四、生态语言学研究的现存问题

通过以上对生态语言学缘起、发展历程的回顾以及对研究现状的综述可以发现，生态语言学已成为一门学科，不过，仍然存在以下三个问题。

（1）研究对象不尽明确。传统的两大主流研究范式都有各自明确的研究对象，"隐喻模式"的研究对象主要集中于社会热点问题，如语言的生存发展状态，语言多样性，语言世界系统，语言的生存、发展、消亡，濒危语言保护，语言进化，语言活力，语言规划，语言与现实世界的互变互动关系，语言多样性与生物多样性的关系，生态系统与文化系统等（黄国文 2016）。"非隐喻模式"主要通过研究语言或语言系统探寻其在生态环境问题中所发挥的作用，尤其是 21 世纪之后的研究突破了环境问题的局限，转而关注语言在人类与其他生物及环境之间生命可持续关系中的作用，因此涵盖了影响生命可持续关系的所有问题（何伟 2018）。然而，这两种研究范式之间存在割裂，即二者研究对象之间的关联性还没有得到学界的关注。另外，Steffensen 和 Fill（2014）提出的"延展性生态假说"（Extended Ecology Hypothesis）以及 Cowley（2017）提出的"根性生态语言学"（Radical Ecolinguistics）并没有明确的研究对象，难以展开具体研究。

（2）研究方法不系统。"隐喻模式"通常使用录音、录像等方式来记录和研究语言，然后对所获数据进行转写、建档、评估和分析。近年来科技的飞速发展为语言生态的研究提供了许多现代仪器，如超声仪、核磁共振仪、电子声门仪等。"非隐喻模式"通过描写和分析语言，主要对语言进行定性研究，也有一些学者通过定量分析对生态语言学研究进行综述。Steffensen 和 Fill（2014）将语言和自然当作统一的整体，将符号生态学、自然生态学、社会文化生态学以及认知生态学这四种研究路径进行融合，倡导语言生态研究整体化。Cowley（2017）主张通过语言研究提高人们的生物生态意识，将语言世界和非语言世界通过"语言使用"（languaging）连接起来。由此可见，目前生态语言学缺乏系统的研究方法，不同研究方法的内在逻辑关系以及如何利用这种关系将其进行融合，是生态语言学学科发展的重要任务。

（3）研究范围边界不清。由于"生态"概念的泛化，任何能够发生相互作用关系的要素都能构成一种"生态系统"，由此推动了许多学科的生态学化，例如生态翻译学、生态教育学（或教育生态学）、生态美学、生态诗学、生态心理学等。然而，不同学界对生态化学科术语的理解不同：生态翻译学被界定为一种具有跨学科性质的翻译理论形态，是一种生态途径的翻译研究或生态学视角的翻译研究，而并不是一个独立的学科（胡庚申 2008）；生态美学被看作生态学和美学相结合而成的新型学科，但由于其尚在形成过程中，还不具备一个学科的特点，只是一种发展中的美学理论形态；教育生态学被看作教育的边缘学科，运用生态学方法研究教育与人的发展规律。由此可见，学界对生态化学科属于一门独立学科、下位学科还是研究理论或方向看法不一。我们认为，生态语言学是一门独立的学科，虽然其具有超学科的属性（何伟、魏榕 2018c），但是研究范围应该是有界的，目前能够确定的研究范围涉及"从生态的视角探讨环境对语言的影响以及从生态的视角揭示语言对环境的影响"（何伟 2018：12）。"生态"作为一个概念可以被泛化，但"生态语言学"作为一门学科是不能被泛化的。

鉴于上述问题，本文认为，生态语言学目前仍然是一门年轻的学科，需要学界的共同关注和努力：在统一的生态哲学观的指导下，通过对研究范式、研究方法以及研究范围的进一步探讨，逐步确立适合生态语言学研究的统一框架、系统的研究方法以及清晰的研究范围，并致力于各种生态问题的解决，促进生态系统的良性发展。

* 本文原载于《浙江外国语学院学报》2019 年第 1 期，收入本文集时略有删改。

参考文献

Alexander, R. J. Resisting imposed metaphors of value: Vandana Shiva's role in supporting Third World agriculture. *The Online Journal Metaphorik*, 2003 (4): 6 – 29.

—— Investigating texts about environmental degradation using critical discourse analysis and corpus linguistic techniques. In A. Fill and H. Penz (eds.). *Routledge Handbook of Ecolinguistics*. New York and London: Routledge, 2018: 196 – 210.

Alexander, R. and A. Stibbe. From the analysis of ecological discourse to the ecological analysis of discourse. *Language Sciences*, 2014 (41): 104 – 110.

Baker, S. *Sustainable Development*. New York and London: Routledge, 2006.

Batardas-Boada, A. The ecology of language contact: Minority and majority languages. In A. Fill and H. Penz (eds.). *Routledge Handbook of Ecolinguistics*. London: Routledge, 2018: 26 – 39.

Chen, S. Language and ecology: A content analysis of ecolinguistics as an emerging research field. *Ampersand*, 2016 (3): 108 – 116.

Cowley, S. Ecolingusitics, the bio-ecology and the fragility of knowing. Presented at the 2nd International Symposium on Ecolinguistics and the 19th Symposium on Functional Linguistics and Discourse Analysis, Beijing, 2017.

Dension, N. A linguistic ecology for Europe? In A. Fill and

P. Mühlhäusler (eds.). *The Ecolinguistics Reader*: *Language, Ecology and Environment*. London: Continuum, 1982: 75 - 82.

Elliasson, S. The birth of language ecology: Interdisciplinary influences in Einar Haugen's "The ecology of language". *Language Sciences*, 2015 (50): 78 - 92.

Fill, A. *Wörter zu Pflugscharen*: *Versuch einer Ökologie der Sprache*. Wien/Köln: Böhlau, 1987.

—— Ecolinguistics: States of the art. *Ass Arbeiten Aus Anglistik Und Amerikanistik*, 1998, 23 (1): 3 - 16.

—— *Ökolinguistik. Eine Einführung*. Tübingen: Gunter Narr, 1993.

—— Language and ecology: Ecolinguistics perspectives for 2000 beyond. In AILA Organizing Committee (ed.). *Selected Papers from AILA 1999 Tokyo*. Tokyo: Waesda University Press, 2000.

—— Ecolinguistics: States of the art 1998. In A. Fill and P. Mühlhäusler (eds.). *The Ecolinguistics Reader*: *Language, Ecology and Environment*. London: Continuum, 2001: 43 - 53.

Fill, A. and P. Mühlhäusler. *The Ecolinguistics Reader*: *Language, Ecology and Environment*. London: Continuum, 2001.

Fill, A. and H. Penz. *The Routledge Handbook of Ecolinguistics*. New York and London: Routledge, 2018a.

—— Ecolinguistics in the 21st century: New orientations and future directions. In A. Fill and H. Penz (eds.). *Routledge Handbook of Ecolinguistics*. London: Routledge, 2018b: 437 - 443.

Finke, P. Politizität Zum Verhältnis von theoretischer Härte und praktischer Relevanz in der Sprachwissenschaft. In Peter Finke (ed.). *Sprache im politischen Kontext*. Tübingen: Niemeyer, 1983: 15 -75.

Finke, P. Sprache als missing link zwischen natürlichen und kulturellen Ökosystemen. In A. Fill (ed.). *Sprachökologie und Ökolinguistik*. Tübingen: Stauffenburg, 1996: 27 -48.

Gerbig, A. The representation of agency and control in texts on the environment. *AILA*, 1993 (93): 61 -73.

Goatly, A. Green grammar and grammatical metaphor, or language and the myth of power, metaphors we die by. *Journal of Pragmatics*, 1996, 25 (4): 537 -560.

— *Critical Reading and Writing: An Introductory Coursebook*. London: Routledge, 2000.

— *Washing the Brain: Metaphor and Hidden Ideology*. Amsterdam: Benjamins, 2007.

— Lexico-grammar and ecoliguistics. In A. Fill and H. Penz (eds.). *Routledge Handbook of Ecolinguistics*. London: Routledge, 2018: 227 -248.

Haarmann, H. *Multilingualismus* 2. Tübingen: Narr, 1980.

— *Language in Ethnicity: A View of Basic Ecological Relations*. Berlin: Mouton de Gruyter, 1986.

Haeckel, E. *Generelle Morphologie Der Organismen*. Berlin: Hansebooks, 1866.

Halliday, M. A. K. New ways of meaning. The challenge to applied linguistics. *Journal of Applied Linguistics*, 1990 (6): 7 - 36.

—— New ways of meaning: The challenge to applied linguistics. In A. Fill and P. Mühlhäusler (eds.). *The Ecolinguistics Reader: Language, Ecology, and Environment.* London: Continuum, 2001: 175 – 202.

Haugen, E. *The Ecology of Language.* Palo Alto: Stanford University Press, 1972.

Mackey, W. F. The ecology of language shift. In P. H. Nelde (ed.). *Sprachkontakt und Sprachkonflikt.* Wiesbaden: Franz Steiner, 1980: 35 – 41.

Martin, J. Positive discourse analysis: Solidary and change. *Revista Cnaria de Estudios Ingleses*, 2004 (49): 179 – 200.

Mowat, R. B. *Diplomacy and Peace.* London: Williams & Norgate, 1935.

Mühlhäusler, P. Preserving languages or language ecologies? A top-down approach to language survival. *Oceanic Linguistics*, 1992, 31 (2): 163 – 180.

——*Linguistic Ecology: Language Change and Linguistic Imperialism in the Pacific Region.* London and New York: Routledge, 1995.

Phillipson, R. and T. Skuttnabb-Kangas. Linguistic imperialism and the consequences for language ecology. In A. Fill and H. Penz (eds.). *Routledge Handbook of Ecolinguistics.* London: Routledge, 2018: 121 – 134.

Sapir, E. Language and environment. *American Anthropologist*, 1912 (14): 226 – 242.

Steffensen, S. V. Language, ecology and society: An introduction to dialectical linguistics. In J. C. Bang, J. Døør, S. V. Steffensen and J. Nash (eds.). *Language, Ecology and Society*: *A Dialectical Approach*. London: Bloomsbury Academic, 2007: 3 – 31.

Steffensen, S. V. and A. Fill. Ecolinguistics: the state of the art and future horizons. *Language Sciences*, 2014 (41): 6 – 25.

Stibbe, A. An ecolinguistic approach to critical discourse studies. *Critical Discourse Studies*, 2014, 11 (1): 117 – 128.

—— *Ecolinguistics: Language, Ecology, and the Stories We Live By*. London: Routledge, 2015.

—— Critical discourse analysis and ecology. In J. Flowerdew and J. E. Richardson (eds.). *The Routledge Handbook of Critical Discourse Studies*. London: Routledge, 2018a: 497 – 509.

—— Positive discourse analysis: Rethinking human ecological relationships. In A. Fill and H. Penz (eds.). *Routledge Handbook of Ecolinguistics*. London: Routledge, 2018b: 165 – 178.

Trampe, W. *Ökologische Linguistik, Grundlagen einer ökologischen Sprach-und Wissenschaftstheorie*. Wiesbaden: Westdeutscher Verlag, 1990.

—— Language and ecological crisis. In A. Fill and P. Mühlhäusler (eds.). *The Ecolinguistics Reader: Language, Ecology and Environment*. London: Continuum, 1991: 232 – 240.

Voegelin, C. F. and F. M. Voegelin. Languages of the world: Native America fascicle one. Contemporary language situations in the New World. *Anthropological Linguistics*, 1964, 6 (6): 2 – 45.

Voegelin, C. F., F. M. Voegelin and Noel W. Schutz Jr. The language situation in Arizona as part of the Southwest Culture Area. In D. H. Hymes and W. E. Bittle (eds.). *Studies in Southwestern Ethnolinguistics. Meaning and History in the Languages of the American Southwest.* The Hague & Paris：Mouton, 1967：403 – 451.

Weinrich, H. Economy and ecology in language. In A. Fill and P. Mühlhäusler (eds.). *The Ecolinguistics Reader：Language, Ecology and Environment.* London：Continuum, 1990：91 – 100.

常军芳, 丛迎旭. 功能语言学视角下的生态话语分析模式建构：以中国环保部长报告为例 [J]. 北京科技大学学报（社会科学版）, 2018 (4)：27 – 32.

戴桂玉, 仇娟. 语言、环境、社会：生态酒店英文简介之生态批评性话语分析 [J]. 外语与外语教学, 2012 (1)：48 – 52.

范俊军. 生态语言学研究述评 [J]. 外语教学与研究, 2005, 37 (2)：110 – 115.

范俊军. 语言活力与语言濒危的评估：联合国教科文组织文件《语言活力与语言濒危》述评 [J]. 现代外语, 2006 (2)：210 – 213.

范俊军. 语言多样性问题与大众传媒 [J]. 现代传播（中国传媒大学学报）, 2007 (2)：71 – 73.

范俊军, 宫齐, 胡鸿雁. 语言活力与语言濒危 [J]. 民族语文, 2006 (3)：51 – 61.

海然热. 语言人：论语言学对人文科学的贡献 [M]. 张祖建, 译. 北京：北京大学出版社, 2012.

韩军. 中国生态语言学研究综述［J］. 语言教学与研究,
    2013（4）: 107-112.
何伟. 关于生态语言学作为一门学科的几个重要问题［J］.
    中国外语, 2018（4）: 1, 11-17.
何伟, 耿芳. 英汉环境保护公益广告话语之生态性对比分析
    ［J］. 外语电化教学, 2018（4）: 57-63.
何伟, 魏榕. 国际生态话语之及物性分析模式构建［J］. 现
    代外语, 2017a（5）: 597-607.
何伟, 魏榕. 国际生态话语的内涵及研究路向［J］. 外语研
    究, 2017b（5）: 18-24.
何伟, 魏榕. 话语分析范式与生态话语分析的理论基础
    ［J］. 当代修辞学, 2018a（5）: 63-73.
何伟, 魏榕. 多元和谐, 交互共生: 国际生态话语分析之生
    态哲学观建构［J］. 外语学刊, 2018b（6）: 28-35.
何伟, 魏榕. 生态语言学: 发展历程与学科属性［J］. 国外
    社会科学, 2018c（4）: 113-123.
何伟, 张瑞杰. 生态话语分析模式构建［J］. 中国外语,
    2017, 14（5）: 56-64.
洪堡特. 普通语言学论纲［M］//洪堡特语言哲学文集. 姚
    小平, 译. 长沙: 湖南教育出版社, 2001a.
洪堡特. 论人类语言结构的差异［M］//洪堡特语言哲学文
    集. 姚小平, 译. 长沙: 湖南教育出版社, 2001b.
洪堡特. 论人类语言结构的差异及其对人类精神发展的影响
    ［M］. 姚小平, 译. 北京: 商务印书馆, 1999.
胡庚申. 生态翻译学解读［J］. 中国翻译, 2008（6）: 11-
    15, 92.

黄国文. 生态语言学的兴起与发展 [J]. 中国外语，2016 (1)：扉页，9-12.

黄国文. 从系统功能语言学到生态语言学 [J]. 外语教学，2017 (5)：1-7.

黄国文. 自然诗歌中的元功能和语法隐喻分析：以狄金森的一首自然诗歌为例 [J]. 外语教学，2018 (3)：1-5.

黄国文，赵蕊华. 生态话语分析的缘起、目标、原则与方法 [J]. 现代外语，2017 (5)：585-596.

李国正. 生态语言系统说略 [J]. 语文导报，1987 (10)：54-59.

李国正. 生态汉语学 [M]. 长春：吉林教育出版社，1991.

连佳欣，吴白音那. 我国生态语言学研究回顾与展望：基于 2007—2016 年期刊文献的分析 [J]. 内蒙古师范大学学报（教育科学版），2018，31 (4)：79-81，92.

潘世松. 语言生态伦理的性质及原则 [J]. 南昌大学学报（人文社会科学版），2014 (3)：151-156.

王馥芳. 生态语言学和认知语言学的相互借鉴 [J]. 中国外语，2017 (5)：47-55.

王晋军. 生态语言学：语言学研究的新视域 [J]. 天津外国语学院学报，2007，14 (1)：53-57.

文兰芳. 语言多样性的生态学意义 [J]. 外语学刊，2016 (1)：28-31.

辛志英，黄国文. 系统功能语言学与生态话语分析 [J]. 外语教学，2013 (3)：7-10.

徐世璇. 语言濒危原因探析：兼论语言转用的多种因素 [J]. 民族研究，2002 (4)：56-64，108.

徐世璇，廖乔婧．濒危语言问题研究综述［J］．当代语言学，2003（2）：133-148.

杨阳．系统功能视角下新闻报道的生态话语分析［J］．北京第二外国语学院学报，2018，40（1）：33-45.

尹静媛．从生态语言学的视角解读《动物之神》［J］．外国语文，2016（6）：69-74.

殷祯岑，祝克懿．官场话语生态的形成过程考察［J］．湖南师范大学社会科学学报，2015（5）：12-19.

袁颖．媒体报道的生态取向：BBC中国雾霾新闻标题的生态话语分析［J］．北京科技大学学报（社会科学版），2018（4）：33-41.

张东辉．生态语言学认识观与语言多样性［J］．前沿，2009（13）：103-104.

张壬午，张彤，计文瑛．中国传统农业中的生态观及其在技术上的应用［J］．生态学报，1996，16（1）：100-106.

张瑞杰，何伟．生态语言学视角下的人际意义系统［J］．外语与外语教学，2018（2）：99-108，150.

赵蕊华．系统功能视角下生态话语分析的多层面模式：以生态报告中银无须鳕身份构建为例［J］．中国外语，2016（5）：84-91.

郑红莲，王馥芳．环境话语研究进展与成果综述［J］．北京科技大学学报（社会科学版），2018（4）：9-16.

祝克懿．当下官场话语与生态文明建设［J］．湖南师范大学社会科学学报，2013（6）：17-20.

祝克懿，殷祯岑．生态语言学视野下的官场话语分析［J］．南昌大学学报（人文社会科学版），2014（4）：137-143.

作者简介

何伟，中山大学博士（2003），北京师范大学博士后（2007），北京外国语大学中国外语与教育研究中心教授、副主任，国际系统功能语言学协会理事，国际生态语言学研究会系统功能语言学学界代表，中国生态语言学研究会会长，中国英汉语比较研究会（一级学会）理事，中国英汉语比较研究会英汉语篇分析专业委员会副会长，中国英汉语比较研究会功能语言学专业委员会常务理事，*Journal of World Languages* 国际期刊创刊及联合主编，*Functional Linguistics* 国际期刊副主编。获得的奖项和荣誉包括：教育部新世纪优秀人才（2009）、北京市优秀教师（2009）、北京市精品课程负责人（2010）、宝钢优秀教师奖（2015）、中国冶金教育系统年度杰出人物奖（2015）、北京市高校青年教师教学基本功比赛优秀指导教师奖（2015）等20种。主持（含完成）多项国家级社科基金项目，近年来发表130多项研究成果。研究方向：系统功能语言学、生态语言学、话语分析、翻译研究等。

高然，北京外国语大学博士研究生，研究方向：系统功能语言学、英汉对比研究、生态语言学。

生态语言学与语言可持续发展

黄国文

一、引　言

语言生态（the ecology of language）和语言可持续发展（linguistic sustainability）是过去 20 多年来生态语言学（ecolinguistics）研究的主要范围，也发表了一些重要成果，其中之一是 Alwin Fill 和 Hermine Penz（2007）主编的题为《可持续语言：应用生态语言学研究》的论文集。关于语言生态和语言可持续发展这类论题，有两种研究视角。一个是隐喻的途径，把语言与语言环境的关系比为生物和生物环境的关系，把语言比作资源，就像把石油看作是一种自然资源一样。另一种研究视角是非隐喻的途径，把语言当作自然的一个组成部分，语言就是资源，语言和其他生物物种一样，在大自然中生活着。因此，自然资源有可持续发展的问题，语言同样有这样的问题。采取隐喻视角的学者很多，代表性人物是美籍挪威学者 Einar Haugen（Haugen 1972），采取另一种视角的学者也很多，代表性人物是系统功能语言学创始人 M. A. K. Halliday（1990/2007，2007）。

本文主要以 Halliday 的系统功能语言学理论作为指导，采用 Halliday 的研究路径和方法，从语篇分析入手，以英国《在线邮报》（Mail Online）的一个语篇为例，讨论语言是怎样影响生态的，以此来探讨语言可持续发展问题。

二、可持续发展

要讨论语言可持续发展，首先必须回顾可持续发展的概念，同时说明什么是我们所理解的语言可持续发展。由于本论文的理论指导是 Halliday 的系统功能语言学（Halliday 1978，1994；Halliday and Matthiessen 1999，2004，2014），所以下面也简单回顾 Halliday 关于系统生态语言学（systemic ecolinguistics）的一些观点。

（一）可持续发展的概念

语言可持续发展，是从普通的可持续发展（sustainable development）中引申出来的。可持续发展这个概念的提出，最早可以追溯到 1980 年由世界自然保护联盟（IUCN）、联合国环境规划署（UNEP）和野生动物基金会（WWF）共同发表的《世界自然保护大纲》。1987 年 2 月，在日本东京召开的第八次世界环境与发展委员会上通过了《我们共同的未来》的报告，后又经第 42 届联大辩论通过，于 1987 年 4 月正式出版发布。

有关可持续发展的定义有很多种，其中，《我们共同的未来》中的定义影响最广：能满足当代人的需要，又不对后代人满足其需要的能力构成危害的发展。它包括两个重要概念：需要的概念；尤其是世界各国人们的基本需要，应将此放在特别优先的地位来考虑；限制的概念，技术状况和社会组织对环境满足眼前和将来需要的能力施加的限制。（见百度百科）

由于可持续发展涉及的领域（包括自然、环境、社会、政治、经济、科技、历史、地理等）很广，所以，不同的研究者就根据自己的研究领域进行再定义，有侧重于自然方面的定义、侧重于科技方面的定义，也有侧重于社会方面的定义、侧重于经济方面的定义、侧重于文化方面的定义等。因此也就有了自然环境的可持续发展、科技可持续发展、社会可持续发展、经济可持续发展、文化可持续发展等。这些不同的表述都是相互联系、相互作用和相互制约的。简单地说，可持续发展就是人与自然和谐共生，其中人类的健康生存最为重要，是发展伦理的终极尺度。具体说来，可持续发展包括以下三个重要假定：①以人为本，全人类利益高于一切；②健康发展，幸福生活高于一切；③为未来着想，在满足目前需要的同时，不能侵犯或剥夺后代人生存和发展的权力。

（二）语言可持续发展

按照可持续发展的基本定义，我们看看可以怎样理解语言可持续发展。从语言可持续发展的角度看，语言是我们生活中不可或缺的部分，所以应该做到语言能满足当代人的需要而又不对后代人满足其需要的能力构成危害；我们自己和后代人都需要语言，我们时时刻刻都要把语言放在特别优先的地位来考虑；同时，我们要认识到技术状况和社会活动对环境满足眼前和将来需要的语言能力的限制。

举个例子说，对于英语是母语的人来说，他们的优势越来越明显。全球化强化了英语的地位和作用，因此英语变成了非常重要的软实力，变成了可以换取经济价值的商品。而对于母语不是英语的人来说，就要花时间、精力、金钱来学习英语，以便能够在"地球村"中工作和生活。因此，从语言可持续发展看，我们应该保护不被认定为大语种的语言（尤其是使用者少或较少的语言），这样才能保证这些语言使用者的需要和他们后代人的需要。从生态的角度看，这是保护物种的多样性；语言的消亡就是多样性的丢失。科学技术的发展对"小语种"的生存和发展也带来了限制和威胁。例如现在智能化的服务所使用的语言只是少数的几个大语种，那么对于本族语是小语种的人，要么就是自我封闭、与世界隔绝，放弃参与智能化和参与地球村的活动，要么就得越来越少或不用自己的母语，最终放弃自己的母语。这样，他们的母语就会慢慢消亡，就像其他物种的消亡一样。这就是物种多样性的流失。

由于语言是文化的载体，语言的消亡就意味着文化的消亡。而对于那些民族来说，自己的语言和文化的消亡，就意味着自己没有了根；不知道从哪里来，就不知道要到哪里去。因此，从语言可持续发展的角度看，我们要保护好各种语言，就像保护自然界中的各种物种一样。研究濒危语言（包括方言）的状况，调查小语种（包括方言）的使用情况，提醒大家一起爱护语言，采取保护语言的措施，把现实的情况放在更大的自然、环境、社会、政治、经济、科技、历史、地理环境中考虑，就是生态语言学要研究的问题之一。

我们对自然、对周围环境、对自己的一言一行的态度，是来自我们对世界的认知和对自己身份的认同和构建。自然环境造就了每一个人和每一个人的语言，这是因为"一方水土养一方人"和"一方水土养一方说某种语言的人"。相反，人的语言影响了自然环境，人的很多破坏生态的行为是语言使用带来的。举个例子，如果我们每天都说"吃鱼翅老的可以长寿，男的可以壮阳，女的可以美容，小的可以聪明成长"，并把吃鱼翅宣传成一种身份的象征（只有有钱人、上层人才能吃到鱼翅），那这种观念就会成为我们行动的指南：有钱人就会天天吃鱼翅（因为老的要长寿，男的要壮阳，女的要美容，小的要聪明成长），越来越多的餐馆就会更多地供应鱼翅，那结果就是越来越多的人为了"长寿、壮阳、美容、聪明成长"而导致更多的渔民采用"割鳍弃鲨"的方法来收集更多的鱼翅卖给餐馆。这种行为的可悲后果是，被割去鱼鳍的鲨鱼会沉入海底，可能是窒息死亡，可能是活活饿死，也可能是因为伤口感染死亡；从鲨鱼被割下鱼鳍的那一刻开始，它将在痛苦中慢慢死去。我们在餐馆里吃的一碗鱼翅，代价是一条鲨鱼的生命；我们的生态环境也就这样被破坏了。我们（黄国文、肖家燕 2017）曾提到，据报道（http://dy.163.com/v2/article/detail/CFETAQNN05248NJC.html, retrieved on August 18, 2018），每年大约有 7000 万条鲨鱼因为人们想取其鱼翅食用而被割鳍，最后死亡，杀害鲨鱼的速度比鲨鱼繁殖的速度快了 30 倍。因此，2006 年，位于美国的"野生救援"（Wild Aid）机构邀请篮球明星姚明为保护鲨鱼做代言人，他在这个公益广告中的话语是："没有买卖，就没有杀害。"据美国《华盛顿邮报》（"In China, victory for wildlife conservation as citizens persuaded to give up shark fin soup" by Simon Denyer, *The Washington Post*, October 20, 2013) 报道，现在"割鳍弃鲨"的情况已经有了改善，鲨鱼因为要被取鱼鳍而被杀害的数量仅 2011—2013 年就降低了 50%～70%，鱼翅也渐渐退出了宴席的餐桌。姚明的一句"没有买卖，就没有杀害"，所产生的效果是巨大的。这就是语言是怎样影响生态的具体例子。

三、Halliday 关于生态语言学的观点

系统功能语言学创始人 Halliday 多次谈到语言与生物和生态的关系问题，他的《意义表达的新方式：对应用语言学的挑战》(Halliday 1990/2007) 一文被普遍认为是一篇影响深远的力作，原因是"它为在系统功能语言学视野下探索如何研究生态语境、语言和语言的影响开了先河"（辛志英、黄国文 2013：8）。他的研究路径被称为"韩礼德模式"（the Halliday approach）（Fill 2001）。

Halliday 采取了与 Haugen (1972) 完全不同的研究范围和研究重点。Haugen 所说的是"语言生态"（the ecology of language），他采用隐喻的视角，把语言和言语社团的关系比喻为生物和自然环境的关系，他所说的"环境"是指"使用某一语言作为语码的社会"，他的研究重点是"任何特定的语言与其环境的相互作用"。相反，Halliday 强调语言在社会环境和文化环境中的重要功能，突出语言在各种生态问题中的重要作用，突出语言学家的社会责任和担当；他提醒语言学家要在环境保护方面做出贡献；他（Halliday 1990/2007：172）还从生态语言学的角度对等级主义（classism）、增长主义（growthism）等问题进行讨论。

在《作为进化主题的应用语言学》(Halliday 2007) 一文中，Halliday 区分了"机构生态语言学"(institutional ecolinguistics) 和"系统生态语言学"。机构生态语言学指的是语言和这种语言的使用者（以及不再使用这种语言的人）之间的关系。例如，对于那些自己的母语不是社会"通用语"或"普通话"的人来说，由于工业化和经济的快速发展，他们的语言（母语）面临着越来越少被使用，最终因没有人使用而消亡的威胁；他们少用或不用母语，是经济等因素造成的。系统生态语言学指的是 Halliday（2007）所说的"我们的意指方式如何左右我们对环境的影响"(How do our ways of meaning affect the impact we have on the environment?)，即语言对人类的行为（包括人类对生态的影响的行为）和生态环境的影响。语言学家要关心生态环境问题，是因为语言对我们生活中的所作所为起着决定性的作用，语言影响着我们赖以生存的生态系统。

系统生态语言学的提出，是基于 Halliday 的语言观和他的马克思主义语言研究倾向（常晨光、廖海青 2010；何远秀 2016）。Halliday（1990/2007：145）告诉我们：语言并不是被动地反映现实，语言主动创建现实；现实并非事先存在的，并非等着被赋予意义；现实必须被主动构建；语言在构建过程中演化且作为构建的中介。语言并不是建立在某个基础之上的上层建筑，它是意识与物质相互影响的结果，是我们作为物质存在与作为意识存在的矛盾体的结果，作为与经验对立的领域。例如，"增长主义"能成为指导我们行为的准则，就是因为在我们的生活中，人们总是认为增长就是好的，增加要比减少好（Halliday 1990/2007：162）。因此，对于一个国家的政府来说,生产总值必须增长,生产力必须增长;对于每个人来说,收入必须增长,好吃的东西要越来越多,道路要越来越宽,车要越跑越快。

我们的意识形态是在特定的环境中慢慢形成的。语言反映了意识形态,而意识形态又影响了人们的一言一行、所思所想,这样就形成了我们赖以生存的"故事"(Stibbe 2015);我们会信奉这些故事,会践行这些故事。

四、个案分析

根据 Halliday(2007)系统生态语言学的观点,语言影响着我们的行为,语言影响着生态。我们的意指方式左右着我们对环境的影响,左右着我们的所思所想和所作所为。因此,每一个语篇都是根据语境(文化语境、情景语境、上下文语境)在特定的社会环境中表达意义的。特定的话语传递特定的意义,话语背后的意识形态也随之传递出来。当我们把"吃鱼翅老的可以长寿、男的可以壮阳、女的可以美容、小的可以聪明成长"的故事传播出去并被广泛接受后,就会导致消费者、经营者、捕捉者把故事所隐含的理念付诸行动,这样大量的鲨鱼就会在被割去鱼鳍后在痛苦中慢慢死去,生态就会受到破坏。

下面我们采用系统功能语言学(Halliday 1978,1994;Halliday and Matthiessen 1999,2004,2014)的语篇分析方法,考察 2017 年 5 月 8 日英国的《在线邮报》刊登的一篇文章。

(一)关于《在线邮报》

《在线邮报》是英国《每日邮报》(*Daily Mail*)旗下的

一个网站,它属于小报(tabloid),据说它是世界上访问量最大的报纸网站,在国际上也很有影响力,它拥有独立的英国、美国、印度和澳大利亚分站。

《在线邮报》报道的内容包括国际新闻、英国本地体育、个人理财、旅游、科学和生活新闻等,其文章往往以图片为主,而不是长篇的新闻;该网站主要组成部分是娱乐新闻,主要报道名人新闻和八卦故事。

《在线邮报》允许用户创建账户并参与对所刊登文章的评论,并且还允许任何人以匿名方式参与讨论。

(二)作为个案分析的语篇

我们要分析的语篇(http://www.dailymail.co.uk/femail/article-4483708/Student-25-given-2-500-month-sugar-daddy-60.html)讲的是英国一个充当"甜妹"的大学生的经历,原文配有很多图片。限于研究内容的范围和篇幅,我们只分析其语言部分。下面是该语篇(By Stephanie Linning for MailOnline. PUBLISHED:09:41 BST, 8 May 2017 | UPDATED:15:44 BST, 14 May 2017)的文字部分。

1. 标题

这篇文章的标题特别长,有几个句子:

Glamorous student, 25, says sugar daddy, 60, who she doesn't have sex with showers her with gifts and gives her £2,500 every month (and she insists her boyfriend, 36, doesn't mind)

· Ilham Chocolat, 25, met her sugar daddy, a 60-year-old doctor, five years ago

·He has given her a £2,500-a-month allowance and taken her to high end hotels

·The doctor also bought her a bar so she could fulfil her dream of being a landlady

·Miss Chocolat insists her boyfriend, 36, is happy with her being a sugar baby

2. 正文

全文一共有 19 个自然段。为了方便后面的讨论，每个自然段都编了号。文章中主要提到三个人：① 名叫 Ilham Chocolat 的"甜妹"，未婚，大学生，25 岁，原先是从非洲多哥移居到意大利，后从意大利的博洛尼亚到英国；②"甜爹"，离异，医生，60 岁；③"甜妹"的男朋友，36 岁。

[1] A glamorous 25-year-old student has revealed how she is showered with money and gifts by a sugar daddy 35 years her senior.

[2] Ilham Chocolat, from Bologna, Italy, says the divorced

doctor buys her "anything she wants or needs" and gives her a monthly allowance of £2,500 so she can treat herself to designer handbags and lavish shopping sprees.

[3] In return Miss Chocolat goes on date with the doctor, from Rome, twice a month but insists they have never had sex. Instead she describes their relationship as a "platonic love".

[4] "He enjoys his time with me," Ilham said. "He said I made him feel like a small boy and full of energy."

[5] Miss Chocolat also insists her 36-year-old boyfriend is perfectly happy with the unusual arrangement.

[6] Regarded as one of the best sugar babies in the business, Ilham will be sharing her secrets to success and advice on snaring a sugar daddy at a special summit in London this month.

[7] Rather unusually, Ilham met her sugar daddy through a friend rather than a specialist dating website.

[8] She said: "I started a relationship with a man without understanding what the name [given to] the relationship was. I was 20 and he was 55."

[9] She continued: "I find men of my age very immature. So, when I met the older man, the doctor, he offered me a figure that I needed in that moment of my life."

[10] "He didn't want anything physical from me. He was very, very smart."

[11] Together they have agreed the relationship will never become more serious, or sexual, largely because of the age difference.

[12] Instead the doctor treats Ilham to high end clothes, stays in world class hotels, and has even bought her a diamond ring.

[13] "He gives me an allowance of 3,000 euros (£ 2,500) a month," she said. "He takes me shopping and anything I want he gets me. Whatever I want or need, I can have."

[14] "If I need 5,000 or 6,000 euros I just ask him."

[15] The most extravagant gift came just a year after they met when the doctor bought her a bar, allowing her to fulfil her childhood dream of being a landlady.

[16] Miss Chocolat has even introduced the doctor to her family, and says they approve of the relationship.

[17] The doctor has also helped Ilham, originally from Togo, launch a charity endeavour which provides washing machines to communities in Africa.

[18] She added: "I want to help Africa and provide washing machines so the people can flourish. I am a philanthropist."

[19] Ilham will share her secrets at Seeking Arrangement's Sugar Baby Summit in London this month.

Taste of the high life: Miss Chocolat and her sugar daddy sip on cocktails in a bar

(三) 分析

这篇文章共由 19 个自然段构成，分为作者（Stephanie Linning）的描述（叙述）和主人公 Ilham Chocolat 的话语（引语）两部分。叙述占了 7 个自然段，转述的话语占 10 个自然段（其中 3 个是间接引语，7 个是直接引语），另外有 2 个自然段由叙述＋引语构成。

第［1］个自然段是间接引语，起点题的作用：一个 25 岁的"甜妹"告诉大家，一个 60 岁的"甜爹"给她好多钱和礼物。

第［2］个自然段是间接引语，对［1］进行细化：来自意大利博洛尼亚的 Ilham Chocolat 说，离异的医生给她买任何她想要的东西，而且还每个月给她 2500 英镑的零用钱，所以她可以买名牌手提包并随便买东西。

第［3］个自然段是叙述＋间接引语：Chocolat 小姐与来自意大利罗马的医生每个月有两次约会，但她特别说，他们之间从来没有性行为。按照她的描述，他们之间是"柏拉图式的恋爱"。

第［4］个自然段是直接引语：Ilham 说，他与我在一起很享受，他说我使他感觉自己像个小男孩那样精力充沛。

第［5］个自然段是间接引语：Chocolat 小姐坚持认为，她 36 岁的男朋友对这个不寻常的安排非常满意。

第［6］个自然段是叙述：Ilham 被认为是圈中最优秀的"甜妹"之一，她本月会在伦敦的一个聚会上和大家分享她怎样成功勾住"甜爹"。

第［7］个自然段是叙述：很奇怪的是，Ilham 是通过一个朋友，而不是通过约会网站，认识这个"甜爹"的。

第［8］个自然段是直接引语：她说，我与这个男人开始这种关系时，还不知道这种关系叫什么。那时我 20 岁，他 55 岁。

第［9］个自然段是直接引语：她继续说，我发觉与我年龄相当的男人很不成熟。这时，我遇到这个年龄大点的医生，他给了我一笔钱，而这时候的我正需要这么一笔钱。（这句话中的 figure 既有"数目"的意思，也有"形象"的意思，一语双关。所以这句话也可以理解为：他的形象正是这个时候的我所需要的，即他扮演了我在生命中的那一刻所需要的角色。）

第［10］个自然段是直接引语：他不想从我这里得到身体上的东西，他是一个非常聪明的人。

第［11］个自然段是叙述：他们两人约定，这种关系永远不要变得认真，或者与性有关，主要是因为年龄的差异。

第［12］个自然段是叙述：医生给她买高档的衣物，入住世界级宾馆，还给她买了钻戒。

第［13］个自然段是直接引语：她说，他每个月给我 3000 欧元（2500 英镑）的零用钱，还带我去购物，我要什么他就买给我什么。我需要什么，就能得到。

第［14］个自然段是直接引语：如果我需要 5000 或 6000 欧元，我就问他要。

第［15］个自然段是叙述：他们认识一年后，医生给她了一件最奢侈的礼物，就是给她买了一间酒吧，圆她从小就想做店主的梦想。

第［16］个自然段是叙述＋直接引语：Chocolat 小姐甚至把医生介绍给她的家人认识，并说家里赞成他们这种关系。

第［17］个自然段是叙述：Ilham原先来自非洲多哥，医生还帮助她举办慈善活动，为非洲的人提供洗衣机。

第［18］个自然段是直接引语：她补充说，我要帮助非洲，给那里的人提供洗衣机，这样他们的生活会过得更好。我是个慈善家。

第［19］个自然段是叙述，内容与第［6］个自然段的叙述相近：Ilham本月会在伦敦的"寻找'甜妹'峰会"上与大家分享她成功的经验。

五、讨　论

下面的讨论主要涉及四个方面的内容：①语篇所要传递的信息，这是对语篇进行分析后的讨论；②破坏性语篇与有益性语篇，这是评价语篇的一种方法，通过语篇传递的信息对其进行价值判断；③语言构建现实，即讨论在过去、现在和未来，语言是怎样影响我们对现实的认知的；④话语与语言可持续发展，探索语言使用与语言可持续发展之间的关系。

（一）语篇所要传递的信息

这个语篇与其说是一篇报道，倒不如说是为"Seeking Arrangement"做的一个广告。整个语篇都在说这个叫Ilham Chocolat的"甜妹"如何成功、如何美好。

1. 核心信息：做"甜妹"是美好的

该语篇要传递的核心信息是：做"甜妹"会获得很多东西（钱和物），可以利己利人，是一种非常美好的事情。下面我们将其归纳成六点。

（1）"甜爹"给她好多钱和礼物，她想要的任何东西"甜爹"都会给她买，可以买名牌手包并随便买东西，除了高档的衣物，还入住高档宾馆，还买了钻戒。他每个月给她3000 欧元（2500 英镑）的零用钱，如果需要更多钱"甜爹"也会给。"甜爹"给她买了一个酒吧，圆她做店主的梦。这些表述见第 [1]、[2]、[10]、[12]、[13]、[14] 和 [15] 个自然段。用了这么多篇幅来强调做"甜妹"所能得到的美好生活，很有诱惑力。

（2）"甜爹"给了她这么多物质的东西和钱，但对她没有任何身体上的要求，他们之间是柏拉图式的恋爱，关系简单，相处很轻松。这些表述见第 [3] 和 [11] 个自然段。

（3）"甜妹"的男朋友不仅不介意她与"甜爹"的这种关系，还非常满意；她家里人也赞同他们这种关系。这些表述见第 [5] 和 [16] 个自然段。

（4）年轻男人不成熟，年龄大的男人又有钱，又没有过分的要求；做"甜妹"不需要有经验，做"甜妹"能使男人感觉自己像个小男孩那样精力充沛；这是利人利己的事。这些表述见第 [4]、[8] 和 [9] 个自然段。

（5）做"甜妹"不仅可以买高档衣物，入住高档酒店，有丰厚的零用钱，还可以帮助别人，成为慈善家。这些表述见第 [17] 和 [18] 个自然段。

（6）这个"甜妹"无疑是有本事的"成功人士"，她本月会在伦敦的集会与大家分享她成功的经验。这些表述见第 [6]、[7] 和 [19] 个自然段。

从上面这六点可以看出，语篇所传递的信息是：做"甜妹"是一件很美好的事情，自己有钱花，有高档的礼物收，有机会住世界级酒店，又不需要身体的付出，男朋友和家人也都高兴，还可以帮助别人（例如，使老男人感觉自己像男孩那样精力旺盛，还有机会做善事），因此，年轻的女孩可以向她学习，听她分享经历。

2. 语言体现意义

以上是从语篇所表达的意义角度分析的，现在我们看看语言形式的使用是怎样体现意义的。先从直接引语和间接引语的使用看。全文19个自然段中，10个使用引语（直接引语：第［4］、［8］、［9］、［10］、［13］、［14］和［18］个自然段；间接引语：第［1］、［2］和［5］个自然段），另外还有2个自然段中也含有引语（第［3］和［16］个自然段中的间接引语），这是通过做"甜妹"的主人公的现身说法，增强可信度，这样才容易使年轻的女孩相信语篇所传递的内容的真实性。

虽然我们没有分析与该语篇所配合的主人公的照片，但在这里也必须指出，所有的照片属于三个方面的内容：①主人公"甜妹"自己不同表情的照片；②"甜妹"与"甜爹"在一起的照片；③各种名牌的手包和高档衣物。从所提供的14张有"甜妹"头像的照片看，不论采用哪种标准，该主人公一点都称不上是"美人儿"。但是，恰恰是这种看起来非常普通的人的照片，才能够诱惑更多的人加入这个行业。有兴趣加入这个行业的女孩读到这样的文字，看到这个普通人的照片，第一个反应应该就是："她都可以，我更可以"。如果是这样，那广告的效果就达到了。

这个语篇的语言选择与意义的表达配合得非常合适。除了上面说的采用直接引语和间接引语来达到主人公现身说法，把一切栩栩如生地描述出来，句子、短语、词组和词的选择也把作者想要表达的意义淋漓尽致地传递出来。几乎每一个句子都有强化语篇内容的表达。

第［1］个自然段：把"甜妹"描述成一个"迷人的"（glamorous）的学生；用动词"洒下"（shower）表示钱和礼物像水那样"哗啦啦"地到来。

第［2］个自然段：明确用"离婚的"（divorced）来说明"甜爹"的身份，言下之意就是"甜爹"和"甜妹"都是单身的、自由的人，不是婚外情，没有违反伦理道德；用"设计师手袋"（designer handbags）和"奢侈购物"（lavish shopping sprees）来说明，一旦做了"甜妹"，一般女孩的虚荣心就可以得到满足。

第［3］个自然段：用"have never had sex"，而不用"have not had sex"，这样更加强调他们之间从来没有身体上的关系，而且把这种关系描述为"男女间没有性爱的纯洁友谊"（a platonic love）。

第［4］个自然段：有了这种"甜爹""甜妹"的关系，60岁的男人感觉自己像个小男孩（feel like a small boy）那样精力旺盛（full of energy）。

第［5］个自然段：虽然"甜妹"跟一个大她35岁的老男人在一起玩耍，但她的男友感到"非常幸福"（perfectly happy）。

第［6］个自然段："甜妹"不自私，要让更多的人也像她一样幸福，所以她要和大家分享"成功的奥秘"（her secrets to success），也教大家怎样做（advice）才能"勾住'甜爹'"（snaring a sugar daddy）。

第［7］个自然段：成为"甜妹"并不难，不一定要找专门的约会网站（a specialist dating website），通过朋友

(through a friend) 就可以搞定。

第[8]个自然段：没有经验的生手不用担心，不知道"甜爹"和"甜妹"是做什么的也没有关系（without understanding what the name [given to] the relationship was）。言下之意是这种事情没有那么复杂。

第[9]个自然段：年轻人跟年轻人不好玩，跟"我"一样大的男孩都不成熟（men of my age very immature）。言下之意是老男人成熟，年轻女孩应该找比她们大几十岁的老男人才好玩。

第[10]个自然段："甜爹"不用"我"的身体做什么（He didn't want anything physical from me）。言下之意是"甜爹"不会要"我"用身体来换取什么东西。

第[11]个自然段："甜爹"和"甜妹"的关系永远不会太认真（the relationship will never become more serious），也不会有性（sexual）关系；这是他们两人约定的（together they have agreed）；这里用的"together"表明他们之间是有商有量的，不是一方的意见强加给对方。

第[12]个自然段："甜爹"带"甜妹"买高档的衣物（high end clothes），入住世界级宾馆（world class hotels），"甜爹"还给她买了钻戒（a diamond ring）。

第[13]个自然段："我"每月的零用钱就高达3000欧元（3,000 euros），他还带"我"去购物（he takes me shopping），"我"要什么他给什么（anything I want he gets me）。

第[14]个自然段：除了他给"我"的，"我"还可以要更多。如果"我"需要5000或6000欧元，"我"就问他要（If I need 5,000 or 6,000 euros I just ask him）。

第［15］个自然段："甜爹"给"甜妹"最奢侈的礼物是一间酒吧，圆了她从小就有的想做的店主的梦想（to fulfil her childhood dream of being a landlady）。特别值得指出的是，原文用了"the most extravagant gift came"，而不是"The sugar daddy gave her the most extravagant gift"，说的是，这么奢侈的礼物一年后就自然地来了，好像一切都是不知不觉的，幸福就降临了。

第［16］个自然段：除了男朋友同意"甜妹"与"甜爹"的交往外，她的家人也是赞成（approve）这种关系的。

第［17］个自然段："甜爹"不仅带"甜妹"去购买高档衣服并入住世界级酒店，还帮她举办慈善活动（helped Ilham… launch a charity endeavour），为"甜妹"非洲家乡的人做善事（provides washing machines to communities in Africa）。

第［18］个自然段：有了"甜爹"的帮助，"甜妹"信心满满，不仅自己生活过得好，还想帮助其他人过好生活（I want to help Africa and provide washing machines so the people can flourish），感觉自己是个慈善家（I am a philanthropist）。

第［19］个自然段：这是语篇所要传递的重要信息："甜妹"本月会在伦敦的"寻找'甜妹'峰会"（Seeking Arrangement's Sugar Baby Summit in London this month）上与大家分享她成功的经验（share her secrets）。言下之意是各位不要错过听她介绍经验的机会。

3. 网友的评论

如前所述，《在线邮报》允许用户参与对文章做评论和讨论，自由表达观点，还允许任何人以匿名方式讨论。但是，网站有两点说明：①评论中所表达的观点不一定反映《在线邮报》的意见（这样说是为了避免法律纠纷）；②这些评论是经过筛选的（其实这说明网站是有选择刊登权的）。这篇文章出版后，到 2018 年 8 月 18 日止，一共有 58 人对其进行评论，绝大多数都是比较负面的评论。主要是五个方面的内容。

（1）对"甜妹"的负面评论：她有那么多钱，为什么没有合适的鞋？（She has all that money, yet can't find shoes that fit properly?）【这是读者从图片看到她的穿着，对她所穿的鞋的评论。】/她根本不迷人！！！（She's not even attractive!!!）【也是读者看照片后的评论。】/在我看来，那个迈克高仕手包是假货！（That's a fake Micheal Kors handbag if ever I saw one!）【这也是看照片后的评论。】/像妓女在告诉别人她们"只是接待生"（Just like the brothel workers tell people they are "just the receptionist".）【这是对报道内容的评论。】/看看她脸书首页的裸体照——我不相信她的故事（Look at her nude Facebook cover picture—I'm not convinced by her story.）【从故事内容联系到她给公众的其他举止，得出的结论是此人不是"良家妇女"。】

（2）不相信故事所讲的：没有性啊？那她干嘛啊？吸他的脚趾？（No sex yeah lol, what does she do? Suck his toes?）【不相信他们之间没有身体的接触。】/先不要说故事中不对的地方，她要买洗衣机给非洲的人？？？洗衣机？？？（Everything else that is wrong with this story aside, she wants to buy washing machines to help Africa???? Washing machines????

【非洲给人的印象是缺水的,在非洲用洗衣机会消耗很多水,所以不可思议。】/ 没有人会那样花钱而不期待回报。(No man would part with money like that without expecting something in return.)【不相信他们之间没有身体的接触。】/ 当然他们的关系是纯洁的和清白的,我相信他很高兴为她的风趣、魅力、超好的幽默感、智商、好学和好性格那样花钱,我也相信猪到处飞(这是不可能的)。请原谅我的讥讽。(I'm certain their relationship is pure and innocent. I'm sure he is more than willing to part with his money for her wit, charm, excellent sense of humour, intelligence, depth of learning and general good character. I'm also sure that pigs fly. Pardon the sarcasm.)【用讽刺的口气和话语,表示作者和"甜妹"都在说谎。】

(3)对"甜妹"男朋友的负面评论:她的男朋友需要爷们儿些。很奇怪他对那种关系是高兴的。(Her boyfriend needs to man up. Very strange that he's happy with the arrangement.)【读者觉得"甜妹"的男朋友没有男子气,竟然会同意这种既有男朋友又有"甜爹"的关系。】/ 他男朋友比"甜爹"还傻。(The boyfriend is a bigger fool than the sugar daddy.)【读者直接说"甜妹"的男朋友是个大傻瓜。】

(4)指出这个语篇是软广告:这只是为低劣的网站做广告。(Just an advert for a very sleazy website.)【读者认为这是广告,所推销的网站档次不高。】

(5)相信语篇中的故事:I'm not pretty or hot. Some months ago I dated to an old man. We used to have lunch, go for a walk, some travelling... exactly like a boyfriend, but without sex and love. We were friends. We talked about our lives. We had fun together. He was quite intelligent, I liked his conversation. He gave me some presents (little things, not luxury stuff). I didn't want to accept more, but everything was ok between us! Before this happened to me, I never thought I could have that kind of relationship. So, maybe this is a similar case. Also, in my case, it was just for some months. I don't know if it could be longer. Sometimes things have a "perfect duration" and you shouldn't hope it lasts forever.【这是最长的评论（跟帖），是完全相信和赞成故事所说的。发帖人用自己的亲身经历告诉别人，该故事讲的是可信的，不过，她的经历没有上面语篇中所说的那么美好。例如，她的"甜爹"所给的礼物是"小东西"（little things），"不是奢侈品"（not luxury stuff）；Ilham Chocolat 和她的"甜爹"的关系已经有五年之久，但这个跟帖"甜妹"只有几个月（for some months），而且不一定能这样发展下去（I don't know if it could be longer）。无论如何，这只是一个与众不同的观点，说明读者对同一个语篇有不同的反应。】

4. 语言的评价手段

整个语篇中出现了很多表达人际评价意义的词语，如第[1]个自然段中的"glamorous"（表示这个女孩是迷人的）、"showered"（表达钱和礼物像水那样"哗啦啦"地落下来）等。其他段落也有表示评价意义的词语，限于篇幅，这里就不讨论了。

我们要特别指出的是，正文中作者两次用了"异常的（地）"（unusual, unusually），分别出现在第[5]个自然段（Miss Chocolat also insists her 36-year-old boyfriend is perfectly happy with the unusual arrangement）和第［7］个自然段（Rather unusually, Ilham met her sugar daddy through a friend rather than a specialist dating website）中。

这两个词（一个是形容词，另一个是副词）都是用于表示人际意义的，即表达说话人（作者）个人对所陈述的内容的态度、观点、看法等。作者认为，一个去做"甜妹"的人可以有男朋友，男朋友还非常高兴，这种安排，对作者来说是有些异常的。但是，作者的言下之意是，这样异常的安排，"甜妹"的男朋友也非常高兴；因此，作者想传达的信息应该是：做"甜妹"可以是两全其美的事情（相当于"既当什么又立什么"），这是多么令人羡慕的事啊。

另一个表示评价意义的"异常地"是对"甜妹"是通过朋友介绍（而不是通过特别的网站）而进入这一行的陈述表明自己的态度。但是，这类朋友也不是到处都有且随便就可以认识的。因此，我们认为，作者的言下之意是：你要做"甜妹"，那就来参加"本月在伦敦的特别集会"（第［6］个自然段：a special summit in London this month），就是"本月在伦敦举行的寻找'甜妹'峰会"（第［19］个自然段：Seeking Arrangement's Sugar Baby Summit in London this month）。由此可见，这篇报道不是简单的故事，而应该是一个软广告，为"Seeking Arrangement"做广告，邀请更多的人来做"甜妹"。

（二）破坏性语篇与有益性语篇

生态语言学家 Stibbe（2015）区分了三类话语：①有益性话语（beneficial discourse）；②破坏性话语（destructive discourse）；③中性话语（ambivalent discourse）。这个区分可

以用道路上的交通灯来比喻：有益性话语就像绿灯，破坏性话语就像红灯，中性话语就像黄灯。有益性话语给人以美好的希望，传播的是和谐的、生态的、正能量的精神，比如说，自然诗歌（nature poetry）和讴歌光明的、绿色的、传播正能量的语篇就属于有益性话语；对这类话语，我们要赞美、宣传、提倡、鼓励。破坏性话语是指那些反自然的、反生态的、不和谐的、负能量的、把人引向歧途的话语。破坏性话语给生态、环境带来污染，误导人们，传播负能量信息；对这类话语，我们要揭露、批评、抵制。处于这两类话语之间的是我们生活中最常见的中性话语，这些话语有生态的、和谐的、正能量的一面，也有反自然的、反生态的、负能量的一面。判断某一语篇是有益性话语还是破坏性话语，根据的是分析者的生态哲学观（ecosophy）（Naess 1995；蒙培元 2004；乔清举 2013；Stibbe 2015）。

按照 Stibbe（2015）的区分，按照我们的生态哲学观和价值判断（黄国文 2017；黄国文、陈旸 2016），上面这个讲述"甜妹"故事的语篇属于破坏性话语，因此我们要揭露、批评、抵制，让其他人知道它会给社会生态带来害处。说这个语篇是破坏性语篇，是因为它宣传的是一种我们无法接受的世界观和意识形态，会把人引入歧途，使人走上邪路。这不是话题的问题，是怎样讲述故事的问题。

如果我们像下面那样来谈论这个话题，那它就是有益性语篇了。试把下面我们修改的语篇与原文进行比较（限于篇幅，我们只试着重写标题和前面 6 个自然段）：

Heart-broken student, 25, says sugar daddy, 60, who promised to shower her with gifts and give her £ 2,500 every month without sex, turned out to be a big cheat (and she had to lie to her boyfriend, who would be mad if he knew the relationship)

- Ilham Chocolat, 25, met her sugar daddy, a 60-year-oldman, five years ago
- He promised to give her a £ 2,500-a-month allowance and take her to high end hotels
- The man turned out to be a big cheat because he didn't keep his promise
- Miss Chocolat lied to her boyfriend about everything with a sugar daddy

[1] A heart-broken 25-year-old student has revealed how she was cheated by a sugar daddy 35 years her senior.

[2] Ilham Chocolat, from Bologna, Italy, says the man promised to buy her anything she wanted or needed and give her a monthly allowance of £ 2,500 so she could treat herself to designer handbags and lavish shopping sprees. But he didn't always keep his promise.

[3] Miss Chocolat went on date with the man, from Rome, twice a month and they had sex every time they met. She describes their relationship as a "buying and selling" one.

[4] "He enjoys his time with me," Ilham said. "He said I made him feel like a small boy and full of energy. But I didn't enjoy myself at all."

[5] Miss Chocolat also said that she had to lie to her boyfriend because he would be mad if he knew her relationship with the sugar daddy.

[6] Regarded as one of the ordinary sugar babies in the business, Ilham will be sharing her bitter experiences and advice on being with a sugar daddy at a special summit in London this month.

如果我们比较原文的有关部分和上面重写的部分，就会明白为什么同样的话题会导致语篇传递不同性质的信息。下面我们逐一分析和比较。

先看标题。原文的标题是根据正文的内容撰写的，重写的标题也是这样。试比较这两个版本一些表达的差异。

原文：glamorous →重写版：heart-broken

原文：sugar daddy who she doesn't have sex with showers her with gifts and gives her £2,500 every month →重写版：sugar daddy who promised to shower her with gifts and give her £2,500 every month without sex, turned out to be a big cheat

原文：and she insists her boyfriend, 36, doesn't mind →重写版：and she had to lie to her boyfriend, who would be mad if he knew the relationship

原文：has given ... and taken →重写版：promised to give...and take

原文：doctor →重写版：man

原文：The doctor also bought her a bar so she could fulfil her dream of being a landlady →重写版：The man turned out to be a big cheat because he didn't keep his promise

原文：Miss Chocolat insists her boyfriend, 36, is happy with her being a sugar baby →重写版：Miss Chocolat lied to her boyfriend about everything with a sugar daddy

标题的改写是为正文的内容服务的，动词的变换和动词时态的改变〔如 showers…gives →promised to shower… give; has given … (has) taken → promised to give … (to) take; insists/is →lied〕起了很大的作用。当然，也有整句改掉的（即：The doctor also bought her a bar so she could fulfil her dream of being a landlady →The man turned out to be a big cheat because he didn't keep his promise）或话题一样但意思相反的（即：Miss Chocolat insists her boyfriend, 36, is happy with her being a sugar baby →Miss Chocolat lied to her boyfriend about everything with a sugar daddy）。

下面看看第〔1〕至第〔6〕个自然段的改写情况。

原文第〔1〕个自然段的"glamorous"变成了"heart-broken"，"she is showered with money and gifts"变成了"she was cheated"。

原文第〔2〕个自然段的"the divorced doctor buys"变成了"the man promised to buy"，"so she can"变成了"so she could"，但改写版增加了重要的一句"But he didn't always keep his promise"。

原文第〔3〕个自然段的"In return Miss Chocolat goes on date with the doctor"改成了"Miss Chocolat went on date with the man"，"but insists they have never had sex. Instead she describes their relationship as a 'platonic love'"改为"and they had sex every time they met. She describes their relationship as a 'buying and selling' one"。

原文第〔4〕个自然段段尾增加了关键的一句："But I didn't enjoy myself at all."

原文第［5］个自然段被完全改写后，意思也完全相反：原文的"Miss Chocolat also insists her 36-year-old boyfriend is perfectly happy with the unusual arrangement."变成了"Miss Chocolat also said that she had to lie to her boyfriend because he would be mad if he knew her relationship with the sugar daddy."

原文第［6］个自然段被完全改写后，意思也发生变化：原文的"the best sugar babies"变成了"the ordinary sugar babies"，"her secrets to success and advice on snaring"则变成了"her bitter experiences and advice on being with"。原文的关键词"best""secrets to success"和"snaring"被改换以后（ordinary，bitter experiences，being with），意思变得完全不一样。

（三）语言构建现实：过去、现在和未来

综上所述，在这两个语篇中，语言不仅仅是描述过去发生的事情，而且是构建现实，根据作者的交际意图把过去的事件构建出来。同一件过去发生的事情，可以通过不同的语言结构和词语构建出不同的过去、现在和未来。这里的两个语篇构建的是两个完全不同的故事。我们说原文是破坏性语篇，是因为它构建的是这么一个现实：做"甜妹"就有高级享受（奢侈购物、入住高档宾馆、丰厚的零用钱），不用付出身体，男朋友和家庭都支持，有机会做慈善，还可以有机会圆自己孩提时的梦想，等等。这样的语篇构建的故事是虚假的、骗人的，一定会误导那些有不劳而获的思想的年轻女子，诱导她们去参加这种活动。相反，改写后的语篇变成了一个"甜妹"的痛苦经历，说的是"甜爹"说话不算数，骗取身体，自己还为这种关系不得不跟男朋友说谎。这个语篇构建的故事会提醒那些有不劳而获的思想的年轻女子三思而后行，提醒她们悬崖勒马；因此，我们觉得它应该属于有益性语篇。

《在线邮报》那个语篇构建的未来是：对于类似 Ilham Chocolat 的人，如果选择做"甜妹"，那就会不愁吃、不愁穿、不愁钱，还可以收到奢侈品和高档衣物，入住世界级宾馆，还不用以身体去换取，还可以有男朋友，与"甜爹"的关系轻松自如，等等。相反，改写的语篇构建的画面完全不一样：原先说好给的礼物和零用钱都不能全部兑现，而且每次都要以身体作为代价，还要对男朋友说谎，跟的是个大骗子，他享受了，但自己不享受这种关系，这种关系不是美好的，等等。

从生态语言学的角度看，语篇所构建的就是一种理念，一种我们赖以生存的方式，一种影响着我们所思所想和一言一行的故事。这就是语言的生态问题，也是 Halliday（2007）所说的系统生态语言学要重点研究的问题。

（四）话语与语言可持续发展

每个人都有自己赖以生存和生活的语言，每个人所使用的语言都对他的背景和身份进行定位、认定和构建。讲话带某一种口音的人是因为"一方水土养一方说某种语言的人"，在南方长大的人与在北方长大的人说话的口音、用词就会存在差异，在美国是这样，在英国是这样，在中国也是这样。讲话带某一行业术语和表达，是因为语言的功能变体，这是"语域"问题（Halliday 1978），同样的，在美国是这样，在英国是这样，在中国也是这样。

我们的语言使用，反映的是我们对世界的认识和认知，是我们的世界观、我们的意识形态的表现。通过自己的语言实践，我们表明了自己的身份、态度、价值取向。我们的语言使用，影响着别人（包括认识的和不认识的人）；我们的语言使用会帮助别人完成任务甚至达到他们的人生目标。我们的话语所构建的过去、现在和未来会对他人的幸福生活带来帮助，同样也会影响、阻碍或破坏他们今后的一切。

作为社会成员，大家使用的语言互相影响、互相作用。对同样一件事情，不同的语言和意指方式就会导致不同的结果。俗话所说的"良言一句三冬暖，恶语伤人六月寒"就是这个意思。正因为这样，我们才要提倡"语言美"和"精神文明"。

从语言可持续发展的角度看，我们要弘扬、鼓励、宣传、使用对我们社会有益的正能量话语，使这样的话语成为我们生活的一个核心部分，成为我们行为的指导。像"保护自然、保护环境、保护生物多样性"或"语言影响生态环境、语言是我们生活的一个重要部分"这种话语，都是有益性话语，我们说多了，就成为我们离不开的理念和生活准则，我们就会信奉和践行。

学习和注意使用有益性话语能够使我们成为一个高尚的人、一个纯粹的人、一个有理想的人、一个有道德的人、一个脱离了低级趣味的人。如果我们身边这样的人多了，社会风气就会更好，我们的生活就会更加安定和幸福。相反，如果我们周围的人整天抱怨，整天吵架，整天大声吼叫，整天传递负能量，我们就会感到困惑、压抑、不舒服甚至对生活没有信心。语言的可持续发展，其中一点就是使用合适、得体、规范和表达正能量的语言。

从另一角度看语言的可持续发展，我们必须保护语言（包括语言所传递的文化和所反映的核心价值观），爱护语言的多样性，尊重语言差异和语言使用的差异，这是人与人之间平等的基本保证。英语现在变成了国际"通用语"（lingua franca），这是国际沟通、各国经济发展需要带来的。我们在强调英语重要性的同时，要有语言可持续发展的意识，要从语言保护的视角为非英语本族语者（以及他们的后代）的过去、现在和将来考虑。经济发展可以改善生活，但物质的丰富并不一定就会带来幸福。语言有生命，语言的生命与它的使用者的生活紧紧连在一起。

语言的可持续发展，就是生活的可持续发展，就是生命的可持续发展。因此，我们要重视语言的可持续发展问题。

六、结 语

语言的生态问题和语言可持续发展问题，都是关系到人类命运的问题；我们要构建人类命运共同体，要坚持人与自然共生，语言问题也是一个值得认真考虑的问题。每个人的语言生活都会受到各种生态因素的影响。本文通过对一个语篇的分析，说明语言是怎样构建过去、现在和未来的，也说明语言是怎样影响我们的所思所想和一言一行的；这个例子还说明了语言是怎样影响我们的生活和我们生活的生态系统的。

语言不仅反映现实，还主动构建现实。因此，语言生态问题就是人类生活的问题。环境影响语言生态，语言生态也影响环境。作为研究语言生态的生态语言学，是个新兴的交叉学科，属于广义的应用语言学研究领域。我们期待有更多有良知、有社会责任感、有忧患意识的语言研究者加入我们的研究队伍，一起"Think and act ecolinguistically"（思，以生态语言学为本；行，以生态语言学为道）（黄国文 2016）。

参考文献

Fill, A. Ecolinguistics: States of the art. In A. Fill and P. Mühlhäusler(eds.). *The Ecolinguistics Reader: Language, Ecology and Environment*. London: Continuum, 2001: 43 – 53.

Fill, A. and H. Penz (eds.). *Sustaining Language. Essays in Applied Ecolinguistics*. Vienna and Berlin: LIT publishers, 2007.

Halliday, M. A. K. *Language as Social Semiotic: The Social Interpretation of Language and Meaning*. London: Edward Arnold, 1978.

— New ways of meaning: The challenge to applied linguistics. *Journal of Applied Linguistics*, 1990 (6). Reprinted in J. Webster (ed.). *On Language and Linguistics*, Vol. 3 in the *Collected Works of M. A. K. Halliday*. Beijing: Peking University Press, 2007: 139 – 174.

— *An Introduction to Functional Grammar* (2nd edition). London: Edward Arnold, 1994.

— Applied linguistics as an evolving theme. In J. Webster (ed.). *Language and Education*, Vol. 9 in the *Collected Works of M. A. K. Halliday*. London: Continuum, 2007: 1 – 19.

Halliday, M. A. K. and C. M. I. M. Matthiessen. *Construing Experience Through Meaning: A Language-based Approach to Cognition*. London: Cassell, 1999.

— *An Introduction to Functional Grammar* (3rd edition). London: Routledge, 2004.

— *Halliday's Introduction to Functional Grammar*. London:

Routledge, 2014.

Haugen, E. *The Ecology of Language*. Palo Alto: Stanford University Press, 1972.

Naess, A. The shallow and the long range, deep ecology movement. In A. Drengson and Y. Inoue (eds.). *The Deep Ecology Movement: An Introductory Anthology*. Berkeley, CA: North Atlantic Books, 1995: 3 – 10.

Stibbe, A. *Ecolinguistics: Language, Ecology and the Stories We Live By*. London: Routledge, 2015.

常晨光, 廖海青. 系统功能语言学理论与实践的辩证关系: 适用语言学探索［J］. 外语与外语教学, 2010（5）: 11 – 14.

何远秀. 韩礼德的新马克思主义语言研究取向［M］. 北京: 中国社会科学出版社, 2016.

黄国文. 生态语言学的兴起与发展［J］. 中国外语, 2016（1）: 扉页, 9 – 12.

黄国文. 生态话语和行为分析的假定和原则［J］. 外语教学与研究, 2017（6）: 880 – 889.

黄国文, 陈旸. 生态哲学与话语的生态分析［J］. 外国语文, 2016（6）: 55 – 61.

黄国文, 肖家燕. "人类世"概念与生态语言学研究［J］. 外语研究, 2017（5）: 17, 30.

蒙培元. 人与自然: 中国哲学生态观［M］. 北京: 人民出版社, 2004.

乔清举. 儒家生态思想通论［M］. 北京: 北京大学出版社, 2013.

辛志英, 黄国文. 系统功能语言学与生态话语分析 [J], 外语教学, 2013 (3): 7 - 10.

Author bio

Professor HUANG Guowen, once a professor of Functional Linguistics during 1996 – 2016 at Sun Yat-sen University, P. R. China, is now a professor of Functional Linguistics and Ecolinguistics and also Dean of the School of Foreign Studies as well as Director of Centre for Ecolinguistics at South China Agricultural University, P. R. China (Guangzhou). He was educated in Britain and received two PhD degrees from two British universities (1992, Applied Linguistics, Edinburgh; 1996, Functional Linguistics, Cardiff). He was a Fulbright Scholar at Stanford University during 2004 – 2005. During 2011 – 2014 he was Chair of the Executive Committee of the International Systemic Functional Linguistics Association. He is Editor-in-chief of *Zhongguo Waiyu* (Foreign Languages in China) (Beijing), and is Co-editor-in-chief of *Functional Linguistics* (Springer) and *Journal of World Languages* (Routledge), apart from serving as adviser or member of editorial boards for a number of international journals. He is the Chinese representative (regional representative) of the International Ecolinguistics Association (http://ecolinguistics-association.org/). His main research interests include systemic functional linguistics, ecolinguistics, discourse analysis and translation studies.

有益性话语中的变与不变：
两首《洪湖水》的和谐话语分析

卢 健　常晨光

一、引　言

　　黄国文教授提出的"和谐话语分析"（黄国文 2016a：10；黄国文、陈旸 2016：60；黄国文、赵蕊华 2017：588-589；赵蕊华、黄国文 2017：16-18；周文娟 2017：25；Zhou & Huang 2017：276-277）与系统生态语言学一脉相承，体现了"天人合一""和而不同""知行合一"的中国智慧，是对中国生态语言学研究"缺乏对语言的批评或对语言的微观研究"（韩军 2013：111）这一现状的积极改善。
　　《洪湖水，浪打浪》《再唱洪湖水》紧扣相距近 60 年的两个不同时代的主题，通过适切的意指方式建构生态和谐的现实，表达对洪湖的赞美与热爱。本文对其歌词进行和谐话语分析，试图探究产生于不同时代的内容连续的生态有益性话语，因历史语境、价值观念和语言系统潜势等方面的异同，体现出何种变与不变，从而为中国语境下有益性话语的判定和建构提供启示。

二、生态语言学视域下的话语分类

生态语言学研究领域存在两种互补的路径和视角。一种看重"语言自身作为生态系统"，另一种看重"语言使用如何作用于环境"（辛志英、黄国文 2013：8）。和谐话语分析模式属于后者，即"系统生态语言学"（Halliday 2007：14），或曰"韩礼德模式"（Fill 2001：43）。它认同 Alexander 和 Stibbe（2014：105）对生态语言学的定义：生态语言学研究语言对人类与人类之间、人类与其他有机体之间和人类与自然环境之间的生命可持续关系的影响；其研究目标是维持生命可持续关系（参见黄国文 2017：5）。

生态观是指看待人类、其他生命体和自然环境之间相互关系的一套原则和理念（Stibbe 2015：202）。语言对生命可持续关系的影响正是通过编码一定生态观的话语来实现的。在生态语言学的视域下，生态观对话语的建构和评估至关重要。Stibbe（2015：14）提出了其生态观，即保护维持生命可持续关系的生态系统，并以"生活！"（Living!）一词概括之。他（Stibbe 2014：121 - 124，2015：24 - 33）根据与分析者生态观的对照情况将话语分为三类：①破坏性话语（destructive discourse），传达的观念违背了话语分析者的生态观；②模糊性话语（ambivalent discourse），在某些方面与分析者的生态观相吻合，而在另一些方面却与之相抵触；③有益性话语（beneficial discourse），体现了与分析者契合的生态观。

上述分类从生态观的维度确立了三个范畴,并鼓励抵制破坏性话语,提倡有益性话语,辩证看待模糊性话语,这是值得肯定的。但正如黄国文、陈旸(2018:3-14)所论,在实际话语分析的过程中常常很难泾渭分明地给某一话语贴上特定的标签。较为合理的操作应该是采纳"连续体"的概念:从生态的角度看,所有的话语存在于一个以典型的有益性话语和破坏性话语为两端的"生态有益度连续体"上,如图1所示。比较而言,"甲话语比乙话语更具生态有益性或生态破坏性"。

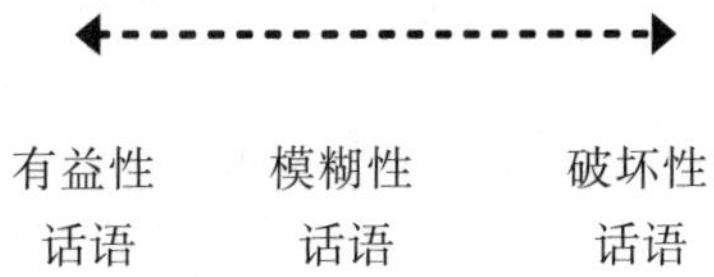

◀-------------------▶

有益性　　模糊性　　破坏性
话语　　　话语　　　话语

图1　生态有益度连续体

再者,仅以分析者的生态观作为分类标准,维度过于单一。正如 Bang 和 Døør (2007:59)以及 Zhou (2017:134) 所言,进入分析者视野的一则话语必然涉及三方面的关系,即作者/说者、读者/听者以及分析者。对话语进行生态分析,判定其在生态有益度连续体上的位置,除生态观外,还应考虑历史语境和话语接受两个因素的作用,三者互为一体,如图2所示。

图2　话语分类的三个维度

话语是语境的产物,其作者都不可避免地受到历史条件的支配和局限;今天的分析者可以赋予昨天的话语以新解,使之具有新的内涵,但不能以今天的观念来苛责昨天的作者。明白这一点,既是话语解读的需要,也是分析者对作者的体念。"语言是我说来给你听的"(陈望道 2009:419),没有接受就没有表达。某一话语产生之后,其预期目标能在多大程度上得以实现,其生命力如何,取决于它能在多大程度上与其读者对象产生共鸣。这种共鸣有赖于语言系统潜势与文化的互动,词汇语法"为某种表意方式提供了可能,而文化则使其具有语境恰适性,从而使这种可能得以实现"(卢健 2017:110)。

三、和谐话语分析框架构拟

和谐话语分析有别于以往的话语分析模式。相较于"批评话语分析"(Fairclough 2003:2-16;Wodak 2011:50-70),它着眼于建构,而不是解构;强调理解主流,而不是局促于边缘;提倡各安其分,各司其职,形成合力,良性互动。相较于积极话语分析(Martin 2012:278-298),它除了关注人类社会,更将眼光放诸整个生态系统的其他生命体及其生存环境,包括其当下和将来,从而由"自我导向"(self-oriented)走向"他者导向"(other-oriented)(Stibbe 2014:119)。作为植根于中国智慧的生态话语分析模式,它跳出"人类中心主义"和"环境中心主义"(赵奎英 2013:13)的二元对立,从"天人合一""和而不同"的思想中吸收养分,提倡人与天地万物共同构成"道德共同体"(乔清举 2013:19),同时承认"爱有差等"(冯友兰 2013:71)的生态现实。

和谐话语分析以"天人合一""和而不同""知行合一"

有益性话语中的变与不变：两首《洪湖水》的和谐话语分析

等思想为哲学基础；它的基础理论是以"语言主动创建现实"（Halliday 2003：145）这一假定为前提，以探究"我们的意指方式如何左右我们对环境的影响"（Halliday 2007：14）为旨归的系统生态语言学；基本方法论是功能语篇分析，包括"观察、解读、描述、分析、解释、评估"六个步骤（黄国文 2006：175）；它重视语言学的"社会理据"和"社会责任"（常晨光、廖海青 2010：13），提倡"思，以生态语言学为本；行，以生态语言学为道"（Think and act ecolinguistically）（黄国文 2016b：11）。综上，我们为该模式构拟出了一个操作框架，如图3所示。

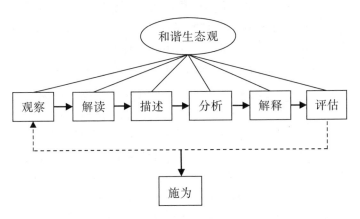

图3　和谐话语分析框架

"和谐"是和谐话语分析的生态观，其内在根据是"天人合一"。"天人本来合一，而人生最高理想，是自觉地达到天人合一之境界。物我本属一体，内外原无判隔。"（张岱年 2015：27）人类、动物、草木、土地、山川等构成"道德共同体"。和谐以"和而不同"为内在规定性,即《国语·郑语》所谓"夫和实生物,同则不继"(左丘明、韦昭 2015:338 - 339;何伟、魏榕 2017:21)。在道德共同体内部,各"成员"各安其位,和睦协调;人承担道德主体责任,认识且服从于自然之道,并助其完善(乔清举 2013:28);人对其他成员的爱是有差等的,即孟子所说的"亲亲而仁民,仁民而爱物"(冯友兰 2013:71)。和谐以"生生不息"为目的。《易传》有云:"天地之大德曰生","生生之谓易"(黄寿祺、张善文 2004:503)。这与上文提到的生态语言学"维持生命可持续关系"的研究目标大体上是一致的。

功能语篇分析的六个步骤依次展开。分析者根据其研究兴趣和目的,通过观察来判断某一话语是否具有分析价值;解读指要弄明白该话语的意义、预期目标及其结果;描述须运用专业术语,有步骤、有系统地进行;分析和解释即在一定理论框架下揭示该话语是怎样表达意义、何以表达那样的意义的;评估是较高的层次,指评判话语的预期目标在多大程度上得到了实现。在和谐话语分析模式中,对和谐生态观的观照贯穿于全过程。另外,我们所分析的既是作为结果的"语篇",也是作为过程的"话语",既作为具体示例,也作为系统潜势。对此,图 3 中用回向虚线箭头呈现。

"施为",即知行合一。"中国哲人探求真理,目的乃在于生活之迁善,而务要表见之于生活中"(张岱年 2015:26);于我们而言,就是要"思,以生态语言学为本;行,以生态语言学为道"。它体现了和谐话语分析重视社会责任的特质。一方面,通过语言学分析揭示话语在生态有益度连续体上的位置;另一方面,探究话语的意指方式及其背后的观念形态，帮助人们认识破坏性话语的本来面目，并为有益性话语的建构提供启示，以促进人们的行为向更加生态的方向发展。

四、两首《洪湖水》的和谐话语分析

两首《洪湖水》分别诞生于1959年和2016年，都以歌唱洪湖为主题。《洪湖水，浪打浪》是歌剧《洪湖赤卫队》的主要唱段之一。它"营造出洪湖的美丽和富庶，刻画了韩英作为洪湖儿女对家乡的无比热爱和由衷赞美"（居其宏2002：65）。词作者为梅少山、张敬安、梅会召和欧阳谦叔，曲作者是张敬安和欧阳谦叔。《再唱洪湖水》的MV于2016年12月3日首发，词作者为陈汉武，曲作者是王原平。王原平在首发式的贺信中称其为"紧扣水乡变迁，紧扣大众心理，紧扣时代特点的代表之作"。作为话语的歌曲本应包括词、曲、演唱（奏）等多个侧面，囿于篇幅和研究目的，本文仅以歌词为分析对象。通过观察、解读，我们注意到这两首歌词具有较高的生态话语分析价值，且表现出某些颇有意义的差异性。

本文的描述、分析在和谐话语分析框架下，以小句的及物性分析（Halliday 1994：108）为主，兼及其他。我们认同赵蕊华（2016：86-90），何伟、张瑞杰（2017：58-59）等将及物性系统进行生态视角下的细化和扩展的做法。需要指出的是，汉语具有一些有别于英语的特点，在分析时应予以注意。

（一）《洪湖水，浪打浪》之分析

《洪湖水，浪打浪》包含16个过程小句。其中［3］、

[4]隐去了动作者,[8]、[9]构成投射关系,[10]的属性可理解为"比天堂美"。其及物性描述如下:

[1]洪湖水(场所)呀浪呀么浪(动作者)打(物质)浪(目标)啊[2]洪湖岸边(被识别者)是(关系)呀么是家乡(识别者)[3]清早(时间)船儿(工具)去呀去撒网(物质)[4]晚上(时间)回来(物质)[5]鱼(存在者)满舱(地点)[6]四处(地点)野鸭和菱藕(存在者)[7]秋收(时间)满畈(地点)稻谷(载体)香(属性)[8]人人(说者)都(程度)说(言语)[9]天堂美(说话内容)[10]怎比(关系)我洪湖鱼米乡(载体)[11]洪湖水(载体)呀长呀么长又长(属性)啊[12]太阳一出(气象)[13]闪呀么闪金光啊(物质)[14]共产党的恩情(载体)比那东海深(属性)[15]共产党(载体)像呀么像(关系)太阳(属性)[16]渔民的光景(载体)一年更比一年强(属性)。

以上描述,有两点值得分析和解释:

(1)话语的语类结构。16个过程构成一个以洪湖为主题,以歌咏为目的的语类结构,层次分明。[1]、[2]一动一静的两个过程生动而鲜明地点出场景;物质过程[3]、[4]再现渔民一天的劳作;[5]、[6]、[7]通过存在过程和含特定环境成分的肯定义关系过程,描写洪湖的富饶和劳动之后的丰收;[8]、[9]、[10]以言语过程和表比较的关系过程表达丰收之后的喜悦;[11]、[12]、[13]再次描写场景,从关系过程到物质过程一静一动,继续渲染喜悦之情,并以"比"和"兴"的艺术形式为后文做铺垫;[14]、[15]为关系过程,渔民将丰收和喜悦归因于"共产党";[16]中的关系过程以"一年一年"为比较参照,既是对现实的肯定，也是对未来的憧憬。至此，话语的语类结构可表示为"场景—劳作—丰收—喜悦—归因—憧憬"。自然的恩赐、渔民的勤劳、政治的清明、将来的可期，生机勃勃的和谐景象跃然纸上。

（2）作为动作者的人类和作为存在者的动物。[3]、[4]中物质过程的动作者在表达层中隐去了，但这并不意味着语义上参与者的缺失。据[16]可知，动作者是洪湖的"渔民"。与之相对，[5]、[6]中的动物"鱼"和"野鸭"则以存在者的角色出现。物质过程的动作者与存在过程的存在者，虽同为参与者，但参与的主动性殊为不同，前者明显高于后者。该话语中对人类和动物一高一低的这种安排，从常规看，并无不妥。我们总是倾向于以"有无意识"为标准来区分人和动物。但较之于将动物建构为强主动性参与者的某些话语，两种意指方式在生态有益性方面高下立判。对此，后文中将结合实例详述。

（二）《再唱洪湖水》之分析

《再唱洪湖水》，不计"渔歌唱晚"等名物化以用作参与者的过程和内容重复的过程，共包含22个小句。作为动作者、行为者和感觉者的"我"或"我们"省略较多。[2]、[19]实质上是表达为物质过程的行为过程，[18]则是表达为物质过程的心理过程。[17]较特别，是所谓的"动结式"，即一个图示（figure）包含两个过程，它们构成"动作—结果"的关系。歌词的及物性描述如下：

[1]再(频度)唱(行为)一曲洪湖水呀浪打浪(范围)[2]梦里(场所)回到(物质)我可爱的家乡(范围)[3]一声声蛙鸣(现象)，一

语言的可持续性

阵阵荷香(现象)，牵起(心理)故事悠长悠长(结果)［4］听(行为)渔歌唱晚(范围)［5］笑(行为)世事沧桑(范围)［6］野鸭(动作者)嬉戏(物质)湖中的月亮(目标)［7］洪湖水(场所)呀浪呀么浪(动作者)打(物质)浪(目标)啊［8］洪湖岸边(被识别者)是(关系)呀么是家乡(识别者)［9］情(载体)悠悠(属性)［10］雁语(载体)长(属性)［11］梦回(行为)田园画(范围)［12］洪湖曲(载体)悠扬(属性)［13］心里(场所)萦绕(心理)我亲爱的家乡(现象)［14］一树树新绿(场所)，一缕缕畅想(伴随)，携手(物质)复兴路上路上(范围)［15］眺(行为)春湖水暖(范围)［16］叹(行为)人间天堂(范围)［17］烟波(动作者/现象)摇醉(物质/心理)唤春的姑娘(目标/感觉者)［18］相思(动作者)动(物质)［19］歌(动作者)飘荡(物质)［20］举(物质)杯(范围)［21］邀(物质)四海(范围)［22］天涯(地点)共(物质)水乡(范围)

以上描述也有两点值得注意：

第一，洪湖的变与不变。《再唱洪湖水》建构了一个风光旖旎、民胞物与的现实。一个"再"字点出了两首《洪湖水》内容上的连续性和话语上的"互文性"。洪湖还是那个洪湖，她依然是"浪打浪"的"春湖水暖"，依然是"渔歌唱晚"的"人间天堂"，洪湖如此多娇，自然引得洪湖儿女魂牵梦绕，这是水乡的不变之处。50多年前，洪湖渔民感念共产党的恩深似海；今时今日，洪湖人民携手走在中华民族的复兴路上，其领导力量依然是共产党。这亦为不变之处。但是，时代的脉搏必然以水乡的变迁来昭示它的跳动。从"梦里""心里""四海""天涯"等范围和环境成分可知，今天的很多洪湖人已不再"清早船儿去撒网，晚上回来鱼满舱"，他们的生产生活方式发生了很大的变化，洪湖更多地成了"举杯邀四海,天涯共水乡"的桑梓之地。此乃水乡之巨变也。

第二,从自我导向走向他者导向。该话语中的人类在面对洪湖时,多以行为过程的行为者和心理过程的感觉者的角色出现。他们或"唱""听""笑""梦""眺""叹"洪湖的田园之美,或因洪湖之美而心心念念,如痴如醉。在这样的建构中,洪湖不再是渔民索取的"目标",而只是人们行为的"范围"和引发特定感知的"现象";人类对自然的干预降到了极低的程度。有趣的是,[6]中的"野鸭"却扮演了物质过程动作者的角色。"嬉戏"与"玩耍""追逐"近义,也可看作行为过程;但"嬉戏"却平添了不少生趣,而且还带了目标"湖中的月亮",俨然成了有意识的动作。[17]的动结式构造亦颇为巧妙,"烟波"既是物质过程的动作者,也是心理过程的现象,"唤春的姑娘"成了目标和感觉者;仿佛那湖才是主动的参与者,那人只是被动的接受者。以上分析和解释告诉我们,在话语建构者的观念中,人类已不是衡量一切的标准,大自然不再是没有生命、没有意识的存在,自然有自然的怡然自得,即"内在价值"。这种从自我导向走向他者导向的观念的形成就是生态和谐的自觉过程。

五、讨论:有益性话语中的变与不变

据本文所提出的话语分类标准,两首《洪湖水》都是生态有益性话语。"生态观"维度的解释已较详尽,此处主要从另外两个维度论证。从"历史语境"来看,《洪湖水,浪打浪》的时代,无论是歌曲创作的 1959 年,还是歌剧《洪湖赤卫队》所反映的土地革命时期,打鱼撒网、春种秋收就是洪湖岸边的生活方式和生存之道。正所谓"亲亲、仁民、爱物"。在当时的生产力条件下,"生生不息"客观上首先是指人类自身的生生不息;且人类的活动尚在自然的承受范围之内,这从"四处""满畈""满舱"等环境成分的选择上可见一斑。渔民热爱这方水土,推崇天道酬勤,歌颂党的领导,期待美好的明天,这些都是积极向上的,因而也是和谐而有益的。《再唱洪湖水》的时代,生产力水平大为提高,经济环境空前开放,人与自然的关系不再像50多年前那样简单而直接。一方面,人们纷纷走向四面八方,谋生手段多样,生活方式多元;另一方面,与经济发展亦步亦趋的生态问题凸显,物质的丰裕也使人们有条件思考人在道德共同体中所应尽的更多责任。抒发对家乡的眷念,鼓励尊重自然的内在价值,提倡减少人类的主动干预,在当前的时代背景下具有切实而重大的生态意义。我们很欣喜地注意到近期有关"洪湖拆围,渔民上岸"的新闻(荆州日报客户端 2017 - 10 - 23)。这是在政府主导下保护洪湖生态所迈出的重要一步,也耦合了和谐话语分析中知行合一的"施为"主张。

如前所述,"话语接受"是话语获得生命力的条件。系统潜势既提供了作者所能使用的意指方式的范围,也意味着读者所能接受的意指方式的范围,文化使双方意指方式的交集获得语境恰适性并得以实现,这便赋予了话语可接受的生命力。两首《洪湖水》都很好地解决了这一问题,从而使话语建构的生态有益性现实最终成为我们信奉并践行的"故事"(stories-we-live-by)(Stibbe 2015:6)。试举一例,两则话语都很善于选择"意象":在我们的文化中,"稻荷芬芳""人间天堂""雁语蛙鸣""渔歌唱晚""田园如画"等都是耳熟能详，并能迅速产生生态和谐美感的意象，易于激发人们心中对自然的道德责任感，进而改善自己的生态行为。

虽然都是有益性话语，但两个文本在生态有益度连续体上的位置有所不同。《再唱洪湖水》较之《洪湖水，浪打浪》生态有益度更高，这表现为编码于话语中的生态意识的程度更高。如上文所论，人类从动作者到行为者和感觉者，动物从存在者到动作者，参与者主动性的一降一升，集中体现了两则连续的有益性话语的一个显著变化。如果说《洪湖水，浪打浪》呈现的是生机勃勃的景象，《再唱洪湖水》则展示了生趣盎然的画面。尽管受到历史语境的局限，但两者毕竟反映了生态意识从自发到自觉的变化。需要说明的是，我们比较两则话语生态有益度的高低，并无意于评判孰优孰劣，生态有益性只是看待话语的一种视角，它并不能揭示话语的方方面面，话语分析不能也不必面面俱到。

六、结　语

本文对 Arran Stibbe 等学者提出的话语分类标准做了补充，主张从生态观、历史语境和话语接受三个维度来考察话语，判定其在生态有益度连续体上的相对位置；构拟了和谐话语分析框架，并据此分析了《洪湖水，浪打浪》和《再唱洪湖水》两首歌的歌词。作为不同历史语境的产物，两首《洪湖水》都是生态有益性话语，都以适切的意指方式建构生态和谐的现实。历时观之，两者反映了生态意识从自发到自觉的变化。两则连续的话语体现出诸多的"变"与"不变"：变的是向洪湖的索取，不变的是对洪湖的依恋；变的是生产生活方式，不变的是对生态和谐的建构；变的是时代的主题，不变的是迈向新时代的主体和领导力量。历史在变与不变的辩证互动中，沿着其自身的逻辑，向更加和谐的新的现实演进。

* 本文原载于《外语教学》2019年第5期，收入本文集时略有删改。

参考文献

Alexander, R. and A. Stibbe. From the analysis of ecological discourse to the ecological analysis of discourse. *Language Sciences*, 2014（41）: 104 – 110.

Bang, J. C. and J. Døør. *Language, Ecology, and Society: A Dialectical Approach.* London: Continuum, 2007.

Fairclough, N. *Analysing Discourse: Textual Analysis for Social Research.* London: Routledge, 2003.

Fill, A. Ecolinguistics: State of the art 1998. In A. Fill and P. Mühlhäusler (eds.). *The Ecolinguistics Reader: Language, Ecology and Environment.* London: Continuum, 2001: 43 – 53.

Halliday, M. A. K. *An Introduction to Functional Grammar* (2nd edition). London: Edwand Arnold, 1994.

— New ways of meaning: The challenge to applied linguistics. In J. Webster (ed.). *On Language and Linguistics: Collected Works of M. A. K. Halliday.* London: Continuum, 2003: 139 – 174.

— Applied linguistics as an evolving theme. In J. Webster (ed.). *Language and Education: Collected Works of M. A.

K. *Halliday*. London: Continuum, 2007: 1–19.

Martin, J. R. Positive discourse analysis: Solidarity and change. In Z. H. Wang(ed.). *CDA / PDA: Collected Works of J. R. Martin*. Shanghai: Shanghai Jiao Tong University Press, 2012: 278–298.

Stibbe, A. An ecolinguistic approach to critical discourse studies. *Critical Discourse Studies*, 2014 (1): 117–128.

——*Ecolinguistics: Language, Ecology and the Stories We Live By*. London: Routledge, 2015.

Wodak, R. Critical linguistics and critical discourse analysis. In J. Zienkowski, J. Östman and J. Verschueren (eds.). *Discursive Pragmatics*. Amsterdam: Benjamins, 2011: 50–70.

Zhou, W. J. Ecolinguistics: Towards a new harmony. *Language Sciences*, 2017 (62): 124–138.

Zhou, W. J. and G. W. Huang. Chinese ecological discourse: A Confucian-Daoist inquiry. *Journal of Multicultural Discourses*, 2017 (3): 264–281.

常晨光,廖海青. 系统功能语言学理论与实践的辩证关系:适用语言学探索 [J]. 外语与外语教学, 2010 (5): 11–14.

陈望道. 关于修辞 [C] //陈望道语言学论文集. 北京:商务印书馆, 2009: 419–420.

冯友兰. 中国哲学简史 [M]. 北京:北京大学出版社, 2013.

韩军. 中国生态语言学研究综述 [J]. 语言教学与研究, 2013 (4): 107–112.

何伟,魏榕.国际生态话语的内涵及研究路向[J].外语研究,2017(5):18-24.

何伟,张瑞杰.生态话语分析模式构建[J].中国外语,2017,14(5):56-64.

黄国文.翻译研究的语言学探索[M].上海:上海外语教育出版社,2006.

黄国文.外语教学与研究的生态化取向[J].中国外语,2016a(5):扉页,9-13.

黄国文.生态语言学的兴起与发展[J].中国外语,2016b(1):扉页,9-12.

黄国文.从系统功能语言学到生态语言学[J].外语教学,2017(5):1-6.

黄国文,陈旸.生态哲学与话语的生态分析[J].外国语文,2016(6):55-61.

黄国文,陈旸.生态话语分类的不确定性[J].北京第二外国语学院学报,2018(1):3-14.

黄国文,赵蕊华.生态话语分析的缘起、目标、原则与方法[J].现代外语,2017(5):585-596.

黄寿祺,张善文.周易译注[M].上海:上海古籍出版社,2004.

荆州日报客户端.十九大代表带来三张大照片,洪湖渔民上岸还一湖碧波荡漾[N/OL].荆州日报,2017-10-23. http://www.cnchu.com/viewnews-240756.html.

居其宏.新中国音乐史[M].长沙:湖南美术出版社,2002.

卢健.《语言与学习面面观》评介[J].中国外语,2017

(5): 108-111.

乔清举. 儒家生态思想通论 [M]. 北京: 北京大学出版社, 2013.

辛志英, 黄国文. 系统功能语言学与生态话语分析 [J]. 外语教学, 2013 (3): 7-10.

张岱年. 中国哲学大纲 [M]. 北京: 商务印书馆, 2015.

赵奎英. 从生态语言学批评看"生态"与"环境"之辨 [J]. 厦门大学学报 (哲学社会科学版), 2013 (5): 9-19.

赵蕊华. 系统功能视角下生态话语分析的多层面模式: 以生态报告中银无须鳕身份构建为例 [J]. 中国外语, 2016 (5): 84-91.

赵蕊华, 黄国文. 生态语言学研究与和谐话语分析: 黄国文教授访谈录 [J]. 当代外语研究, 2017 (4): 15-18, 25.

周文娟. 中国语境下生态语言学研究的理念与实践: 黄国文生态语言学研究述评 [J]. 西安外国语大学学报, 2017 (3): 24-28.

左丘明. 国语 [M]. 韦昭, 注. 上海: 上海古籍出版社, 2015.

作者简介

卢健, 博士, 华中农业大学外国语学院副教授。研究方向: 功能语言学、生态语言学。

常晨光, 博士, 中山大学国际翻译学院院长、教授, 澳大利亚研究中心主任。研究方向: 功能语言学、语篇分析、澳大利亚研究。